. . . . and the leaves of the tree were for the healing of nations . . . .

Revelations 22:2

The
MASTER BOOK
OF HERBALISM

PAUL BEYERL

Illustrations by
Diana Greene

PHOENIX PUBLISHING CO.
P.O. Box 10, Custer, Washington 98240

NOTE

The information published herein is presented
from an historical and folkloric perspective
only and should not be used as a substitute for
treatment by a physician or other health care
professional(s).

This edition printed 1996

PHOENIX PUBLISHING, INC.
Portal Way
P.O. Box 10
Custer, Washington USA 98240

Distributed in Canada by
PHOENIX PUBLISHING INC.
821 - 254th Street
Langley, BC V4W 2R8

ISBN 0-919345-53-0

Cover design and artwork by Bob Birtch
Printed in the U.S.A.

This book has been manufactured on recycled paper using vegetable based inks.

DEDICATION

I should like to dedicate this book to the following:

To Jim, who has put up with countless hours typing, and been supportive of me in my work;

To my publisher Doug Brown, who gave me encouragement and the means by which this has come to pass;

And to the family I have through the Rowan Tree, which has grown around me as I grow in years, and is a joyous experience for all of us.

I also dedicate this book to each of you, for your interest in herbs is like a small light which will light the way into a new age, made better by each of us caring and loving enough to desire to help, and to heal.

CONTENTS

Illustrations have been provided for plants easily found wild in North America.

INTRODUCTION:

THE WORKING BOOK OF
THE TRADITIONAL HERBALIST

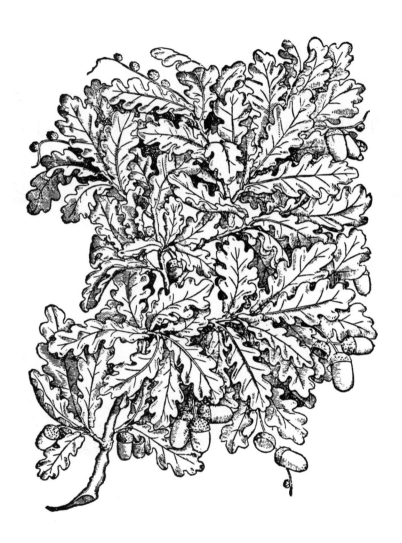

THE WORKING BOOK OF
THE TRADITIONAL HERBALIST

 should like to introduce you to this book, for it has a very personal meaning and purpose for me. It is an herbal in the Traditional sense, in that it encompasses many aspects of herbs and their uses, and is in accordance with those principles which have come down to us through the ages. It is far from complete, being the first attempt at taking my own, personal herbal which I have assembled through these years and making it available to the general public. I believe that the working book of an Herbalist is never complete, but continually grows as new material is added, reflecting the personal growth and experience of the Master Herbalist's own practise. Even as I complete this manuscript, I have found additional ancient lore and more practises which I can only save for a revision at a later date.

In this process, I encourage all readers to feel free to send me their own personal correspondences and findings, and in a few years to come, perhaps we can see a greatly expanded revision come into print.

There is a wealth of books on the market which give us hundreds upon hundreds of herbs and their medicinal uses. Grieve alone records around eight hundred herbs. For this reason, I have limited the number of herbs in the remedial herbal of this book in order that the student may draw upon a reasonable number of choices. When faced with hundreds, it boggles the mind. I feel that the needs of all those seeking information about herbs call for more completely indexed books which reflect greater information about Native American practises, both religious and remedial; herbal practises which come to us from Africa and all lore, whether handed down through family or in print, not readily available to the general public. Mrs. Grieve did a remarkable service for the herbal community in preserving such a wealth of information, and should be regarded by all of us as approaching near sainthood. Perhaps by working together in the spirit of the new Aquarian Age, we can pool our information and save it for the future.

THE NATURE OF HERBS

I quote from *Revelations* the following: "And the leaves of the tree were for the healing of nations," (22:2), for this is our heritage as we move into a growing awareness of the powers of herbs. There is a tendency to bring to mind a small number of kitchen herbs (small, green, growing things), yet the realm of the Herbalist encompasses nearly all plants and trees which grow upon the Earth. We may use roots, bark of trees, whole plants, leaves, flowers and the choice goes on and on. It is important to know how these creatures (for they truly have being as do all living things) have come to us.

Plant life came from the great maternal oceans, even as did we, going back many ages when all life was birthing in the great seas of the Earth. For the Herbalist, this is a very significant and symbolic connection between human and plant life. From tiny, one-celled plants, they grew and changed and at some miraculous time was chlorophyll evolved. At this time did the kingdom of plants gain the ability to manufacture their own food with the aid of the radiant energies of the Sun. This, however, was not enough, for in more time they also evolved sexual reproduction, for this life was good and was in need of procreation.

In the study of plants, it is possible to see an incredible variety of reproductive processes. It was beautiful, this process of perpetuating life, and led to spores, seeds, and flowers, all of which have fascinated the human mind for ages. Still not content, plants did not want to spend eternity bound to the ocean, and at some point in time moved onto the dry land. This was no simple process, for the root systems had to undergo extraordinary change. There was a terrifying amount of sunlight without the protective waters to keep them from scorching and parching, and even worse, they were no longer able to flow with the tides and currents, to move with seasonal change. Once rooted, they were stuck permanently in that patch of ground.

Herbs are things of mystery, each a miracle of life itself, experiencing growth, being, and reproduction. Some grow to incredible height, and live far longer than any human. Others are so tiny we tend to miss even their being. From spore to exquisite flower, each is worthy of consideration.

CHLOROPHYLL

As Mr. Huxley says in his book *Plant and Planet:*

The great invention of the plant kingdom, the factor which differentiates it totally from all animals of whatever complexity, apart from a few borderline cases among single-celled organism is chlorophyll. Whether it is a one-celled algae or a giant forest tree, a plant will contain this substance.

This process of chlorophyll manufacture allows the plant to take certain rays of the sun and combine them with water and carbon dioxide to create, nearly alchemically, glucose. In the process, oxygen is given off which is required by the animal kingdom in the beautiful symbiotic process in which we share the geosphere of the Earth. This process is called photosynthesis.

It is a striking fact that part of the chlorophyll molecule is nearly identical to a molecule of blood pigment, the primary difference being iron in blood is replaced by magnesium in plants. Another fact which may derive from our common origin is the chloroplast (that part of the plant which is the converter), changing the rays of the sun, or solar energy, into chemical energy. Plants have been the first, by many ages, to be solar converters. A little known fact occurs when the process is reversed, as the day moves into night. This is when plants turn their 'converters' around, to change the chemical energy into growth. At this point, there are a number of plants which emit light, which accounts for the magick of twilight.

SENSORY PERCEPTIONS

Plants respond to light. We see this in the manner by which they position their leaves, turning them either towards or away from the sun, dependent upon their specific needs. Their roots grow towards water. They have the ability to perceive, although the 'how' of it continues to elude scientists.

Many of them are capable of tactile perception. The tendril of some vines is so sensitive to touch that in one variety, the plant begins coiling within twenty seconds, completing one grasping turn in less than four minutes. There are the Mimosas, who cause their leaves to droop, nearly instantly, at the slightest touch or by the trembling of the ground from approaching herds of plant-hungry animals, looking dead and withered and thus guaranteeing their survival. One outstanding scientist, J. Chandra Bose, has carried out numerous experiments to prove his belief that plants do, indeed, have a developed and functional nervous system. Russian scientists published a report in 1970 which suggests that the nervous system of plants is very similar to that of humans. They have even suggested a location for the center of this system (the root neck).

Backster and Henson created something of a literary uproar with their experiments, wiring plants with electrical currents, dumping

7

poisons on them and provoking them, as they recorded the sensations of the plants with galvanometers. This has led to books dealing with the need to talk to your plants, and for a couple of years most television talk shows devoted one or more segments to that phenomenon. In the past couple of decades there have been instances in which plants have led to the apprehension of criminals.[1] The most interesting is one in which plants were wired with lie detector equipment, and reacted very strongly when the guilty party entered the room. We have also found articles reporting the reactions of plants to the killing of tiny brine shrimp, all done scientifically, with the plants 'wired' and the shrimp placed in boiling water. The resulting graphs of the galvanometer show very intense reactions by the plants. All of this has led to exhortations for all of us to 'talk' to our plants, and do everything but take them to lunch. Even Luther Burbank, that giant of horticulture, was certain that his plants grew better because he used his mind to direct positive forces towards them.

A BRIEF HISTORY

What causes all of this interest, and how long has it been going on? Because the work of the Herbalist is so ancient as to have existed long before recorded history, and because in many eras it was a tradition handed down orally or in secret books from one to another, we can only imagine how it came to be. There are many who feel that the medicine man or wise woman evolved out of the simple food grower or shepherd. These were the ones who watched nature in her daily manifestation and observed how the animals and birds turned to plants in their hungers and in their illness. Imagine the amazing thoughts and questions which would come from making the potent observation that an animal had healed itself by eating a particular herb, and seeing this process repeated again, and again, giving it the substance of proof. It it holds true for animals, why not for humans?

It had to have been a very experimental science, and only those healers with powerful senses of intuition could circumvent direct learning from an already-proven healer. Perhaps this is an explanation for the Herbalist being so connected with religion and magick. The remedies we know of which date back thousands of years are still, in most cases, very accurate, now that we have scientific proof. An example is Hyssop, long thought very powerful against wounds and infection, and thought of as having great spiritual and physical powers to protect against infections. It has been used for purification for a long time. Modern research shows us that Hyssop, if allowed to mold, produces penicillin. The Traditional Herbalist, however, cannot wait for science to dissemble every molecule of the plant, but must rely on the ages-old body of available knowledge.

Some of the oldest printed matter, and I use the word printed not in the literal sense, is over 4500 years old. The oldest herbal, to my knowledge, is the *Pen Tsao*, the great book of healing written by the Chinese.

We have found clay tablets from Sumeria which show that herbal work was used in conjunction with astrology, and we know from records that Thosthmes III, Great Pharoah of Egypt 2500 years ago, was interested enough in herbal knowledge to send forth an expedition of scholars and herbalists to Syria to bring back their science, already considered advanced. All major works of religion contain references to herbs, and it would appear that they have always been with us.

How old is the oldest herbal? Around the same time Thosthmes III was gathering herblore for his people, the Greeks were beginning to treat herbs with great seriousness. Because much of their society was based upon written material, they began to organize the study. Hippocrates systematically placed about four hundred herbs into medicinal categories so that their use would be more readily understood. Plato and Aristotle worked with herbs, the latter considered an expert in astringents and demulcents. But a significant date in herbals is found when Pliny published his *Natural History*, which is rather like an encyclopedia of its time, dealing with herbs and many other aspects of nature. Because the knowledge was already so evolved, we find most of the herbals since are generally revisions, rewritten books and new attitudes towards the same ancient skills.

A more recent figure is Culpeper, born of a clergyman's family in London in 1616. This is a story of an Herbalist which we find repeated in many versions throughout time in which they are radical, holistic, ahead of their time, and subsequently subject to persecution. Culpeper was studied in different forms of medicine, particularly that which came down from Hippocrates. As such, he was also a competent astrologer. He studied healing systems of the Middle East, and was a prolific author in his day, publishing many books and treatise on the subject. Culpeper fought the system, and spent much of his life traveling the British Isles, ministering to the poor and collecting plants in their natural habitat. He was good at this work, but when it came to social graces he was blunt and lacking in tact. At that time the 'establishment' was the College of Physicians, the counterpart of the American Medical Association today.

During Culpeper's time, physicians were moving from astrology, for it had acquired a bad reputation from the Middle Ages. Culpeper worked hard to show that astrology was a useful tool even as Hippocrates had said, and died at a young age (38) from tuberculosis contracted from his patients, unable to fight it off due to his own poverty and exhausting schedule.

9

THE HERBALIST TODAY

Does this mean that our fate today is the same? I should hope not, yet there are similarities. We are on the brink of a New Age, and from all appearances, it will include herbs as a major source of healing powers for both body and for spirit. These past few decades have seen a great resurgence in this field with many books appearing on the market. Health food stores proliferate and there are a growing number of herb shops and co-ops with herbs. The nature of Aquarius dictates that the future will hold small communities of people with inner members serving the needs of others. There is no reason that Herbalists and Physicians cannot co-exist in harmony. I believe the trend toward nurse practioners and physician's assistants is an indication of this potential. I am fortunate to know several local doctors, all older and reputable, who have high regard for my own work and have shared information with me about the connections between herbs and pharmaceuticals. It was still very recently a part of medical training (herbal uses being an essential part of the medical student's learning) well into the twentieth century. Only recently has this been abandoned, left to those of us who regard the Herbalist as an essential person for the survival of humanity.

It is somewhat radical in nature, this profession, for we are healers without legal license to practise, and needs dictate that we approach our work as holistic healers advising preventative treatment. Diagnosis has become very complex, as has the nature of disease. Although certain herbs may have been used to treat infectious diseases in the past, this does not mean that they are totally effective today, for modern society has bred new and complicated viral plagues resistant to herbs and even existing pharmaceuticals. Many of the modern diseases require modern methods and taking chances can lead to serious complications. Human life is very precious and the Herbalist must never overstep the boundaries of caution. Should a death result from improper herbal treatment, there could well be an uproar from the general public and we could all be labeled as 'quacks', for the press is very quick to react.

Our motivation must be through love, and those who desire to practise as Herbalists are advised to pursue along with their studies, an 'accepted' profession such as medicine or chiropractics. It may not be an ideal situation for us, but it is workable, and as beings in a society, we must live with those laws. There is a strong need for us to evolve a profession of our own in order that those of us who become adept in our fields can practise herbal medicine. But to do so involves such ethical questions as licensing, evaluation of ability and the like. We could well turn into another system such as the A.M.A., and the herbal profession attracts few who enjoy being part of large bureaucracies.

I feel that our most important work today is not in healing but in collecting all the information we have at hand and seeing that it is preserved for the future generations. We have the advantage of the publishers; knowledge we put in print has a high chance for survival into the future. The prospect of herbalist as recognized practitioner is unlikely in our lifetime, yet our work is still geared to those generations of life which will come into the future ages. We must learn our materials well and also do our own, personal work to stimulate interest and acceptance. This book is my own contribution towards that work.

THE TRADITIONAL HERBALIST

By the title Traditional Herbalist, I refer to those studies which encompass the tradition established by Hippocrates, the founder of modern medicine. In studies, this includes the working with remedial herbs and also the use of astrological prognosis. This is not a look merely at 'the way things were', for it is a continually growing art and must be seen as relevant to the future. The personal working herbal of any Herbalist is a collection of notebooks, a library of printed books, card files, and jars and gardens of herbs. It is never complete, for none of us shall live long enough to complete the monumental task it would entail. Thus, the Traditional Herbalist is one who is part of a large connection with others, all working toward common goals.

There are ethics associated with this title which may be found in the appendices as "The Laws of the Traditional Herbalist." They involve keeping an open mind about life itself, and being able to perceive the common threads and patterns woven into all existence. They involve the philosophical perspective of being able to break down the meanings of life into simple symbols found in use since all recorded time. These 'laws' reflect personal attitudes and a commitment that the Herbalist live a life above reproach and have a professional attitude and demeanor which should be found in all physicians, counselors, and priests. It is mandatory that the Herbalist never play God, but see the herbs as a gift of nature to be used when the balance is kept. Someone who would be greedy with nature, only taking and not giving, is not worthy of the title.

The Traditional Herbalist follows in the tradition of Paracelsus, who is discussed later in this book. His philosophy of the physician was one who was "ordained by God," and is not to be lightly taken. We have great work before us, and it requires intense study and total commitment.

11

THE HISTORY OF THIS BOOK

I was fortunate as a child the day my parents moved to a new house. I found among the neighbors of this rural village, the woman next door. She was wonderful, for she was an adult and I a child, and we met and talked and she treated me as an intelligent human. Her name was Yetive, and she knew a great deal about herbs, having more in her garden than I had ever before experienced. Indeed, previous to her, I was largely unaware of the existence of herbs.

She knew much about the native plants of the areas, and in years to come we made expeditions into the woods although we never had adequate opportunity to explore this. I was caught up in my schooling and too separated by distance from the time I left high school. I have never forgotten her, nor she me, although she looks at my magickal training with apprehension. This, also, I feel is part of the life of a Traditional Herbalist.

Years later, I had a summer to spend living in the Northern areas of Minnesota during which time I studied the herbs and wildflowers as they grew, sketching them and watching their cycles. And later in time, a man who was one of my mentors at the time said, "What this community needs is an herbalist." Something inside me stirred and within a day, I felt that the words had been prophetically directed at myself, for it was the answer I had been seeking all my life. I set out to acquire both books and jars of herbs, and in looking for the books was continually frustrated. Grieve's two volumes were filled with information, but there was no index, only hundreds upon hundreds of herbs. Only in careful rereading of her text have I been able to use her books as part of my working herbal. As I went, I was guided by my strong Virgo tendencies and assembled many notebooks and card files with all my research carefully organized and readily available.

I first began teaching herbal healing in 1976-1977. As I grew, my books became better organized and they have become the textbook from which I hold discourse. For many years I wanted to publish my own herbal as my contribution and gift to people for the joy I had reaped from my own work. There was always more research to be done, and at last, the past spring, I realized that the process of collecting information was endless and I needed to stop right where it was and write it all down. Because of this, there are many inconsistencies in spelling, for I am well-read in Anglican and American English and there are many ways to spell names of herbs and words of the profession. You will note that I use both 'herb' and 'herbe' in my text. The former is to indicate remedial use and the latter, the magickal/religious uses available. All of you must give thanks to the editor, for I am not even consistant in this, having been given

12

the freedom by my publisher, to write and write. If I had been intent upon producing a word-perfect manuscript, I would have been years in the working and this book would never have been complete.

HOW TO USE THIS BOOK

There are two main divisions in this book. First is the Remedial Herbal, which is intended as a guide to the study of herbs for healing. It is not a large list of herbs and by no means complete, but it gives the student enough herbs to use as a beginning, covering a wide range of applications. The introduction to this section will give you the means to make the various types of remedies common to the Herbalist: the infusions, poultices, decoctions, et al. I have not attempted to provide specific recipes for they must be tailored to the individual and can, as a result, be misleading. Do not combine herbs unless you have first learned them as individual entities.

Keep a notebook of your own and see it as a tool which grows as you do. Collect your tools and take care of them. Protect, also, your knowledge, for that is your most precious possession.

With each herb, I have provided a Commentary which gives you useful or interesting information about the particular herb. This will also serve your interest in pursuing those traditional Herbalists, and for these comments I turn to Grieve, Culpeper, and Gerard. Turn to their books and read the rest of what they have to say about each herb, and turn to other Herbalists as well. In most cases, there is a good description of the herb and lore is included. Should you want more extensive lore, turn to the Magickal Herbal, for there it is given in more detail.

In addition to the index at the end of this book, I have provided a "Guide for the Remedial Herbal," in order that the student find cross reference for all herbs included in this section. This guide is to show you where to turn to find more information and should never be the basis for your preparations. It is only a guide.

In the appendices is "Remedial Herbal Classification," which will help you in learning the vocabulary of the Herbalist. In some schools of work these words are not consistent, which you will find for yourself as you explore many of the books available. Treat this, also, as a guide rather than exact definitions. Each Herbalist will require a personal feeling and meaning for the terms, being able to use them as a means of determining the appropriate herb for any situation.

There is a second herbal in this book, the Magickal Herbal. Here there is a long list of herbes and their lore. I feel this is perhaps the more significant part of this book, for within the lore can we find the means by which people have tried to define the special energy of each herbe. It is fascinating reading and as resource material, will round out your appreciation of the history we have at hand.

There are many correspondence tables in order that those who study the path of the Traditional Herbalist can easily find planetary associations for various herbs. Again, this is an incomplete list and this work is a continuing process.

AND FINALLY . . .

I should like to make a wish, and it is this: that each of you find some of the same joy in this book, for it has a profound meaning for me. Seeing it come to pass and typing it all out has brought me in touch with many things tucked away in my notes but not in my head. In closing, I should like to share with you these words which come from the Mystery School of the Rowan Tree, which I wrote of our studies:

> Then you shall be taught to be wise,
> so in the fullness of time
> you shall count yourselves
> among those
> who serve the Ancients;
> And you shall grow to love
> the music of the woodlands,
> to dance to the Sound of His Pipes,
> in step with cloven hooves
> & the forest song . . .
> And you shall learn
> the Mystery of Rebirth,
> filling your heart with Her moonlight,
> growing in harmony with the Earth,
> as Her child,
> protective of your Mother . . .
> And you shall grow in wisdom,
> And you shall grow in compassion,
> And in love shall you heal the sick,
> pursuing the arts of healing,
> the lore of the Mother's herbs . . .
> Learning the psychic arts,
> to cure,
> to nurture,
> to help Her children grow . . .
> And in wisdom you shall give counsel,
> knowing the skills of divination,
> seeing how the children

best flow in Universal Harmony,
understanding planetary cycles,
and knowing prophecy . . .

Blessed Be,

Paul V. Beyerl

May your songs fill the night, and your love pour out as the laughing of a stream . . . May your chants be butterflies in the breeze, the cry of the lone bird, the might of thunder, the sigh of a new-born baby . . .

Midsummer, 1982

Minneapolis, Mn.

INTRODUCTION TO THE REMEDIAL HERBAL

THE REMEDIAL HERBALIST

With the growing interest in herbs, one of the primary questions I am asked is how one gets started working with herbs. Aside from an understanding of herbs, which is a continually growing process, there are certain tools and essentials necessary. Of course, the primary ingredient for the Herbalist would be the actual herbs themselves. Those herbs listed in the Remedial Herbal are representative of what we have available. They are selected from well over a thousand choices, based upon availability and usage. When the time comes for you to choose herbs to begin to work with, you must first check your local stores. Look in the health food stores, although those sources tend to be more expensive. For those who live in areas supplied with co-ops, they tend to offer a good supply, usually less expensive although limited in quantity. In the list of resources, you will find a number of mail order sources.

One of the most enjoyable ways of collecting your herbs is to grow your own, which requires some garden or ample window box space. It is also possible to go out into the wild (which in urban areas can include river-front areas, parks, and wildlife preserves) and gather your own. There are quite a few herbs indigenous to North America included in the Remedial Herbal.

In either case, once you have your herbs, you must come up with a means of keeping them readily available and stored so that they retain freshness as long as possible.

HERB STORAGE

You will find, over and over, that all of the books recommend using glass containers for storing your herbs. You may also use a ceramic container that has been well-glazed. Once you begin to collect a variety of herbs, the treasure hunt for containers is on. You will be able to hunt among garage sales, used stores, and attics. An ideal container will have a large opening in order that your measure or scoop will easily fit into the jar and bring out the herb without spilling it all about. The large opening also makes it much easier to fill the jars.

Sunlight is very harmful to herbs unless they are still growing. The rays of the sun, when in direct contact with the herb, will cause a chemical breakdown of many of the constituents in the same manner that they can cause wood or fabric to bleach out. Look for jars that are colored. Not only do they give added protection, but a collection in the Herbalist's closet of blue, green, and brown jars is beautiful to behold. Store all your herb jars out of the sun. If you have a closet to spare, fit it with shelves, but otherwise use a vacant cupboard. If all else fails, set them on shelves and have a heavy curtain which can be draped across the front. Have the shelving located so that it will never be in the way of direct sunlight. Remember that the path of the summer sun is much different from the winter season.

Ask for wonderful containers for presents. You know how difficult it is to answer that question, "what do you want for your birthday?" Well, as a practising Herbalist, it is fair game to ask for containers. There are some beautiful jars in antique shops, and most of us would love a collection of aesthetically pleasing containers. This is one way to accomplish that art. It is much superior to the extensive collection of baby food jars I started out with, thanks to the goodness of my sister and her two little boys.

An ideal container would be well-sealed, and for jars this means a screw-top lid. Those that do not seal this tightly may be used for storing roots, for the root is less likely to suffer chemical breakdown. Dried resins are another form of herb which is less fussy about air contact.

Label all of your jars. Good intentions are of no help when it is impossible to distinguish one chopped, light-green leaf from another. The ability to easily distinguish one from another merely by taste and smell only comes with experience, and I know of no experienced Herbalist that does not use labels. Labels are easily found at any office supply or dime store. For the artistic, design your own and have them copied. These you may attach with tape. A label should give the common name of the herb, and it is good to add the latin name. This is one of the easiest ways to learn the true names. For the Traditional Herbalist, adding the planetary correspondence is of immense value. If you have gathered the herbs yourself, add the date to the label. This you will find very useful in months to come.

THE MORTAR AND PESTLE

Once you have some herbs, perhaps the most fun tool is the mortar and pestle. A question which comes up continually is, "which is which?" The mortar is the cup-shaped tool, and the pestle is the 'pounder-grinder'. To the Traditional Herbalist, they represent a coming together of feminine (the mortar) and masculine (the pestle) which result in healing and creativity.

In nearly all herbal preparations, it is important to grind the leaves, seeds, roots, etc., thoroughly. This is essential in those preparations which will be brought in contact with a solvent such as water or alcohol. As the herb grows, the constituents are stored within the cellular structure of the plant. When the herb is dried, this all contracts, leaving the important elements trapped within the cell membranes. In order to release these constituents from the herb, maximum contact with the solvent solution is essential. Thorough grinding with the mortar and pestle increases the surface area of the herb many-fold, exposing as much of the solid material to the liquid as possible. Thus, when you filter out the residue, you have remaining in the infusion or decoction the maximum amount of volatile oils.

There is also much intrinsic value in the actual labor you put into your preparation. You are mixing your concentration, awareness, and the actual physical energies of the labor with the preparation. This combination of inner energy and physical energy leads to a more profound working relationship of the Herbalist to the work being done and are, in a sense, a magickal alchemy, for the Herbalist is also an ingredient in the remedy.

The best mortar and pestle sets are those made of very durable materials. I prefer the thick, rock-hard ceramic sets used by chemists and pharmacies. They are relatively easy to find for purchase and have an unglazed interior which provides maximum friction for the grinding. A smooth finish in the cup is not of much value, for it inhibits the grinding. There are some sets made of wood, very attractive, and nice to have also. You may find that they have a lacquered finish both in and out and then are of little value, for the varnish will come off into your mixture. Some woods will also retain oils from the herbs and keep the scent and color of previous mixtures. Try a set out without the herb, but work the pestle around and see if it will grind with friction. Some sets are beautiful, particularly handthrown sets of pottery, but are of little value to the Herbalist. However, it is great fun to have a collection of mortar and pestle sets.

Remember that many of the herbs are very tough. It takes a solid pestle to also function as a pounding tool in order to break down many of the dried roots used by the Herbalist. Another suggestion is to purchase some sort of grinder. The crank-type of meat grinder used in kitchens may be very useful, and in our herb shop we have an iron wheat mill, which is also a crank grinder. It is excellent, and can grind any root. Caution must be given in any attempt to grind resins such as frankincense or myrrh. They will not grind. They will gum up your tools. If you need them finely ground, the easiest approach is to purchase them that way.

PHILTRE

Another tool of the Herbalist is a philtre, which is a nicely archaic word for a strainer. If I were to use the word strainer, it brings to mind one of those metal mesh things used in the kitchen. However, this is inappropriate for the Herbalist, for the metal is capable of chemical action with the solution and what you end up with could be quite different indeed.

The philtre is needed to strain out the used plant substance from the herbal solution as is done in the making of an infusion. After all of the desired constituents (or as much as time allows) have been dissolved, it is necessary to use the philtre to separate the solid material from the solution. This leaves us with a nice, clear liquid which is more easily ingested into the person's system.

The best philtre is made of several layers of cloth of a natural, undyed fabric, such as linen or cotton. Cheesecloth or gauze may also be used. A slightly less effective philtre is a bamboo tea strainer, although an amount of finely ground herb will pass through. I know of several herbalists who use a coffee filter and the plastic cone (but only one which has never been used for coffee). Be certain to avoid metal strainers, for they can lead to the formation of hazardous metallic oxides in your preparations.

INFUSER

Another essential tool for the Herbalist, an infuser, might be something as simple as a teapot, or it might be a complex 'steeper'. Simply put, an infuser might be whatever is necessary in order to steep the herbs in boiling water. At the same time, care must be taken in order that the volatile oils do not all escape in the steam. There should be a fairly tight seal so that no steam is allowed to escape.

Again, you are cautioned against the use of metals, for many of the herbal constituents will react when in contact with metal. The ideal container is glazed with enamel. One combination I use most often is a small enamel saucepan with a small plate for a lid. It seals tightly, and is easy to handle. I also have a nice imported one from India which has a small basket which sits in the water, holding the herbs. Although far more pleasing to my aesthetics, it isn't nearly as convenient.

The herbs may be either within a sack of gauze, a basket, or just loose within the container, for they will be filtered in any case. Actually, having them loose is the best, for you can swirl them about, providing maximum contact with the water. Without motion they can

22

easily float to the top and sit inactive doing a poor job of passing the oils into the solution. To avoid problems, have a number of infusers at hand. A good Herbalist has the ability, and frequently the necessity, to make several infusions at the same time.

How long should you leave the solution in the infuser? Of course, this will vary with the type of preparation, but a handy rule of thumb is until the solution is a comfortable drinking temperature, often ten to fifteen minutes.

MEASURE

Many old recipes call for a measure of this and a measure of that. What is a measure? There appears to be no precise or consistent quantitative answer to the question. For most Herbalists, a measure is a constant amount. Thus, the ratio of ingredients to each other is maintained. The ideal measure of an Herbalist is a very personal tool. My personal favorite is a solid silver spoon from the 1933 World's Fair in Chicago. I· have had this for over twenty years and am very comfortable with it. I have others, and they vary in the amount each holds, but the same measure is used throughout a preparation and the ratio is maintained. Choose your measure with care, following all recommendations for material. Always avoid aluminum.

MISCELLANEOUS TOOLS

The closet of the Herbalist is filled with a delightful variety of tools. There should be an ample supply of gauze, adhesive tape, and the expected first aid bandages, etc. For working with oils, one will find an array of little bottles, old perfume bottles of interesting shapes and colors which have been thoroughly cleaned. A couple of eyedroppers are essential, and can be purchased from a druggist. Make certain that the rubber 'squeezer' can be removed for complete cleaning. A glass funnel is another likely tool.

Herbalists who collect their own herbs will have a special hand-trowel or shovel for digging. A special knife is also needed for cutting the stems and branches. For the Traditional Herbalist, it will have a white handle and a single-edged, very-sharp blade. Remember that in any craft, the skilled worker will have one tool for each specific purpose and will not abuse the tool in other uses. A master carpenter would never use his good screwdriver to open a can of paint.

Other things might include string for tying the bunches of herbs together, labels for marking the containers, and an index card file used for recording all preparations, clients, and noteworthy experiences (such as how to locate that mysterious patch of bloodroot which can be found only in May).

All tools must be properly cleaned before their first use. They should be completely washed with pure soap and water and rinsed so none of the residue remains. If you use a funnel, be certain that the bore, or long tube, is clean each time you are done. Store all your tools carefully to avoid breakage. An Herbalist with faulty tools is severely limited.

PREPARATIONS

The true Herbal Craftsperson will meditate as the work is done, and when the herbal mixture is complete, will meditate upon the completed work. Only then is learning continued.

This process can be done by keeping a notebook or card file of all your preparations. It is an essential record to have, for it will record your growth in wisdom and in the ways of the Herbalist. Trust not to memory, not even if your daily tonic includes rosemary tea!!

The water for the following preparations is heated to boiling and then poured over the herb. The herbs are not boiled in the water, for this will cause a breakdown of the vitamins and nutrients, so essential to the healing process.

INFUSION

This is the process of drawing out of the herb all those properties wanted for the healing. The water will act as the fixative, taking the herbal constituents into solution with it. Be aware that not all constituents are water soluble. Some may be removed only by means of alcohol and will be discussed later.

Think of the infusion as a strong tea. Most recipes you will find call for a full ounce of herb to one pint of water. In practise, this is often stronger than needed and most of the Herbalists work with lesser doses for an infusion. You may lessen the amount of herb to a half an ounce, and in the case of minor ailments, you may begin remedial work with even a quarter of an ounce.

Some say you should let the herb steep for half an hour, many say fifteen minutes. The longer I study herbals, the more I realize that there are no perfect formulas for our methods. You will experiment on your own. Some herbs will be extracted in water sooner than others, and in time your intuition is what you must trust.

It is unlikely that the person will be able to drink comfortably any infusion which has not rested for at least fifteen minutes. You may also, however, make strong teas as remedies, and these are what the lesser times and quantities of herb would yield. This is also a recommended approach for the beginner.

DECOCTION

A decoction will require the same tools as for the infusion. The difference is that we are either extracting the constituents from a much more solid herb, such as thick pieces of root which cannot be ground, or because the particular remedy calls for a far stronger dose of constituent.

In the case of a decoction, it is all right to boil the herb. In fact, this is the process. Be certain that the steam will not carry away all your volatile oils. Some recommend one ounce of herb to one pint of water. Some say one part herb to twenty parts of water.

In the making of a decoction, the flavor will be much stronger, and these are the preparations which truly are best when aromatics are added. You might try using three parts herb and one part compatible aromatic.

If you will have more than one ingredient in the decoction, begin with the toughest. First place in the boiling water the toughest roots, then the seeds, then stems. If there are to be leaves, they can be added when the mixture is removed from the heat and allowed to steep. In making a decoction, begin with the water cold.

POULTICE

In applying herbs externally, this is the means for bringing the afflicted part of the body in contact with the herb. This is one of the messier preparations, but essential among the arts of healing.

Tools needed include your infuser, a slotted wooden spoon, or other tool to scoop the wet, gooey herb out of the water, and gauze.

Pour boiling hot water over the herbs, just enough to cover the herbs, or to evenly moisten them. We are not trying to extract any of the constituents but merely to wet all of the herb so that the constituents will remain in the herb. When it is evenly wet, remove it with the strainer, and place it between layers of gauze. This is then directly applied to the afflicted area with the moisture of the herbs passing into the person, carrying their healing virtues.

This is a very simple remedy, even though it might occasionally drip down one's elbow.

OINTMENTS

An ointment is made by macerating an herb in a fixative such as lanolin, vegetable fat or petroleum jelly[2]. This process is accomplished by heating the fixative until it is quite warm and immersing the ground herb into it. Once immersed, the mixture can be heated gently more than once and allowed to cool. All of the constituents which are soluble in fat will be extracted.

Once you feel satisfied that the maximum amount of constituents have been extracted, the entire works can be filtered. They should be warm when put into the philtre, for even that way they will strain quite slowly. Once filtered, the ointment should be placed into a storage container and allowed to cool. This same process may be used to make salves.

WASHES

Occasionally the Remedial Herbal will recommend using an herb as a wash. This is a simple procedure, for you make either a tea or an infusion, but the resulting solution is used externally.

TINCTURE

This is the preparation most recommended when long-term storage is required. A tincture requires alcohol (a 75% grade) which can be safely ingested. Into a jar which can be tightly sealed, place one to four ounces of herb, eight ounces of alcohol, and half as much water. Seal the jar and keep it safely out of the light for two weeks. Each day, at least once, check it, and make sure that you loosen the mass of herb inside the jar by swirling it about. Continue this process for two weeks and the alcohol will extract the constituents without need of heat. This preparation is best begun on the new moon and completed on the full.

MACERATE

This term was used in the description of ointments and is also relevant in the making of oils. It means that the herb is steeped in a fat substance, such as lanolin or other fixatives for ointments and salves, or also applies to the steeping in oil. Herbal oils can be made for massage to use as liniment by using an oil to extract the constituents. Traditionally, olive oil is an excellent fixative, but it usually smells like olive oil and many today prefer pure sunflower or sesame oil as they are odorless and colorless. You may macerate the herb either with heat or with patience. With heat, bring the mixture gently up to hot and then allow it to cool. This can be done several times. When you feel it is ready, then you may philter it all. The other approach is to let it sit, usually for two weeks, but easily for a month. No heat is needed, but it does take patience.

There are many oils which are suitable as fixatives, and you might also choose one for its own herbal properties.

FIXATIVES

At this point I should like to mention fixatives, for they often are a source of confusion for the beginner. There are many available, from the vegetable shortening you use in your kitchen to exotic types, like coconut fat. Older Herbalists once used lard, for that was the most readily available. It is worth a tour of your neighborhood. See what is available. Your grocer will have a variety of oils. Some are pure and highly recommended, others are kitchen brands and less recommended, but are still usable. The grocer carries solid fixatives from lard to shortening. Your druggist is another source. Lanolin is very expensive and is purchased, usually, in a tube. This means you must have another container at hand when the mixture has been made.

HARVESTING

One of the greatest joys of the Herbalist is harvesting. For some, this is an exciting trip to the local herb shop, and bringing home a collection of tiny bags to open and empty into the containers of your herb closet. For others it means waiting for the delivery man to bring your mail order, a box which, when opened, fills the room with the heavenly scents of herbs.

However, at the moment, I am referring to gathering the live plant. As mentioned in Tools, you need a digger and a cutter. Depending upon your aspirations as an Herbalist, you may choose anything from a pair of scissors to a knife with a white bone handle, used only for the cutting of herbs. The latter is highly desirable, and those who possess such a tool would agree.

There are many myths and legends in the gathering of herbs. For the Traditional Herbalist, all the proper magickal etiquette would be observed. It is most recommended that everyone aspiring to be an Herbalist, even if not interested in magick, go out sometime and try gathering herbs in the appropriate manner (discussed later in this book.) It is a very interesting process, and only then can the individual truly judge the centuries-old process.

In any case, the following suggestions are to be taken. Most Herbalists will tell you to gather your herbs in the morning. Wait until the sun has dried the morning dew, for moisture on the herbs increases the chance of mold forming, and then all effort has been lost. If at all possible, avoid rainy seasons, but if your weather is bad all year, then need, not reason, must determine the season.

Many will suggest phases of the moon. One of the most workable suggestions is to gather those herbs used to remove disease (antiseptics, astringents, expectorants, for example) during the waning moon, which means from full to new moon when it is increasingly more visible in the mornings. Collect those herbs which bring health (tonics, stimulants, and the like) during the waxing moon, when it grows to full. Obviously, some herbs serve both purposes, and the adept Herbalist would collect comfrey as an expectorant beneath the waning cycle and the comfrey for tonic during the waxing moon. This also requires two containers appropriately labeled.

If you are gathering the flowers, they are best taken when they have just opened, still fresh and vital. This, of course, may mean that the lunar cycle must be disregarded.[3] Flowers decrease in value when they are past their prime.

Bark would be best taken in the spring or in the autumn. Make certain that the shrub or tree is mature enough to withstand the collecting and never, never take an amount that brings harm to the plant. Bark will take a long time to completely dry.

Roots may be gathered when the plant passes into its dormancy. Sometimes this is not practical, and in the case of herbs grown for their root, you may gather them when it is appropriate in your gardening. If you are gathering them in the wild, do so only as one would thin a crop, always leaving enough so that your harvest will not be felt the following year.

A book for the identification of wildflowers is most helpful when gathering in the wild as it aids in finding herbs as they grow in your own area. Annuals may be collected all the way to the ground. If the roots are desired, remove the entire plant. Biennials may be gathered, leaving at least half of the stem the first year. Enough must be left to replenish the root and give it nourishment. Perennials may be taken depending upon the amount growing. Never cut them to the ground, for this often endangers the root.

Gather the seeds only when they are ripe and mature, for then they will contain the maximum amount of constituent.

One rule which is essential to the Herbalist is to leave behind some small gift for the Earth whenever your harvest Her herbs. A small sea shell is an example of a wonderful gift. It may be buried in the soil if a root has been dug, or left in the patch to show that your heart understands the laws of conservation. The Traditional Herbalist has at least one container filled with little cockle shells and things which will thank the Earth for her bounty. Never, never take more than you will use in the coming year, for you may return each year when the harvest is properly done. Should you need more, then you must turn gardener and work to propagate and develop the patch and in the meantime purchase commercially the herbs for the rest of your need.

HERB DRYING

There is nothing more pleasing to the Herbalist than to walk into a room and find bunches of herbs suspended from the ceiling, hanging and drying, filling the air with a light, clean scent. There is something very special about gathering your own herbs, and in some schools of thought the process of gathering becomes a very serious ritual in the meaning of life.

The ideal place to dry your herbs is a dark, very dry and well ventilated room. Depending upon the structure of the species of herb, it will take anywhere from several days to many weeks for the herb to be completely dry. If you think your plants have dried, remove a leaf and crush it between your fingers which will quickly show you whether it is dry or not. Thicker parts of the herb will take considerably longer, even a year or more for heavier roots. If you haven't the time, slice the roots first lengthwise, and then they will dry faster.

The maximum temperature is about 93 degrees Fahrenheit (about 35 Celsius). Temperatures above that level will cause a breakdown of constituents. There are some sources, including Culpeper, that suggest drying your herbs in the sun, but this is very hazardous to the constituents and not at all wise. The only cases in which this is suggested is for certain magickal uses which require special forms of gathering.

Older herbals often picture colonial kitchens with wonderful bunches of herbs hanging about the kitchen. In those days the kitchen was warm, dry, and had very little sunlight entering it. This also served, in part, as a deterent for insects, for tansy and other herbs were common and discouraged flies and other insects from hanging around.

If you need to dry seeds, do it in a paper bag pricked with a pin, for they also need ventilation. A bag made of cheesecloth is another means.

In drying your herbs, do remember the temperature requirements. Many think instinctively that an attic is ideal for it is warm and dry and provides an out-of-the-way space. These become too hot, however, and dried green leaves with no medicinal value are worth little to the Herbalist.

HERBALS

Every Herbalist worth his or her healing abilities has an herbal. I am not referring to the type (including this) that you purchase in a store, but one of your own making. Each of us learns from our own experience. Obviously, I am unable to present a perfectly complete herbal. Mrs. Grieve has recorded in her two volumes around eight hundred herbs, and to attempt to surpass that would prove unnecessary. In the Remedial Herbal of this book I present less than a hundred herbs, but they are seen as a starting place from which you expand your own knowledge and collect those pieces of information and lore relevant to your personal work.

The herbal of the Herbalist may include one or more notebooks, a couple of card files, and pictures, charts, and scraps of paper kept and saved. This book I am writing for you is the result of seven notebooks, four card files and countless other references.

In the beginning, I most strongly suggest acquiring a copy of Grieve's (more information given in the bibliography). With her excellent book you can find nearly any herb in use about fifty years ago. Most of the herbs we work with have been in use for many hundreds of years, some for even thousands. Another excellent source is Culpeper and between the two you have an excellent historical perspective which in itself provides immense value. If you can afford it, Gerard's book is in print through Dover, and is like a wandering through wonderland for the Herbalist. Our knowledge in the arts of healing is first drawn from those who have gone before, and then from our own experience. In the case of this book, as you continue through its pages, you will see how those many sources led to varied spelling, a combination of Anglican and American, for in the multitude of herbals we find both, and many other variations.

ADVICE

Before you continue, and before you begin your journey into the world of herbs, I should like to caution you. In many areas practising as an Herbalist may be illegal, perceived as practising medicine without a license. Never, never overstep your bounds. Never do more in the beginning than work to ease the discomforts of colds, influenza, and the like.

The realm of diagnosis is not necessarily that of the herbalist. It is very unwise to attempt to diagnose an illness. Always recommend that your patients see a doctor. Then an excellent approach is that they supplement their medication with the herbal preparations. In those situations, it is often found that recovery of health is very quick. Work with your herbs to prevent illness.

Every Herbalist must have a thermometer at hand. Learn how to read it, for any changes in body temperature must be watched. Do not rely on your sense of touch, for that is comparative and unreliable. Fever is tricky, for it is the body's way of waging war against bacteria. Germs cannot survive a high temperature, and the increase in body heat is one means of trying to kill them off during a crisis. Fever also has unpleasant side effects such as thirst, constipation, and when climbing unchecked may cause brain damage and death.

Health is a most serious matter. Never play doctor. Do promote health, and do love the joys of herbs. They do heal, and as you grow in wisdom, so shall you grow in their use.

A GUIDE FOR THE
REMEDIAL HERBAL

A GUIDE FOR THE
REMEDIAL HERBAL

ABDOMINAL PAIN   peppermint

ABORTIFACIENT   bay laurel (berries), cohosh (large doses)

ABSCESSES   chamomile (facial), chickweed, comfrey, cubebs (prostrate), elm (slippery)

ACNE   agrimony, chamomile, cleavers, dandelion, elder, lavender, mistletoe berries

AGING   slippery elm

ALCOHOLISM   angelica, cayenne, ginger (alcoholic gastritis)

ALIMENTARY CANAL   marshmallow, peppermint (esp. for pains)

ALKALOID   a clear, chemically complex organic base, usually a mixture of nitrogen and oxygen

ALTERATIVE   aloe, betony (wood), burdock, cleavers, clover, cohosh (black), elecampagne, fireweed, golden seal, marshmallow, mountain grape, red clover

ANAESTHETIC   (see anesthetic)

ANALGESIC   alleviates pain without loss of consciousness, similar to anodyne

ANEMIA   blackberry, marshmallow

ANESTHETIC   clove (oil), kava kava, mandrake (caution), peppermint (oil)

ANEURISM   aconite

ANODYNE   aconite, camphor, chamomile, elder flower, hops, kava kava, lady's slipper, lavender, mandrake, motherwort, peppermint, skunk cabbage, valerian, white willow, witch hazel

ANTHELMINTIC   blue cohosh, elm (slippery), ferns, male fern, St. John's Wort, tansy, wormwood

ANTIBACTERIAL   see antiseptic; sage, uva ursi

ANTIBILIOUS   mayapple

ANTIBIOTIC   (see antiseptic), aloe

ANTIEMETIC   (see nausea), (see stomachic), cinnamon

ANTIPERIODIC   white willow

ANTIPYRETIC   (see febrifuge), fenugreek, pomegranate (rind)

ANTISEPTIC   anise (oil), aloe, avens, basil, benzoin, camphor
(mildly), chamomile, cinnamon (oil), clove (oil),
elecampagne (excellent), eucalyptus (powerful), garlic
(used extensively; use the raw juice), kava kava, onion,
pennyroyal, peppermint (oil), sage, skunk cabbage,
thyme

ANTISPASMODIC   blue cohosh, catnip, chamomile, clover, cramp
bark, cumin, fireweed, lobelia, mistletoe, motherwort,
pennyroyal, peppermint, red clover, rue, skunk cabbage,
thyme, valerian, verbena

APERIENT   cleavers, dandelion, dock, elder flower, feverfew,
golden seal, parsley (root)

APHRODISIAC   damiana, kava kava

APPETITE   chamomile (mix with ginger), blessed thistle, hops,
mints, mountain grape, rosemary, tansy

AROMATIC   allspice, anise, basil, betony (wood), caraway, clove,
dill, eucalyptus, fennel, golden rod, lavender, lovage,
mugwort, peppermint, sage, St. John's Wort, wintergreen, yarrow

ARTERIES   foxglove

ARTERIOSCLEROSIS   foxglove, mistletoe

ARTHRITIS   "Mary Cook's remedy:[4] 2 handfuls mullein leaves, steep
½ hour and strain; add 1 tbsp. mayapple root and ½ cup
Virginia snake root; heat ½ hour without boiling.
Use 1 quart water. Take 1 tbsp. daily," aloe, bayberry,
comfrey, cramp bark, garlic, hops, kava kava, sage,
skunk cabbage, tansy, thyme

ASTHMA   anise, asafoetida, bloodroot, coltsfoot, comfrey, feverfew, heart's ease, skunk cabbage, elder bark,
elecampagne, garlic, horehound, hyssop, lobelia
verbena

ASTRINGENT   agrimony, alum root, avens, bayberry, blackberry,
celandine, chamomile, cinnamon, cinquefoil, cleavers,
cohosh (black), comfrey, dock, elder flowers & leaves,
elecampagne, eyebright, fireweed, golden rod, golden
seal, ground ivy, hawthorn, horsetail, ivy, marigold,
mullein, myrrh, nettles, plaintain, pomegrante (rind),
raspberry, rosemary, sage, St. John's Wort, self heal,

shepherd's purse, uva ursi, verbena, white willow, wintergreen, witch hazel, yarrow

BACK TROUBLE   agrimony in vinegar

BALDNESS   yarrow

BEARBERRY   (see uva ursi)

BED WETTING   kava kava, St. John's Wort

BLADDER & INFECTIONS THEREOF   burdock, dandelion, ground ivy, irish moss, St. John's Wort, uva ursi

BLEEDING   (see astringent, haemorrhage, haemostat, styptic), avens, cleavers, comfrey, fireweed, nettles, sage, St. John's Wort, shepherd's purse, witch hazel (internal), yarrow

BLOOD   agrimony, angelica, betony (wood), burdock (one of the best purifiers), cleavers, hops, sage

BLOOD PRESSURE   bay laurel, bloodroot (lowers it), foxglove (increases it), mistletoe, tansy (for high blood pressure)

BOILS   burdock, dandelion, fenugreek, hops, slippery elm

BOWELS   (see aperient, cathartic, laxative), witch hazel

BREAST FEEDING   blessed thistle

BRONCHIAL TUBES   (see expectorant)

BRONCHITIS   angelica, anise, asafoetida, benzoin, bloodroot, clove, clover, coltsfoot (smoking herb), camphor, cubebs, elecampagne, elm (slippery), eucalyptus (use the vapors), feverfew, garlic, golden seal, lavender, lobelia (caution), marshmallow, orange peel, mullein, red clover, rue (make a compress for chest, may mix this with mustard), horehound, verbena

BRONCHORRHOEA   myrrh

BRUISES   (see vulnerary), burdock, comfrey (poultice), golden rod, lobelia (tincture), marjoram, marshmallow, thyme, wolfbane (arnica, not aconite)

BURNS   aloe, burdock, cleavers, comfrey, elm (slippery), plantain (fresh if possible), sage (fresh)

CALCIUM   coltsfoot, comfrey, dandelion

CANCER   barley (eaten regularly), bloodroot (caution), celandine (greater), cleavers, dock, poke (good for uterine and breast cancers), red clover (esp. for skin cancers), spurge

CARDIAC   aconite (for cardiac arrest), balm, bloodroot (caution), camphor, cramp bark, elder bark, elm (slippery; may be mixed with bugleweed), eucalyptus (stimulant), foxglove (caution), hawthorn, heart's ease, hops, horsetail, kava kava, lily of the valley (caution), marigold, mistletoe (strengthens pulse), rosemary (calms irregularities, makes a good tonic), skunk cabbage, tansy

CARMINATIVE   angelica, anise, balm, basil, caraway, catnip, cinnamon, clove (a good choice), cubebs, cumin, dill, fennel, feverfew, ginger, hyssop, lavender, lovage, myrrh, pennyroyal, parsley, peppermint, rosemary, sage, tansy, thyme, valerian

CATARRH   inflammation of mucuous membranes; often requires expectorant herbs

CATHARTIC   (see laxative, purgative, bowels. This is often drastic in action), fireweed, mayapple, spurge, unicorn root

CATHARTIC EXPECTORANT   bloodroot

CHILDBIRTH   (see labor), motherwort

CHILDREN   dill (makes a good fixative for most medications)

CHILLS   catnip, cayenne, bayberry, pennyroyal, peppermint, rosehips, wintergreen

CHLORIDE   dandelion

CHOLERA   peppermint

CIRCULATION   camphor (stimulant), foxglove, mistletoe, nettles

COLD SORES   cleavers

COLDS   angelica, anise, avens, bayberry, benzoin, boneset, catnip, cayenne, cleavers, coltsfoot, comfrey, elder blossoms (served hot with peppermint), elecampagne, horehound, hyssop, liquorice, mugwort (especially at the onset), nettles, onion, orange, pennyroyal, pepper-mint (for less severe cases), rosemary, rose hips, sage, thyme, yarrow

COLIC   pains in abdomen or bowels due to obstruction (e.g. constipation or toxemia), angelica, anise, asafoetida, catnip, chamomile, ginger, peppermint, rosemary, rue, unicorn root, avens

COLITIS   avens, elm(slippery), golden seal, mullein, witch hazel, wormwood

COMPLEXION   elder flowers, nettles

CONGESTION   (see expectorant), balm, elm (slippery), elecampagne, feverfew, marshmallow

CONSTIPATION   (see demulcent, emollient, laxative, aperient, et al), chickweed (decoction), dandelion (make a broth of the root), elm (slippery, an enema is the best treatment), sage

38

CONSUMPTION   elecampagne, elm (slippery), horehound, liquorice, nettles, St. John's Wort, comfrey

CONTAGION   angelica (to prevent the spread of disease, burn as incense in the room)

CONVULSIONS   (see antispasmodic), chamomile, cramp bark, mistletoe, valerian

COPPER   chickweed, dandelion

CORNS   spurge (with caution)

COSMETIC   aloe (see skin)

COUGH   agrimony, angelica, anise, coltsfoot, comfrey, cramp bark, dock, elm (slippery), elecampagne, garlic, ground ivy, horehound, liquorice, marshmallow, rue, red clover, thyme

CRAMPS   (see antispasmodic), cramp bark, peppermint (especially for those of the stomach), wintergreen

CROUP   aconite, bloodroot, eucalyptus (external use only), marshmallow, rue

CYSTITIS   cubebs, uva ursi

DANDRUFF   fenugreek, marshmallow (use as a wash for the scalp), rosemary (combine with borax and use cold as a rinse)

DELIRIUM TREMENS   chamomile, hops, mistletoe, sage

DEMULCENT   aloe, barley, chickweed, coltsfoot, comfrey, elm (slippery), ferns, Irish moss, heart's ease, liquorice, marshmallow

DEOBSTRUENT   plantain

DEPRESSION   tansy

DIAPHORETIC   angelica, balm, blue cohosh, boneset (especially when served warm in an infusion), burdock, catnip, celandine (greater), elder leaf, elecampagne, garlic, ground ivy, hyssop, lady's slipper, lobelia (use only with caution), marigold, motherwort, mugwort, pennyroyal, rosemary, skunk cabbage, tansy (especially for low fevers), verbena, yarrow

DIARRHEA   agrimony, avens, bayberry, blackberry, camphor, dock, chamomile (as a tincture for children), cinquefoil, comfrey, ginger, mullein, St. John's Wort, shepherd's purse, pomegranate (rind), white willow bark

DIGESTION   (see carminative, stomachic), angelica, boneset, burdock (tonic for chronic ailments), caraway, chamomile (especially with ginger), clove, fennel, hops, wormwood (in light doses for debilitated cases)

DIGITALIS   see foxglove

DIPTHERIA   lobelia

DIURETIC   agrimony, benzoin, blue cohosh, burdock, celandine
(greater), chamomile, cleavers, dandelion, damiana,
dog's grass, elder bark, elecampagne, elm (slippery),
foxglove (this is quite strong for most cases), garlic,
golden rod, ground ivy, hawthorn, hops, horehound,
ivy, lady's slipper, lily of the valley, lovage, mugwort,
onion, parsely, plantain, pomegranate, shepherd's
purse, uva ursi, valerian, wintergreen

DOUCHE, VAGINAL   marshmallow

DROPSY   blue cohosh, garlic, hawthorn, mayapple

DRUNKENESS   cayenne

DYSENTARY   avens, bayberry, blackberry, bloodroot, comfrey,
marshmallow, St. John's Wort

DYSPEPSIA   (impaired indigestion) sage, white willow

EARACHE   bay laurel (use the oil), chamomile (steep the whole herb)

ECZEMA   (a standard mixture is equal parts of burdock, marshmallow, and yarrow), bloodroot, burdock, celandine
(greater), dandelion, heart's ease, horehound, marigold,
mountain grape

ELDERLY   (see also aging), boneset (used for trouble with digestion),
chamomile (use as a digestive tonic), slippery elm (use to
maintain regularity)

EMESIS   clove

EMETIC   bayberry, bay laurel, blessed thistle (use as a standard for
emergencies), bloodroot, boneset (in large quantities),
chamomile, elder bark, fireweed, heart's ease,
mandrake, mayapple, poke, surge (this can be
dangerous), unicorn root (fresh)

EMMENAGOGUE   angelica, bay laurel, blessed thistle, bloodroot,
blue cohosh, catnip (best if you use the fresh juice),
chamomile, elm (slippery), feverfew, golden seal, horsetail, lady's slipper (use with extreme care), marjoram,
marshmallow, mistletoe, motherwort, mugwort, myrrh,
pennyroyal, peppermint, rue, sage, tansy (this is
excellent and safe), verbena, wintergreen

EMMOLIENT   barley, comfrey, elder leaf and bark, elm (slippery),
heart's ease, fenugreek, Irish moss, liquorice,
marshmallow, mullein

EMPHYSEMA   angelica, mullein

ENEMA   elm (slippery)

EPILEPSY   blue cohosh, garlic, heart's ease, lobelia
             (use with extreme care), marigold, mistletoe, mugwort,
             valerian

EXPECTORANT   agrimony, angelica, anise, benzoin, bloodroot,
             barley, blue cohosh, clove (oil), coltsfoot, comfrey,
             elder flower & leaf, elecampange, elm (slippery), ferns,
             feverfew, garlic, heart's ease, horehound, hyssop, lobelia
             (caution), myrrh (only if there is no fever), St. John's
             Wort, sage, skunk cabbage, thyme.

EYES   agrimony, chickweed, elder flowers, eyebright (this is
             often mixed with golden seal), golden seal

FASTING   fennel (makes the process feel better), horehound
             (used for cleansing during the fast)

FATIGUE   fennel, lavender (use the oil in a bath)

FEBRIFUGE   avens, balm, boneset (will taste more tolerable if mixed
             with sage), cinquefoil, elder flower, fenugreek, sage,
             verbena, wormwood

FEVERS   (see diaphoretic, febrifuge, sudorific) aconite
             (recommended for fevers accompanying a very severe
             cold, but must be used with caution), angelica, avens,
             balm, blessed thistle, boneset (this is excellent), catnip,
             (good in all cases, and excellent for children), cinquefoil,
             elder (primarily the flowers), fenugreek, lovage,
             marigold, motherwort (especially when fever-induced
             delirium is present), pomegranate (rind), yarrow

FIXATIVE   elder flowers (especially for burning oils which cannot
             be consumed internally)

FLATULENCE   (one of the 'nicer' names for intestinal gases)
             (see carminative, stomachic) allspice, angelica, anise,
             caraway, cinnamon, clove, fennel, peppermint, unicorn
             root, wormwood

FLEAS   pennyroyal, fennel

FOMENTATION   (an application of both heat and moisture, usually
             to reduce pain, swelling, and inflammation) comfrey,
             blessed thistle

FOOD POISONING   blessed thistle (to induce vomiting)

FRACTURES   comfrey

FRECKLES   elder flowers (is said to lighten them)

FUNGUS GROWTHS   bloodroot

GALLSTONES   celandine (greater)

GALL BLADDER   dandelion

GANGRENE   elm (slippery, mix with wormwood and powdered charcoal, and apply externally)

GARGLE   eucalyptus (makes an excellent antiseptic), lavender, myrrh (good for most oral problems), sage (best for bleeding)

GASTRIC TROUBLE   elm (slippery), mayapple

GENITO-URINARY TRACT   kava kava

GERMICIDE   (see antiseptic, antibacterial), clove, lavender

GLANDS, SWOLLEN   elm (slippery)

GOITRE   nettles

GONORRHEA   cubebs (taken in capsule form after the first state of the most active symptoms have appeared), kava kava

GOUT   chamomile (especially when mixed with ginger), kava kava, tansy

GUMS   dock (for bleeding), sage (one of the best for bleeding), pennyroyal (for infections)

HAEMORRHAGE   St. John's Wort (immediately contact a doctor), shepherd's purse (considered good, but also contact a doctor)

HAEMORRHAGE, INTERNAL   agrimony, cinnamon (especially of the womb), comfrey (use a decoction full strength for lungs, stomach, bowels; mix with witch hazel), mistletoe, shepherd's purse. This is a serious condition, and improper treatment by an Herbalist may result in a loss of the patient. Always call an Emergency Squad, doctor, or ambulance immediately, and treat the patient herbally as you are waiting.

HAEMOSTAT   (see styptic; used to stop bleeding; some consider haemostats less strong than styptics, but others see them as interchangeable terms), marigold, mistletoe, nettles, sage, shepherd's purse, St. John's Wort, white willow, yarrow

HAEMORRHOIDS   comfrey, cubebs, celandine (lesser; this is perhaps one of the most reknown herbs for this condition; make a lotion and apply directly), chickweed (will cool and comfort), mullein, verbena, yarrow (use this in those cases involving bleeding; use at decoction strength)

HAIR   nettles (to stimulate growth), rosemary (to condition and stimulate growth), yarrow (said to prevent baldness)

HAY FEVER   (a mixture of orange peel, tansy & yarrow), eyebright, mullein, yarrow

HEADACHES   anise, basil (tea), betony (wood), catnip (especially for nervous headaches), ground ivy, ivy, lavender, mistletoe (use carefully), marshmallow (for sinus headaches), rosemary, rue (rub the fresh leaves on the temples, or chew them), verbena, white willow (this is excellent)

HEARING   blessed thistle

HEARTBURN   chamomile (especially with ginger), peppermint

HEART FAILURE   aconite (carefully), camphor (to stimulate when caused by severe, infectious fever; use capsules or in an emergency, inject 3-5 grains dissolved in sterile olive oil)

HEART MURMUR   rosemary

HEPATIC   (a mixture of agrimony and boneset is excellent), celandine (greater), dock, dog's grass, ivy, mayapple, St. John's Wort, tansy, verbena

HEPATITIS   agrimony, celandine (greater), dandelion, dock

HERPES   bloodroot, calendula

HOARSENESS   chickweed, garlic, liquorice

HYDRAGOGUE   (used to remove excess water or fluid from the system) mayapple (use with care)

HYSTERIA   blue cohosh, catnip, chamomile, hops, lavender, motherwort, pennyroyal, rue, St. John's Wort, tansy

INDIGESTION   (see digestion, carminative, stomachic)

INFECTION   (see inflammation, antiseptic, antibacterial) ferns (for chest infections), hyssop (use as a dressing for wounds, etc.), mandrake (external use only), pennyroyal

INFLAMMATION   chamomile (use a hot fomentation), chickweed (ointment), hops

INFLUENZA   (indicating the serious influenzas, rather than the light overnight stomach flus, which can be treated with stomachics and antispasmodics) balm, blackberry (especially with loose bowels), blessed thistle (during recovery), boneset (take as a warm tonic every ½ hour), cinquefoil, coltsfoot (if it settles in the chest), cleavers, elder, peppermint (especially when mixed with yarrow, boneset, and elder)

INSANITY   catnip

INSECTS   (see pesticide) anise (especially when mixed with
carbolic and sassafras oils), lavender, plantain, pennyroyal

INTESTINAL INFLAMMATION   chamomile (fomentation), comfrey,
golden seal, marshmallow

IRON   chickweed, comfrey, dandelion, nettles

IRRITANT   (see rubefacient) cayenne, nettles

JAUNDICE   agrimony, burdock, celandine (greater), dandelion,
dock, dog's grass, parsley, St. John's Wort

KIDNEY   (see diuretic) burdock, celandine (greater, especially
for stones), dandelion, hawthorn (for infections), Irish
moss, parsley, pomegranate, tansy, uva ursi, yarrow,
nettles, verbena

KIDNEY STONES   cleavers, celandine (greater), dandelion, dog's
grass, golden rod, horsetail, parsley (root)

LABOR   blue cohosh (use in complications to hasten delivery
if the mother is too ill or exhausted to bring delivery
herself), motherwort, mugwort, peppermint, raspberry,
skunk cabbage

LARYNGITIS   benzoin, blackberry, fireweed, liquorice

LAXATIVE   (see aperient, bowels, cathartic, purgative) boneset,
dock, elder berries, golden seal, mandrake

LEPROSY   frankincense, garlic, myrrh

LEUCORRHOEA   cubebs, kava kava, myrrh

LINIMENT   (macerate the following herbs in oil) cayenne,
chamomile, ivy, peppermint, sage, skunk cabbage,
wintergreen

LIVER   agrimony, boneset, dandelion, dog's grass, golden seal,
hops, mayapple, parsley (root), sage, St. John's Wort,
verbena

LUNGS   (see expectorant, pectoral, pulmonary) angelica (for
congestion), cohosh (black), coltsfoot, comfrey,
elecampagne, elm (slippery), eucalyptus (especially for
infections), horehound, marshmallow, rosemary (smoke
with coltsfoot)

MAGNESIUM   dandelion, peppermint

MEASLES   elder flowers, golden seal, marigold, sage, yarrow

MEMORY   rosemary

MENTAL HEALTH   blessed thistle, sage, rosemary

MENSTRUAL CYCLE   (see emmenagogue), cohosh, feverfew, mugwort, rue, wintergreen

MIGRAINE   rosemary

MISCARRIAGE   unicorn root (for chronic cases)

MOUTH   pennyroyal, sage (both for infections)

MUCOUS   pennyroyal (for internal discharge), wintergreen

MUSCLES   cayenne (use as a liniment)

NARCOTIC   (some of these herbs are dangerous only in quantity, others should not even be approached; all of these need to be studied carefully) bayberry, bay laurel, celandine (greater), lavender, mandrake, mistletoe (especially berries), nutmeg, poke, rue, skunk cabbage, unicorn root

NAUSEA   basil, cloves, betony (wood), chamomile, hops

NERVINE   basil, betony (wood), catnip, chamomile, cramp bark, hops, lady's slipper, lavender, mandrake (with care), mistletoe, motherwort, mugwort, parsley, pennyroyal, red clover, rosemary, rue, St. John's Wort, tansy, verbena

NERVOUS DISORDERS   basil, camphor, catnip, chamomile, cramp bark, hops, lady's slipper, lily of the valley, mistletoe, peppermint, rosemary, rue, sage, valerian, verbena, wormwood

NEURALGIA   chamomile, lavender (oil, used externally), mistletoe, valerian

NIGHTMARES   catnip (collect the flowering tops and make a thick mixture), chamomile (very effecive)

NITROGEN   clover

NOCTURNAL INCONTINENCE   (see bed wetting) kava kava

NOSEBLEED   yarrow

NURSING   blessed thistle (to increase milk flow)

NUTRIENT   elm (slippery), blackberry, coltsfoot, comfrey, dandelion, nettles

NUTRITIVE   (see nutrient) barley, Irish moss

OBESITY   nettle seeds

OPTHALMIA   (herbs which affect the eyes), (see eyes) eyebright, lobelia, golden seal, verbena

ORAL   sage (all purpose for infections)

PAIN   (see anodyne, anesthetic, neuralgia), (sciatica which is

45

	pains in the legs), barley, lady's slipper, motherwort
PALSY	lavender, mistletoe
PARALYSIS	lavender (oil, externally), wolfsbane (arnica)
PECTORAL	anise, benzoin, cinquefoil, clover, coltsfoot, elder flowers and bark, elm (slippery), eucalyptus, eyebright, ferns, feverfew, horehound, hyssop, liquorice, red clover, sage, St. John's Wort
PESTICIDE	elder, fennel, pennyroyal
PHLEGM	(see expectorant), angelica
PILES	(see haemorrhoids)
PLAGUE	blessed thistle, ivy
PLEURISY	angelica, elm (slippery), verbena
PNEUMONIA	aconite
POISONOUS	aconite, bloodroot, bay laurel (in quantities of leaves and berries), celandine (greater), foxglove, mistletoe (berries)
POTASSIUM	coltsfoot, dandelion, peppermint
PREGNANCY	golden seal
PROSTRATE	cubebs (especially for abscesses), pumpkin seeds (these should be steeped overnight, and taken as a tonic)
PSORIASIS	blackberry, burdock, cleavers, fireweed, horehound, marigold, marshmallow, mountain grape
PULMONARY	(see pectoral), aconite, agrimony, angelica, coltsfoot, comfrey, elecampagne, liquorice, marshmallow
PULMONARY COMPLAINTS	hyssop, Irish moss, St. John's Wort
PULSE	aconite, bay laurel, foxglove (normalizes), lily of the valley
PURGATIVE	(see aperient, bowels, cathartic, laxative), aloe, celandine (greater), damiana, elder bark, heart's ease, horehound, mandrake, poke
RASHES	hops, plantain
REFRIGERANT	catnip, chickweed, plantain
RHEUMATISM	aconite, angelica, basil, bayberry, betony (wood), blue cohosh, boneset, comfrey, cramp bark, fireweed, garlic, hops, hyssop, kava kava, lavender, mandrake, poke, sage, tansy, thyme, verbena, wintergreen
RINGWORM	bloodroot
RUBEFACIENT	cayenne, elecampagne (very mild), nettles, rosemary (very mild), rue, thyme, wintergreen
SCALP	rosemary (especially when mixed with borax for

cleansing)

SCARLET FEVER   catnip (mix with saffron), elder flowers

SCIATICA   aconite (expecially when caused by rheumatism), elecampagne, rue (use externally)

SCROFULA   bloodroot, coltsfoot

SCURVY   burdock

SEBORRHEA   agrimony, cinquefoil, elecampagne, burdock

SEDATIVE   chamomile, cohosh (blue), cramp bark, hops, lady's slipper, lobelia, mandrake, parsley, valerian (one of the best), witch hazel

SILICA   comfrey, dandelion

SINUS   (see catarrh), coltsfoot, golden seal, marshmallow

SKIN   agrimony (acne, etc.), anise, benzoin, burdock (good) all-purose remedy), chickweed, cinquefoil, cleavers, dandelion (good astringent lotion), elder flowers, elecampagne, heart's ease, hops, lobelia (use a tincture), marigold, pennyroyal, plantain, self heal

SLEEP   (see sedative), agrimony, anise, clover (red), hops, lady's slipper, rosemary, valerian (one of the best), verbena

SMALLPOX   catnip (mix with saffron), marigold

SMOKER'S COUGH   anise, elecampagne, horehound

SOPORIFIC   (similar to sedative, causes sleep through quieting the nervous system) hops, mandrake

SORES   (see vulnerary) chickweed (use as an ointment), plantain

SPLEEN   dandelion, vervain

SPRAINS   (see vulnerary) comfrey (fomentation), lavender (use oil externally), lobelia, marjoram, marigold, marshmallow, wolfsbane (arnica), tansy (one of the best all-purpose herbs is comfrey, which may be used either internally or externally)

STERILITY   mistletoe (to cure infertility)

STIMULANT   angelica, anise, balm, bayberry, bay laurel, blessed thistle, boneset, catnip, cayenne, cinnamon, clove, cubeb, cumin, damiana, dandelion, dill, elder flowers, elecampagne, eucalyptus, garlic, golden rod, ground ivy, hops, hyssop, kava kava, lily of the valley, lovage, marigold, mistletoe, mountain grape, mugwort, myrrh, nettles, pennyroyal, peppermint, raspberry, rosemary, rue, tansy, valerian, wintergreen, wormwood, yarrow

STOMACHIC   angelica, basil, boneset, catnip, caraway, cinnamon, chamomile, cloves, dill, elm (slippery), golden seal, hops, lovage, myrrh, peppermint, rosemary, rue (small doses), sage, thyme, wormwood

STYPTIC   avens, horsetail, sage, self heal, witch hazel, yarrow

SUDORIFIC   avens, hyssop

SULPHUR   coltsfoot, garlic, Irish moss

SUNBURN   aloe, elder flower

SWELLING   comfrey (fomentation), witch hazel

SYPHILIS   dragon's blood, mountain grape, spurge

TEETH   myrrh (makes a good toothpowder), sage (for bleeding), wintergreen

TENSION   (see nervine)

TETANUS   lobelia

THIRST   liquorice

THROAT   agrimony (gargle when the throat is irritated or has mucous draining through it), anise, avens, bayberry, blackberry, chickweed (when hoarse), cinquefoil (this makes a good gargle), eucalyptus (gargle when in need of an antiseptic), fireweed (for sore throats), hawthorn (good for most sore throats), liquorice, rosemary (can be smoked with coltsfoot), sage (gargle for sore throat)

TONIC   agrimony, aloe, angelica, avens, basil, blackberry, blessed thistle, boneset, burdock, caraway, catnip, cayenne, chamomile, chickweed, cinquefoil, cleavers, clover, coltsfoot, comfrey, damiana, dandelion, dog's grass, elecampagne, eyebright, fenugreek, golden seal, ground ivy, hawthorn, hops, horehound, lily of the valley, mistletoe, motherwort, mountain grape, mugwort, nettles, parsley, peppermint, raspberry, red clover, rosemary, rose hips, sage, self heal, tansy, thyme, uva ursi, verbena, white willow, wintergreen, witch hazel, wormwood, yarrow

TONSILITIS   lobelia, sage

TOOTHACHE   chamomile (use the whole herb), clove (apply the oil to the pained area), lavender (use the oil), sweet marjoram

TUBERCULOSIS   eucalyptus, garlic, mullein

TUMORS   witch hazel

TYPHOID FEVER   elm (slippery), sage

ULCERS   aloe, chickweed, clover, comfrey, elm (slippery), fenugreek, marshmallow, plantain, sage, spurge, verbena, witch hazel. (Remember that there are both internal and external ulcers, and not all herbs are used in both cases.)

URINARY ORGANS   angelica (avoid in cases of diabetes), dandelion (works as a gentle stimulant), dog's grass, ground ivy, kava kava, marshmallow, mistletoe, uva ursi (especially good in cases of inflammation)

URETHRITIS   cubebs, cohosh (blue), dandelion, ground ivy, uva ursi (works upon the inner membranes as an antiseptic)

UTERINE INFLAMMATION   blue cohosh

UTERUS   boneset

VAGINITIS   kava kava

VARICOSE VEINS   witch hazel (external application)

VENEREAL DISEASE   bloodroot (even works to a degree on herpes), damiana, heart's ease

VERTIGO   mistletoe

VITAMINS   blackberry, cayenne (C), coltsfoot (C), comfrey (B12), dandelion (A, E), nettles

VOMITING   (see emetic to induce; antiemetic to stop), basil, cinnamon, mayapple (to induce)

VULNERARY   aloe, agrimony, barley, basil, bay laurel, chamomile, comfrey (poultice), dog's grass, elder, elm (slippery), fenugreek, golden rod, golden seal, ground ivy, hops, horehound, hyssop, ivy, marigold, mullein, plantain, red clover, raspberry, onion, self heal, tansy, thyme, wolfsbane (arnica), yarrow

WARTS   celandine (greater), spurge (use very carefully)

WHOOPING COUGH   blackberry, clover, comfrey, garlic (external), marshmallow, red clover, thyme

WORMS   (see anthelmintic)

WOUNDS   (see vulnerary), aloe, comfrey, elm (slippery), golden seal, marigold, self heal, thyme

HERBS

——— ACONITE ———

. . . signifying corruption, poison, or death, which are the certaine effects of this pernicious plant: for this they use very much in poisons, and when they meane to infect their arrow heads, the more speedily and deadly to dispatch the wilde beasts, which greatly annoy those mountains of the Alpes . . .

— Gerard

The shape of the flower is specially designed to attract and utilize bee visitors, especially the bumble bee. The sepals are purple — purple being specially attractive to bees — and are fancifully shaped, one of them being in the form of a hood.

— Grieve

LORE

Nearly all of the lore associated with Aconite can be traced to its poisonous qualities. Some of the other names this plant is known by will give you an idea of its energies: Wolfsbane is a very common name, for it is said to cure werewolves and kill wolves. It has been called Monkshood because of the curious shape of the flowers. In Greek mythology, Medea used this herb to take vengeance upon Theseus after he had conquered the Amazons. She was known for her use of herbs, magick and the ability to kill. Aconite has other associations with forms of witchcraft.

Aconite is an intriguing plant to the Herbalist. Gerard devotes many pages to some of the varieties . . . winter, mithridate, yellow, etc. Aconite is one of the herbs we can grow easily in northern climates for it is very hardy, a perennial which endures a rough winter. But it is an herb we must grow with great caution, for the warnings of its poison are very true. It is for this that we find great difficulty in locating this plant, short of finding it, digging it up and bringing it home.

Aconite will grow three or more feet high, with deep, shiny leaves and vivid bunches of flowers.

REMEDIAL

The toxic substance of this herb must be thoroughly understood. The root contains an alkaloid, although the entire plant is usually used. One fiftieth of a grain can kill a small bird in seconds, and even but half of that amount will cause a sensation upon your skin which can be felt throughout a day. With minute amounts causing such intense reaction, it would be essential to know the exact amounts which exist in the grown herb. With any poisonous herb, realize that weather and soil conditions can cause fluctuation in the constituents. Unless the gardener were greatly skilled and grew this herb where it would be well- protected, I would not recommend even growing it as part of a collection. Even for those who grow it, strong caution should be given against using it.

When taken internally, Aconite will lower both the rate and strength of the pulse. It is used to treat serious problems with pneumonia, feverish colds, and croup. It has been used as an anodyne for heart conditions, and stronger amounts have been used to bring back the pulse in cardiac arrest. Externally it is used primarily also as an anodyne in such problems as rheumatism and deep pains.

- Anodyne, cardiac, pulmonary.

———— AGRIMONY ————

It openeth and cleanseth the liver, helpeth the jaundice, and is very beneficial to the bowels, healing all inward wounds, bruises, hurts and other distempers.

— Culpeper

The decoction of the leaves of Egrimony is good for them that have naughty livers . . .

— Gerard

It belongs to the Rose order of plants, and its slender spikes of yellow flowers, which are in bloom from June to early September, and the singularly beautiful form of its much-cut-into leaves, make it one of the most graceful of our smaller herbs.

— Grieve

54

Agrimony is a perennial, and its bunches of leaves grow from a deep and tough root. It sends a tall column of flowers which has, in the past, led to the name of Church Steeples. It is soft and downy to the touch, actually more pleasant to the finger than it is to the tongue. There are many references to it historically, it even being one of the plants highly respected by the medical community. Due to its flavor, it has no use in the kitchen.

LORE

Most of the lore associated with Agrimony is in the property of aiding sleep. There are several approaches, one being an herbal pillow, and Grieve reports a curious poem which says that it will put a person to sleep, and sleep of such a nature that it will remain until the Agrimony is removed. There is no basis for belief in this poem, yet there appears to be a large number of persons who use it for sleep (not the comatose variety as in the poem) and find it to work refreshingly well. It is also known as a Counter-magick Herbe.

REMEDIAL

Agrimony holds high esteem as an herb of healing powers. Even its name, agrimonia eupatoria, may be translated as argemone, which means it may heal the eyes, and eupatora, based upon the legendary king and healer Eupator. It is one of the herbs which contains tannin, and this volatile oil is a large part of its healing virtues.

Internal uses include drinking it to aid in the discomfort of a bothersome cough, for which purpose it should be flavored with honey to make it palatable. It may also be used as a gargle for a sore throat. Agrimony is also taken internally to heal the liver. Its primary use today is in cases of hepatitis and the resulting jaundice. Although it is said to cure jaundice, it would appear that it primarily assists the liver in healing itself, so that the jaundiced condition would improve.

Externally, a wash of agrimony is very useful in treating oily skin and the problems of acne. The astringent properties of the tannic acid are also considered useful in strong poultice mixtures for drawing out venomous insect bites and inflamed sores.

- Hepatic, expectorant, astringent.

——— ALOE ———

Hearbe Alloe hath leaves like those of Sea Onion, very long, broad, smooth, thick, bending backwards, notched in the edges, set with certaine little blunt prickles, full of tough and clammie juice like the leaves of the Houseleeke.

— Gerard

The true Aloe is in flower during the greater part of the year and is not to be confounded with another plant, the Agave or American Aloe . . . which is remarkable for the long interval between its periods of flowering.

— Grieve

The Aloe is very distinctive and with its current popularity, easy to recognize. The leaves appear to grow one from the other in alternate directions, sometimes slowly spiraling upwards. They are in two shades of green, the lighter appearing in mottled spots. The prickles are not hazardous and the plant feels cooling to the touch. They adapt easily to growing conditions, accepting a variety of indoor temperatures and light variables.

LORE

Grieve reports various uses of the Aloe as a Religious Herbe, particularly in Eastern countries. The Aloe has strong associations with Mohammed, being taken to his shrine. It is then hung over the doorway of the traveler upon returning home, for it will bring protection. It is also perceived as being a Funereal Herbe, being planted upon graves to bring peace until the resurrection. These customs may well be due to the unusual character of the this succulent which can survive with little water and in the most difficult of conditions.

Aloes also have a magickal reputation of bringing success, and have even been used in some places as an herb which will bring love to the lonely.

REMEDIAL

Aloes are known for their juice, or gel. This valuable healing lotion has been in use since ancient times, mention being made even in the bible: (Nicodemus brings with him a mixture of myrrh and aloe). The gel is useful for most needs of external healing, and its soothing properties have also brought it into use as a cosmetic.

Aloes have been used in the treatment of arthritic pain, for skin irritations such as sunburn, chaffing, or roughness. It has been used as a hair shampoo, alone with water. The juice is mildly antibiotic, astringent, anodyne, and a tonic for healing. Aloe is currently being explored in the treatment of ulcers, both external and internal. They are commonly kept growing in or near a kitchen for the treatment of cuts and burns. The simplest manner of treatment is to break off a small piece of the leaf and smooth the oozing gel upon the troubled area of skin. For internal use, a commercial preparation of dried aloe is recommended.

- Demulcent, stimulating purgative, tonic.

———— ANGELICA ————

. . . others more moderate called it Angelica, because of its angelical virtues, and that name it retains still, and all nations follow it so near as their dialect will permit.

— Culpeper

The stems are stout, fluted, 4 to 6 feet high and hollow. The foliage is bold and pleasing, the leaves are on long, stout, hollow footstalks, often 3 feet in length, reddish purple at the much dilated, clasping bases; the blades, of a bright green colour, are much cut into, being composed of numerous small leaflets . . .

— Grieve

Related to parsley, Angelica is neither an annual nor a perennial, for it takes, instead, several years to grow from seed into a mature, flowering plant. The flowers are spectacular, big spherical clusters, made up of small flowerlets all coming out from a central point on the stalk. They reach up tall and regal in the garden.

The root of the Angelica is much used as a flavoring ingredient in candies and baked goods. It has a wonderfully singular taste, somewhat pungent; more pungent are the seeds which are used in the making of vermouth and other alcoholic beverages.

LORE

Angelica has a history steeped in lore, religious use, and magickal practises. Grieve gives us a large amount of information about this herb. One of the more charming customs is in Eastern Europe, where Angelica is carried into the markets accompanied by ancient chants learned in childhood. These verses are so ancient as to be unintelligible, but are passed on orally as melody and syllabic sounds.

Although the lore of Angelica predates Christianity, it quickly became associated with the Annunciation and with St. Michael. It has long been associated with protection from all forms of evil, and was considered a most important herb in the protection against the plague.

REMEDIAL

In all cases should internal use of Angelica be avoided if the person has diabetes, for it contains sugar which will pass into the system.

However, this is a valuable herb for cleansing the lungs. It is very useful in the treatment of colds, persistent coughs, and conditions which cause a buildup of phlegm in the lungs. It has been used to treat chronic bronchitis and to ease problems of emphysema.

Its properties as a diaphoretic make it valuable in feverish conditions, particularly when involved with a severe cold. It has also been much used in the treatment of indigestion and upset stomachs.

• Diaphoretic, expectorant, stimulant, tonic, carminative, pulmonary, emmenagogue.

——— ANISE ———

The stalke of Annise is round and hollow, divided into divers small branches, set with leaves next the ground somewhat broad and round: those that grow higher are more jagged, like those of young parsley, but whiter: on the top of the stalkes do stand 'spokie' rundles or tufts of white floures, and afterward seeds, which hath a pleasant taste as everie one doth know.

— Gerard

It is a native of Egypt, Greece, Crete and Asia Minor and was cultivated by the ancient Egyptians. It was well known to the Greeks, being mentioned by Dioscorides and Pliny and was cultivated in Tuscany in Roman times. In the Middle Ages its cultivation spread to Central Europe.

— Grieve

The smell and flavor of Anise are made singular by the presence of a volatile oil called anethol. Anise is much used in the baking of cookies, and is also used in the making of Anisette, a liqueur flavored with the seed. The plant is best grown from seed, and as it is gentle and delicate, prefers a long season filled with lots of bright sun.

LORE

Anise has had a variety of magickal uses, from that of preserving youthful looks to keeping one safe in pleasant dreams. It was included in wedding cakes by the Romans in order that they could eat lots of cake without acquiring an upset stomach. It is said that inhaling the smoke from it when burnt will stop a headache, and that drinking it before bed will bring restful sleep.

REMEDIAL

Anise Seed is excellent for those hard, dry, raspy coughs in which it is difficult to bring up the phlegm. It can be made into cough drops, a delightful way to ingest Anise and soothe the throat.

Many Herbalists consider Anise an essential ingredient in any remedy for coughs, colds, and the like, as it not only does much good for the throat and lungs, but is also so pleasantly flavored as to be one of the rare herbs which tastes wonderful.

It is also good for calming the stomach, and will calm gas and nausea. An extract of the oil is an excellent antiseptic and can also be included in facial mixtures to improve the condition of the skin.

- Carminative, pectoral, aromatic, antiseptic, stimulant.

———— AVENS ————

The root in the spring-time, steeped in wine, doth give it a delicate flavor and taste, and being drunk fasting every morning, comforteth the heart, and is a good preservative against the plague or any other poison.

— Culpeper

The decoction of avens in wine is commended against cruditie or rawnesse of the stomacke, paine of the Collicke, and the biting of venemous beasts.

— Gerard

It has thin, nearly upright, wiry stems, slightly branched, from 1 to 2 feet in height, of a reddish brown on one side.

— Grieve

It is not much in the way of flowers, there being but one per stem, and is smaller than one would expect. However, the root is used more than the herbaceous part. They are tough and require a considerable amount of drying time for the collector. Other uses of Avens include the flavoring of ales and the placing of roots in linen closets for the pleasant scent and protection from insects and moths.

LORE

Its uses as an Herbe of Protection are reflected in some of the other names for Avens such as 'the Blessed Herb' and 'Herba Benedicta'. It was used to protect the wearer from all forms of negative energy.

As Grieve reports from the *Ortus Sanitatis*, a book printed but one year before Columbus' discovery of North America, "Where the root is in the house, Satan can do nothing and flies from it, wherefore it is blessed before all other herbs, and if a man carries the root about him no venemous beast can harm him."

As did many other herbs, it gained Christian associations. As it grows leaves in three, it became associated with the Trinity, and the five petals of its small flowers are said to symbolize the wounds of Jesus, as do numerous other five-petalled flowers.

Those who observe tradition will collect the roots from the ground at the beginning of Spring.

REMEDIAL

The astringent properties of the root are most useful in the treatment of diarrhea, dysentery, and other conditions leading to loose bowels. It may be used in the treatment of colitis, but only as a temporary measure until the exact cause itself can be corrected.

Avens is also used in the treatment of sore throats and various combinations of colds and fevers. It also is one of those herbs known as a styptic and has great value in its ability to stop bleeding.

- Styptic, astringent, sudorific, tonic, antiseptic, febrifuge.

—— BALM ——

This herb is so well known to be an inhabitant in almost every garden, that I shall not need to give any description thereof, although the virtues thereof, which are many, should not be omitted.

— Culpeper

Bawme is much sowen and set in gardens, and oftentimes it groweth of it selfe in Woods and mountaines, and other wilde places: it is profitably planted in gardens, as Pliny wroteth . . .

— Gerard

The genus 'Melissa' is widely diffused, having representatives in Europe, Middle Asia and North America. The name is from the Greek word signifying 'bee', indicative of the attraction the flowers have for those insects, on account of the honey they produce.

— Grieve

This plant grows knee-high in ideal conditions. The leaves are sometimes confused with those of catnip, although they are more of a

61

light-green in color. The plant may be easily identified by lightly crushing a leaf, for it will give off a fresh, lemon scent. It is sometimes called lemon balm.

LORE

Balm has been used in charms to attract love. It has also been recommended to be placed in one's bath for the same purpose.

REMEDIAL

Balm is well-used in conditions of chest congestion and colds which settle in the lungs. It has also been used in mild cases of influenza as it generates mild warmth and induces perspiration. It is excellent for the treatment of mild feverish conditions. In the middle ages, it had a reputation as a mild stimulant for cardiac conditions, but the introduction of other herbs led to its primary uses as a diaphoretic, carminative and mild stimulant.

- Febrifuge, diaphoretic, stimulant, carminative.

——— BARLEY ———

The continued usefulness hereof hath made all in general so acquainted herewith, that it is altogether needless to describe it . . .

— Culpeper

Barley hath an helme or straw which is shorter and more brittle than that of wheat, and hath more joints; the leaves are broader and rougher; the eare is armed with long, rough, and prickly beards or ailes . . .

— Gerard

Malt is produced from barley by a process of steeping and drying which develop a ferment 'diatase' needed for the production of alcoholic malt liquors, but in the form of Malt Extract it is largely used in medicine.

— Grieve

Medicinally, the part used is the grain with the tough skin removed. In the process, the grain becomes more rounded and takes on a lustrous patina. This product is known as Pearl Barley.

REMEDIAL

Barley has a slight reputation as an herb of healing, as mentioned by Culpeper in the above quotation. It is often combined with other herbs, for it brings to the mixture properties of a nutritive herb, and is very soothing to the internal organs of the body.

It is used in nearly any internal discomfort, and will enhance the ability of the body to pass on waste through the bladder functions. Perhaps the widest use today is for its nutritive properties, making it excellent for the recovering patient.

Barley may be mixed with other herbs to use externally as a poultice, comfrey being one of the best for the treatment of wounds and sores. It has been combined with chamomile in the treatment of pain, either from sores or in joints and muscles.

It was once mixed with poppies to take away pain, although in such form provided merely the medium for the opiate effect of the poppies. Barley itself has no anodyne properties.

- Demulcent, nutritive, expectorant.

——— BASIL ———

This is the herb which all authors are together by the ears about . . .

— Culpeper

Both Bush and Garden Basil are natives of India, from whence it was introduced in 1573 . . .

— Grieve

Both the green and deep purple varieties are proud and shiny. It has many leaves, of the ovate variety, and may grown easily in a small amount of garden space or in a window box. Basil will send up a small thin stalk, reaching to the sky, and this will slowly fill with pale purple flowers which have a very light scent. There are two types of Basil, bush and garden, and either will scent your garden with the pungent aroma of the volatile oil. It is a good herb for the kitchen, useful as a Greene Herbe in salads, soups, eggs, with nearly any red meat, in all tomato sauce, and in general cooking.

LORE

In its original soil, it was revered as a Religious Herbe, sacred to deities of the Hindu faith and interwoven in the everyday life as a Funereal Herbe. Areas of Europe, even though removed from knowledge of each other, all found Basil as a symbol of love. Grieve tells of customs among the Moldavians, the Cretes, and the Italians in which Basil is strongly linked with romance.

Basil is used today as a Magickal Herbe associated with the rites of initiation; with the need for courage in times of great difficulty, and in aiding the soul on its journey to the next place of being. It is of delightful value in bringing compassion to those who share a meal, and is an herb which can bring kitchen magick to the cook.

REMEDIAL

Basil is excellent externally for minor wounds, scratches, abrasions, and bothersome bites and stings. The volatile oil of this herb is very soothing and promotes quick healing.

Basil may also be ingested easily and safely, the infusions of it being excellent to soothe irritated nerves, especially those which lead a tense, out-of-balance stomach. Infusions of Basil have been said to ease the aches and pains of rheumatism.

Basil is known in times past to have been used as a snuff among those plagued with headaches.

- Aromatic, tonic, carminative, anodyne, antiseptic.

——— BAYBERRY ———

The wax was first introduced into medicinal use by Alexandre in 1722. It is removed from the berries by boiling them in water, on the top of which it floats.

— Grieve

This is a shrub found primarily in the Northeastern reaches of North America. It prefers moist soil and is found in thick patches growing near swamps. It is prevalent along Lake Erie, growing from waist-height upwards, sometimes reaching over one's head by a foot or more. It has speckled, green leaves and clusters of little berries.

LORE

Bayberry has been used in folk practise to attract money, either by carrying some of the bark or dried berries as an amulet, or by tucking a dried leaf into one's wallet or purse. Some work the same magick by burning candles made of Bayberry and meditating upon images of plentiful money.

REMEDIAL

Bayberry is very useful in treating diarrhea and dysentery. It is a strong astringent, and should be used in mild doses. There is a slight narcotic property to the wax which is also useful in quelling those disturbances. Because large doses of Bayberry will induce vomiting, these should be avoided.

Bayberry is also useful in the treatment of chills and bad colds for it is also a strong stimulant, bringing a sense of heat and vitality to the body. It is sometimes recommended that Bayberry be combined with cayenne. In a decoction, Bayberry is excellent for treating a sore and infected throat. Externally, Bayberry is macerated to produce an oil from the berries and leaves which is most useful in the treatment of rheumatism, arthritis, and conditions requiring a liniment.

- Stimulant, emetic and astringent.

——— BAY LAUREL ———

The oil takes away the marks of the skin and flesh by bruises, falls, etc. and dissolveth the congealed blood in them.
— Culpeper

It is reported that common drunkards were accustomed to eat in the morning fasting two leaves thereof against drunkennesse.
— Gerard

The Sweet Bay is a small tree, growing in Britain to a height of about 25 feet, but in warmer climates reaching as much as 60 feet.
— Grieve

65

We are very familiar with the narrow, pointed, drab-green leaf we find in pot roasts and meat dishes. Bay as a kitchen herb is widely used with beef dishes. The leaves are very tough and shiny, holding tight within the volatile oil.

LORE

Bay has a history of use in attracting love and good wishes. It holds prominence among the Greeks who used it to show honor for victorious athletes and was a Religious Herbe for the priestesses at Delphi, where they chewed them as they proclaimed their insights and visions. The herb has been much used to recognize those who have achieved enlightenment.

REMEDIAL

Apart from cooking in which one leaf is adequate to flavor the entire dish, there is little internal use for Bay.[5] The volatile oil can induce strong reactions for the body in large doses, for it is a strong stimulant and has some narcotic properties. The large doses will be unpleasant, causing increased blood pressure, pulse and a likelihood of vomiting. The berries are also potentially dangerous and may induce abortion for an expectant mother. The berries should be avoided.

The primary use of bay, medicinally, is to employ the oil as a remedy for bruises, damaged muscles (in cases where the skin has not been broken), and as an anodyne for earache.

- Diaphoretic, emmenagogue, stimulant, narcotic, emetic.

——— BENZOIN ———

Benzoin is a balsamic resin. Normally the trees do not produce it or any substance analogous to it, but the infliction of a wound sufficiently severe to injure the cambium results in the formation of numerous oleoresin ducts in which the secretion is produced; it is, therefore, a pathological product.
— Grieve

Benzoin is usually purchased in either of two forms. One is the dried resin, ground into a finely granulated powder, somewhat pink to tan in color. The other is as a liquid, easily purchased at a pharmacy. It has a very distinctive odor.

LORE

Benzoin is much used in incense mixtures in contemporary practise. Its primary values are seen as aspects which strengthen the mind and aid in its functions. It has use as a Religious Herbe, a Visionary Herbe, and one used extensively in promoting self-growth and inner development.

REMEDIAL

Used externally, it makes a fine cleansing agent for the skin, working to rid the skin of bacteria, and to cleanse irritated patches of skin. Benzoin is more widely used as a pectoral, and for this the tincture is the best agent. Benzoin is added to vaporizers so as to be inhaled for lung congestion, bronchial infections, deep chest colds, and the like. It has a very clean and healthy smell.

- Antiseptic and pectoral.

——— BETONY, WOOD ———

Common, or wood betony, hath many leaves rising from the root, which are somewhat broad and round at the end, roundly dented about the edges, standing upon long foot stalks, from among which rise up small, square, slender, but upright hairy stalks, . . . whereof are set several spiked heads of flowers like lavender . . .

— Culpeper

There is a conserve, made of the floures and sugar good for many things, and especially for the head-ache.

— Gerard

This form of Betony is called 'Wood' due to its preferred environment. It seems to very much like growing as a woodland flower, although it also enjoys meadows and brushy places. It is found widely throughout England.

LORE

Wood Betony enjoys a history as a Countermagicke Herbe, and was often planted in churchyards for protection. It has been worn as an amulet and there are many historical references to its uses. Grieve tells us of several customs surrounding its use, but one of the most fascinating is this:

> *Many extravagant superstitions grew up round Betony, one, of very ancient date, was that serpents would fight and kill each other if placed within a ring composed of it; and others declared that even wild beasts recognized its efficacy, and used it if wounded, and that stags, if wounded with a dart, would search out Betony, and eating it, be cured.*

REMEDIAL

Betony was a Religious Herbe of the Celts, theory being that its name evolves from 'bew-ton,' meaning good for the head. Wood Betony has been used in the treatment of headaches. It is still widely used as a nervine for its gentle calming effects. It is said to improve the blood when taken regularly as a tonic, and is helpful in the treatment of rheumatism, working through the circulatory system.

- Tonic, nervine, alterative, and aromatic.

—— BLACKBERRY ——

It is a plant of Venus in Aries . . . If any ask the reason why Venus is so prickly? Tell them 'tis because she is in the house of Mars.

— Culpeper

The leaves of the Bramble boiled in water, with honey, allum, and a little white wine added thereto, make a most excellent lotion or washing water to heale the sores in the mouth, the privie parts of man or woman, and the same decoction fastneth the teeth.

— Gerard

The Blackberry, or Bramble, growing in every English hedge-row, is too well known to need description.

— Grieve

Blackberries are definitely 'brambly' in nature. The stems, or canes, can easily grow four to five feet long, stretching out and tangling with other canes, to form thick patches in the wild or hedges which are tortuous to pass when cultivated. The stalk is very prickled, and the leaves grow in threes. The berries are only a deep, red-black when ripe, passing through pale green, then shades of ever-deepening red as they grow to maturity.

LORE

As mentioned in the description, passing through or beneath a tangle of Blackberry is quite difficult. It must be for this reason that old lore says that "creeping 'neath the Bramble is a sure prevention against disease." They also say that Blackberry collected at just the right phase of the moon is a powerful charm against evil things which may be written against you, negative energies, or people working psychically to harm you. They usually neglect to mention the time, which would most likely be when the Moon and Venus are conjunct in Aries. And then one may wonder if it should be waning or waxing . . .

REMEDIAL

Blackberry is a must for the cabinet of the Herbalist. It is one of the most useful herbs in the treatment of diarrhea and particularly when that condition results from influenza. The leaves may be used and the berries, which are valuable and rich in vitamins, are also useful in treating persons who are run-down and anemic.

Blackberry has been used as a gargle for sore throats and laryngitis. A strong infusion of Blackberry will help to clear up psoriasis, a nervous condition of the skin.

- Astringent, tonic.

— BLESSED THISTLE —

Mars rules this Thistle. It is cordial and sudorific, good for all sorts of malignant and pestilential fevers . . .
— Culpeper

Blessed Thistle taken in meat or drinke, is good for the swimming and giddiness of the head, it strentheneth memorie, and is a singular remedie against deafness . . .
— Gerard

It is said to have obtained its name from its high reputation as a heal-all, being supposed even to cure the plague . . .
— Grieve

Blessed Thistle looks quite like a member of the Thistle family. It grows about knee-high, and branches out to support a weighty load of blossoms and leaves. The flowers reflect the color of the sun, and grow amid prickles and thistle-hairs.

LORE

Blessed Thistle has been used as a Religious Herbe, used to invoke the God Pan. It has gained a reputation as an Aphrodisiac, and in times past was used widely to remove the bad energies of a hex. It still finds use as a Magickal Herbe today, primarily as an Herbe of Protection.

REMEDIAL

Avoid large doses of this herb, for it is a strong emetic. In fact, it is that property which makes this a needed herb in the cabinet of the Herbalist: it brings about vomiting with minimal discomfort and can be used in emergency cases where a toxic substance has been ingested and must be removed by causing the person to vomit up the contents of the stomach. It certainly is better than the suggestion of drinking soapy water!

Mild doses of Blessed Thistle are useful when the stomach is recovering from a siege of the flu, or is in a similar weakened state. It will stimulate the appetite and keep the stomach balanced and content.

- Tonic, stimulant, emetic, emmenagogue.

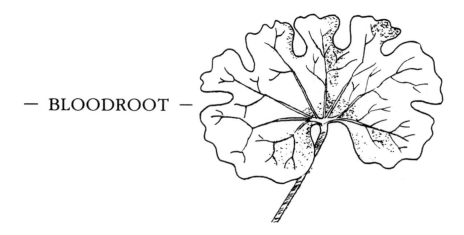

— BLOODROOT —

The root has long been used by the American Indians as a dye for their bodies and clothes and has been used successfully by American and French dyers.

— Grieve

Bloodroot is a magnificent spring flower, found in gently wooded areas throughout North America. A large leaf comes up and out of the soil and holds within it a beautiful creamy-white flower. The leaf is slightly scalloped and both are likely to succumb to the heat of summer. It may only be gathered in the spring unless you have marked a patch, for both leaf and flower are gone by the heats of August.

LORE

Because of the alkaloids Bloodroot is poisonous and has some lore associated with its deadly character. One of the names it is called is 'sweet slumber'.

REMEDIAL

Bloodroot may be used externally. The root should be used and decocted into a strong liquid with water. This may be applied to an area infected with ringworm and will surely cure the disruption.

Mild doses have been used in cases of severe bronchitis, asthma and croup. Extreme caution must be maintained, and this herb should only be used by an experienced Herbalist. It will have a reaction with the heart and is used in certain heart diseases. This herb is best grown for the collector and its use studied rather than practised.

• Cardiac, emmenagogue, emetic, expectorant.

— BONESET —

Throughwort or Boneset is a very common and familiar plant in low meadows and damp ground in North America, extending from Nova Scotia to Florida.

— Grieve

Boneset is a perennial, often mistaken for a weed, for it grows freely throughout the Eastern half of North America. It grows about knee-high, the top branching off for many flowers, clustered in bunches of more than a dozen, white and lightly-scented. It can vary considerably according to the region.

LORE

This is an herb used extensively by Native Americans. Its name is said to have come from the days of the early settlers and pioneers when a rampant influenza swept the plains, inflicting its victims with excruciating pain, as if all the bones were broken; Boneset was used to treat this flu.

REMEDIAL

Boneset is one of the best herbs to use in the treatment of influenza. It helps to lower the temperature of a fever and induces perspiration so that the person is able to recuperate more quickly. Large doses should be used with care, for it can work as either an emetic or laxative. Taken regularly, it has been used to treat rheumatism and colds.

In cases of severe influenza, it helps in preventing severe debilitation, working also upon the stomach, liver and bowels.

It may be served as a moderate-strength tea, cooled for the person, valuable in this manner for also increasing the amount of liquid brought into the system.

• Stimulant, tonic, diaphoretic, febrifuge, emetic, and laxative.

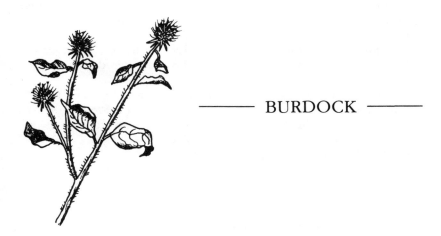

——— BURDOCK ———

It is so well known even by the little boys, who pull off the burs to throw at one another, that I shall spare to write any description of it.

— Culpeper

73

...The juice of the leaves given to drinke with honey, procureth urine, and taketh away the paines of the bladder.

— Gerard

Burdock has very large leaves, somewhat heart-shaped, the underside much paler than the topside. A large stem rises up from the center of the leaves, often reaching many feet in height. Clustered along it, the burrs begin as flowers of a bright and joyful purple, drying to the brown burrs which are so wellknown.

LORE

Shakespeare makes several references to the burrs in "Troilus and Cressida" and in "King Lear." As quoted in Culpeper, the burrs are often playthings of children, for they stick with surety wherever thrown, if there be fabric, anything rough, or even a person upon which to catch.

REMEDIAL

The root is primarily used, being collected and dried. It is very fibrous and tough, and much time should be allowed for it to dry. It is considered one of the best purifiers of the blood in the herbal kingdom.

Unripened burrs, and to a lesser degree the leaves, are used to treat infections of the kidneys. They ease the process and tone-up the organ.

Externally, Burdock, both root and leaves, has been used for all types of scaly skin disorders, such as psoriasis and eczema. Many Herbalists consider Burdock a necessary ingredient for any skin ailment. It has also been used to treat jaundice.

• Alterative, diuretic, diaphoretic, tonic.

——— CARAWAY ———

The root is better food than the parsnips; it is pleasant and comfortable to the stomach, and helpeth digestion.

— Culpeper

Caraway is another member of the group of aromatic, umbelliferous plants characterized by carminative properties, like Anise, Cumin, Dill and Fennel. It is grown, however, less for the medicinal properties of the fruits, or so-called 'seeds', than for their use as a flavoring in cookery, confectionery and liquers.

— Grieve

Caraway will complete its maturation in two years and then need to be planted anew. It looks somewhat like dill as it grows, with finely cut leaves and tall, thin stalks for the fruit. It is native to Europe and Asia.

LORE

Caraway has been an herb of weddings, used both in the cooking, and sometimes thrown at the guests for good luck. It also has a magickal use today as an herbe to consecrate religious instruments.

REMEDIAL

Caraway is a mild tonic and is very good for the digestion. It aids in calming indigestion and gas, and the oil extracted from the fruit is the best for this purpose. A tea made of Caraway, when cooled, is excellent for children.

• Aromatic, stomachic, carminative, tonic.

——— CATNIP ———

The later Herbalists do cal it 'Herba Cataria,' and 'Herba Catti,' because the Cats are very much delighted herewith, for the smel of it is so pleasant to them, that they rub themselves upon it, and wallow or tumble in it, and also feed on the branches and leaves very greedily.

— Gerard

There is an old saying about this plant: 'If you set it, the cats will eat it, If you sow it, the cats don't know it.' And it seems to be a fact that plants transplanted are always

destroyed by cats unless protected, but they never meddle
with the plants raised from seed, being only attracted to it
when it is in a withering state, or when the peculiar scent of
the plant is excited by being bruised in gathering or
transplanting.

— Grieve

More than once I have transplanted a small catnip plant only to
find soft paw marks and a hole where I had set the plant. Catnip can
grow fairly tall, over knee-high, although it can be found nearly
anywhere growing wild, in which case it is usually smaller. It has soft,
downy leaves, heart-shaped and serrated. It sends up little spikelets of
flowers of a pale color, nearly white. The scent of the plant is
memorable, particularly if you are a cat.

LORE

Catnip is used as a tea to calm a person with troubles. It has also
had a minor usage in folk charms. In some areas it appears as a
Religious Herbe.

REMEDIAL

Catnip is highly recommended in treating colds. It will bring a
sense of warmth to the body, bringing perspiration to bring the body
back into balance. It is excellent in the treatment of fevers, and so
palatable that it has a history of being used commonly as a tea.

The lore of Catnip's calming abilities seems to hold true even
though it contains properties as a stimulant. In Wales, Catnip has
been used as an antispasmodic. It has been said that Catnip is good for
all sorts of nervous disorders, even, according to some, that of
insanity.

Catnip is excellent for treating nervous headaches.

• Nervine, stomachic, carminative, tonic, diaphoretic, refrigerant, antispasmodic, stimulant.

——— CAYENNE ———

Cayenne or Capsicum derives its name from the Greek,
'to bite,' in allusion to the hot pungent properties of the fruits
and seeds. Cayenne pepper was introduced into Britain from

76

India in 1548, and Gerard mentioned it as being cultivated in his time.

— Grieve

Cayenne looks typically like a pepper plant. It grows into a sturdy, perennial bush usually knee to waist high, but can reach an astounding height of six feet. Because the volatile oils within ground Cayenne are very subject to deterioration from sunlight, it must be stored in a dark container.

LORE

Potter relates the curious custom of adding Cayenne to bird seed in order to improve the color of the canary's feathers. Some sources say that Cayenne is a remedy for the ravages of drunkenness.

REMEDIAL

Cayenne is a most powerful stimulant. Great care must be taken in using this herb for it also has the properties of a rubefacient, able to irritate the skin or membrane to the point of redness and tenderness.

Cayenne may be used as a 'sure-fire' treatment for severe colds and chills, sometimes administered in hot water with a bit of lemon. This stimulates body heat, vitalizes the blood circulation, and produces perspiration.

Cayenne is also very high in its content of vitamin C.

• Stimulant, tonic, rubefacient.

——— CELANDINE, GREATER ———

This hath divers tender, round, whitish green stalks, with greater joints than ordinary in other herbs, as it were knees, very brittle and easy to break, from whence grow branches with large tender broad leaves divided into many parts . . .

— Culpeper

The Celandine is a herbaceous perennial. The root is thick and fleshy. The stem, which is slender, round and slightly hairy, grows from 1 ½ to 3 feet high . . .

— Grieve

This is the Greater Celandine, not to be confused with the Lesser Celandine. It is found in areas which have found civilization encroaching upon nature. It grows in waste areas, in out-of-the-way places, and may be found as a weed within urban areas. The constituents of this herb give it a most unpleasant flavor, which should not discourage the herbalist from its value.

LORE

There appears to be no Magickal usage ascribed to this herb. It shares a similar growing cycle with Celandine the Lesser.

REMEDIAL

The volatile oils of this herb are powerful medicants, one of which is narcotic and poisonous in pure, extracted form. It is primarily used to remove unwanted conditions from the body, both internally and externally.

The juice of the herb, orange in color and unpleasant, has been used to remove warts, and also in treating eczema, both as ointment and wash.

Celandine the Greater has been used to treat gallstones and kidney stones, to dissolve them and ease their passing out of the body. In Russia, this herb is widely used in the treatment of cancer; Grieve reports that this appears to be effective in many cases.

It has also been used in the treatment of jaundice, working to heal the liver and cleanse it of disease.

- Narcotic, diuretic, purgative, diaphoretic.

——— CELANDINE, LESSER ———

I wonder what ailed the ancients to give this the name of celandine, which resembleth it neither in nature or form; it acquired the name of Pilewort from its virtues . . .

— Culpeper

The Lesser Celandine hath greene round leaves, smooth, slipperie, and shining . . . the stalks are slender, short and for the most part creeping upon the ground: they bring forth little yellow flowers . . .

— Gerard

Wordsworth, whose favourite flower this was (in recognition of which the blossoms are carved on his tomb), fancifully suggests that the painter who first tried to picture the rising sun, must have taken the idea of spreading pointed rays from the Celandine's 'glittering countenance'. "

— Grieve

The name of Celandine for both this herb, the Lesser, and another herb, Celandine the Greater, has been the source of much confusion throughout the ages. This herb is Celandine the Lesser, and was observed by the Celts to respond to sun and rain, opening and closing. Lesser Celandine appears to have instilled a greater sense of wonder, for it is the only herb of these two to have folklore and magickal usage attached to its history. This is an herb of the Springtime, for it appears early, grows fully, and, soon into the summer, passes into its dying cycle to hibernate for the following Spring.

LORE

One of the names for this herb is 'Ranunculus', which means 'tiny frog'. This herb is found growing in the same terrain as the frog: rich, water-fed soil near lakes and streams.

Celandine the Lesser is said to enhance dreams, making them pleasant in nature, delightful and relaxing. It also enjoys use today as a Religious Herbe, in accordance with its relationship to the Spring season, and enjoys current use as a Visionary Herbe.

REMEDIAL

This is an herb which has a long and proven history as a remedy for the treatment of hemorrhoids, or 'piles', as they were once more commonly called. Lesser Celandine is one of many startling examples of the accuracy of the Doctrine of Signatures, set forth by Paracelsus. This herb was given the name of Pilewort, for its tuberous root system looks like swollen and inflamed hemorrhoids or piles. Lesser Celandine was considered one of the best herbs for this condition. It is an excellent astringent, and may be taken either internally as an infusion, or externally, as either an ointment or as a suppository.

Heat finely-chopped Celandine the Lesser with paraffin wax, macerating it until all of the volatile oils have been absorbed, then thoroughly straining out all solids with a philtre. As the wax cools, it may be shaped into small suppositories, which are most effective against hemorrhoids.

• Astringent.

79

——— CHAMOMILE ———

When walked on, its strong, fragrant scent will often reveal its presence before it is seen. For this reason it was employed as one of the aromatic strewing herbs in the Middle Ages, and used often to be purposely planted in green walks in gardens. Indeed, walking over the plant seems specially beneficial to it . . . 'Like a camomile bed — The more it is trodden The more it will spread . . .

— Grieve

Chamomile grows over a wide range of areas, wild forms of it being most common around farmlands. In wild form, it appears to be a daisy-like plant, but growing on a stalk about a foot high, and rather than the solid leaves of a daisy, covered with fine, needle-like (but very soft!) leaves. It will spread out and fill a space. It is most distinguished by its strong scent. It has flowers with little white petals and a yellow centre, and its scent should be learned by the Herbalist, for that is the surest way to identify this herb.

LORE

Chamomile has been in use since the most ancient of times. It is found throughout ancient Egyptian medicine where it was dedicated to the Sun god for its curing powers. Much of its lore comes from the position it can hold within a garden, for it brings health to the other plants in the gardens and is said to cure nearly any plant that it grows next to. It is said even to keep its neighboring plants free of insects. It has stirred imagination, due to its dependable healing powers, and attracted such diverse names as the 'Whig Plant', and 'Plants' Physician'.

Current practise includes use as a Religious Herbe.

REMEDIAL

The most wide-spread use is due to the properties Chamomile has as a nervine. There are many family stories of babies raised with Chamomile tea in their bottles as a means of soothing them, keeping them calm and also curing them of colic and upset stomachs.

80

Chamomile is also known for its use in the treatment of pain. It has been used as a lotion to treat toothaches, earaches, and the pains of neuralgia. It is one of the safest, most pleasant of sedatives available. It is completely harmless, yet will relax, soothe, and comfort the patient into a good night's sleep.

Chamomile may be macerated with an oil to use as a liniment for all types of sore muscles, joints, aches, sprains, bruises and the like. It is also used externally as a wash, aiding the skin to remain healthy and keeping it free from acne and blemishes.

The tea is good for the stomach, toning the organs, and also treating symptoms of indigestion and heartburn. For a patient who has been ill for a time it will also restore the appetite.

Some say that it has been useful in dissolving kidney stones.

• Stomachic, tonic, anodyne, sedative, nervine, astringent, antispasmodic.

—— CHICKWEED ——

The juice, or distilled, water, is of much good use for all heats and redness of the eyes, to drop some thereof into them...

— Culpeper

The leaves of Chickweed boyled in water very soft, adding thereto some hogs grease, the pouder of Fenugreek and Lineseed, and a few roots of the marsh Mallowes, and stamped to the forme of cataplasme or pultesse, taketh away the swellings of the legs or any other part . . .

— Gerard

The fresh leaves have been employed as a poultice for inflammation and indolent ulcers with most beneficial results . . .

— Grieve

Chickweed is well known by most gardeners, for its low-growing bright-green foliage is quick to spread throughout an open, cultivated space. It is not a sturdy plant, which is the probable reason Mother Nature has evolved it into a very quickly growing plant. It branches all about and has tiny flowers. It is easy to collect, for it pulls loose from the ground with ease.

LORE

A very old custom is that of giving Chickweed to birds as birdfood. The preferred part is the seed. Chickweed, according to Grieve, is a favorite for a variety of household pets, including rabbits, and we find gerbils and hamsters also love it.

REMEDIAL

Chickweed is rich in both copper and iron and makes an excellent tonic. It is widely used externally for most discomforts of the skin. The nature of Chickweed most desired by Herbalists is its cooling nature, and it is called for in many ailments, including hemorrhoids and inflamed sores of the body.

The pure juice has been used to treat sore eyes. This should be done carefully, by soaking a pad in the juice, and applying that to the closed eye.

- Demulcent, refrigerant.

———— CINNAMON ————

The tree which hath the Cinnamon for his barke is of the stature of an Olive tree having a body as thick as a mans thigh, from which the Cinnamon is taken, but that taken from the smaller branches is much better . . .

— Gerard

Grows best in almost pure sand, requiring only 1 per cent of vegetable substance; it prefers a sheltered place . . .

— Grieve

Commercial Cinnamon is collected from young shoots. The outer bark is removed and discarded and the inner bark is taken, dried and sold in either of two forms: 'sticks', which are unprocessed, long, curled pieces of the bark, and the finely-ground powder which is the more common.

LORE

In the East where Cinnamon was originally grown, it was used as a Religious Herbe, burnt as an incense to purify the temples. It enjoyed use then as a Magickal Herbe, which is still the custom today.

REMEDIAL

Cinnamon is very effective in treating disturbances of the stomach. It is best used when mixed with other stomachics and astringents, and is used to alleviate gas and cramps caused by gas and works also to stop vomiting.

- Stimulant, astringent, carminative, stomachic, antiseptic.

——— CINQUEFOIL ———

It spreads and creeps far upon the ground with long slender strings like strawberries, which take root again and shoot forth many leaves made of five parts . . .

— Culpeper

They grow in low and moist meadowes, upon banks and by high waies sides . . . These plants do floure from the beginning of May to the end of June.

— Gerard

Bacon says that frogs have a prediliction for sitting on this herb: 'The toad will be much under Sage, frogs will be in Cinquefoil'.

— Grieve

The leaf of Cinquefoil grows in five distinct leaflets, hence its other common names of 'Five-Leaf Grass' and 'Five-Finger Grass.' There are many varieties of Cinquefoil, Gerard recording thirteen in his herbal alone. Cinquefoil sends out tall stalks, each with a bright yellow flower. It has been a primary herb of Herbalists since the time of Hippocrates.

LORE

During the Middle Ages, Cinquefoil acquired quite a reputation as a Magickal Herbe. It is said to be an herb frequently chosen by Witches for their spells, and was one of the ingredients in the reknowned flying ointment.[6] Grieve also records a most unusual recipe used by fishermen to enhance their bait and guarantee catching a lot of fish. Cinquefoil is one of the ingredients.

REMEDIAL

Cinquefoil is a most effective herb in treating nearly all types of fevers. It both reduces the temperature and makes the person more comfortable. It works well in fevers associated with mucous, such as many forms of influenza and inflammatory fevers. Bacterial infections may be treated with Cinquefoil. It is an excellent choice for treating diarrhea.

Externally it is employed as a lotion to treat skin ailments which require an astringent. It is also used as a gargle, although the constituent giving the astringent property has the expected, bitter taste.

• Astringent, pectoral, febrifuge, tonic.

——— CLEAVERS ———

This plant has many common names, as Goose-grass, Catchweed, Bed straw, etc. It is an annual succulent plant, with a weak, procumbent, quadrangular, retrosely-prickled stem . . .

— Culpeper

The juice which is pressed out of the seeds, stalks, and leaves, as Dioscorides writeth, is a remedie for them that are bitten of the poisonsome spiders . . .

— Gerard

The seeds of Clivers form one of the best substitutes for coffee; they require simply to be dried and slightly roasted over a fire, and so prepared, have much the flavour of coffee. They have been so used in Sweden.

— Grieve

There are over three hundred members of this herb, and of them, more than a dozen which are known as Cleavers. It has, as Culpeper says, quadrangular stalks, and the leaves are quite small. It has little barbs, and by this method is able to have its seed transported throughout the country.

LORE

There is little lore to be found for this herb, although at some times in history, it carried with it an extensive reputation as an herb which could heal nearly any complaint.

REMEDIAL

As a tonic, Cleavers was one of the very popular herbs for Spring tonics. When taken internally, it purifies the blood and cleanses the internal system of many diseases.

It has had extensive use externally, used in treating various skin disorders. It may be used in treating acne, and is also good in clearing the ravages of psoriasis.

It is a very strong diuretic, and as such should not be used by

85

those who have diabetes. For others, it will often clear a disease and flush it out through the kidneys. In mild doses, it is excellent in the treatment of colds and influenza.

Cleavers is an herb to keep in mind, for it has been used in some of the more unusual cases, said to dissolve kidney stones, and also to work against cancer.

The entire herb is used in some areas to inhibit bleeding, and may be crushed thoroughly and applied to cold sores, blisters, and burns.

- Astringent, tonic, diuretic, alterative, aperient.

——— CLOVER ———

It grows in almost every place in this country.
— Culpeper

The floures grow on the tops of the stalkes in a tuft or small Foxtaile eare, of a purple colour, and sweet of taste.
— Gerard

A perrenial, but of short duration, generally abundant on meadow land of a light sandy nature, where it produces abundant blossom, forming an excellent mowing crop. Not of great value as a bee plant - the bees not working it for so long as they will the white variety . . .
— Grieve

It is unlikely that this book will not have a reader unfamiliar with Clover. Generally the Red Clover, which has the purple-colored flowers, is used more in remedial work, although Culpeper records only the White Clover. Generally all of the herbaceous portion of the plant is collected and dried, being cut off at ground level.

86

LORE

Known by one of its other names, 'Trefoil,' this herb is found in many books recording magickal lore of herbes. It is one of the traditional herbes of magick, being used as a Religious Herbe, and an Herbe of Consecration. It is, of course, also used for good luck, when you find a four-leafed variety.

REMEDIAL

Clover is used in conjunction with other herbs for severe problems with the bronchial area of the body such as whooping cough or bronchitis. It has also been used to remove disease from the digestive system.

In some parts of the world, Clover has been used externally in the treatment of cancer. There are some herbalists who report moderate success in using it internally in cancer therapy, increasing the dose from the usual once ounce per pint of water to about triple.

• Alterative, pectoral, antispasmodic, tonic.

———— CLOVES ————

Where there is neither grasse, weeds, nor any other herbes growing . . . by reason the tree draweth unto it selfe for his nourishment all the moisture of the earth a great circuit round about, so that nothing can there grow for want of moisture . . .

— Gerard

The spice was introduced into Europe from the fourth to the sixth century.

— Grieve

The Clove is a tropical evergreen growing not too tall, and having a beautifully cone-shaped growth. Cloves contain a large amount of essential and volatile oils used primarily in medicines.

LORE

Cloves do not have ancient lore. They remained in use primarily as a spice, and rarely strayed out of the kitchen. Today, however, they appear to be part of the Aquarian age, and enjoy current use as a Magickal Herbe and Visionary Herbe.

REMEDIAL

The best known and most widespread use of oil of Cloves is in the treatment of the pain from a toothache. The ground Cloves may be taken internally, calming the stomach, relieving gas.
- Ground Cloves: stomachic, aromatic, carminative.
- Oil of Cloves: antiseptic, expectorant, anesthetic.

———— COHOSH ————

A native of North America, where it grows freely in shaded woods in Canada and the United States. It is called Black Snake Root . . .

— Grieve

There are two types of Cohosh currently in use, one known as Black, which is described in the quote from Grieve, and the other known as Blue. The Black variety grows in wooded places, growing from a thick rhizome. A graceful plant, it sends forth a feathery strand of blossoms, sometimes reaching three feet in length. Black Cohosh is sometimes known as Squaw Root, for its properties are an emmanagogue.

Blue Cohosh is actually unrelated to Black Cohosh. It is found more in Swamp areas, and grows small yellow-green flowers and fruit resembling small peas. The root is thinner and longer than Black Cohosh.

REMEDIAL

The primary use today of both varieties of Cohosh is an emmenagogue. Blue Cohosh is employed in cases of difficult delivery of the fetus, particularly when the mother is approaching exhaustion from labor or hasn't enough strength to facilitate birth. Black Cohosh is sometimes thought to ease problems with the menstrual cycle.

Both Cohosh herbs are diuretics, and the Blue may be used in cases of infection and inflammation of the urinary system. The roots of the Blue were used by Native Americans as a sedative, and may be used in epilepsy.

The Black variety also carries with it the ability to cause phlegm to be coughed up from the lungs.

- Blue: emmenagogue, sedative, diuretic, diaphoretic, anthelmintic, antispasmodic.
- Black: astringent, diuretic, alterative, expectorant, emmenagogue.

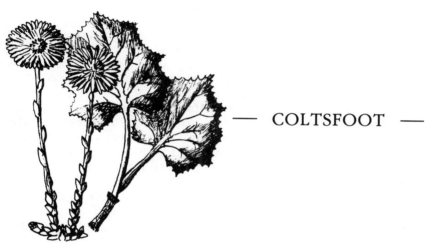

— COLTSFOOT —

This shooteth up a tender stalk, with small yellowish flowers somewhat earlier, which fall away quickly, and after they are past come up somewhat round leaves, sometimes dented around the edges, . . . with a little down or frieze over the green leaf on the upper side, which may be rubbed away, and whitish or mealy underneath.

— Culpeper

The fume of the dried leaves taken through a funnell or tummell, burned upon coles, effectually helpeth those that are troubled with shortnesse of breath, and fetch their winde thicke and often, and breaketh without perill the impostumes of the brest. Being taken in manner as they take Tobaco, it mightily prevaileth against the diseases aforesaid.

— Gerard

The name for Coltsfoot, 'Farfara', is said by Gerard and Grieve to come from a reference to the Poplar tree. The shape is similar to the hoof of a colt, and is sometimes described as if a bunch of large poplar leaves were growing out of the ground. The leaves grow to the size of a large palm without the fingers. It is a perennial.

REMEDIAL

Coltsfoot contains many useful vitamins, among them calcium, potassium, sulpher, vitamin C, and tannin, but is best known for the amount of mucilage within the herb. Grieve tells us that the name 'tussilago' means 'cough dispeller', and this appears to be the most widespread use of the herb.

Coltsfoot has a reputation as a 'smoking herb', as it has been an ingredient in the British Herb Tobacco mixture, along with buckbean, eyebright, betony, rosemary, thyme, lavender, and chamomile. It may also be inhaled or smoked on its own, being an excellent remedy for asthma, bronchitis, various congestions of the lungs, and excess phlegm. Coltsfoot may also be taken as a strong tea mixture or as an infusion for the above conditions.

In the case of a chest cold or an influenza which leads to chest or bronchial congestion, Coltsfoot is a sure remedy for breaking up the phlegm and helping the person to clear it through coughing. Although there is social pressure against coughing up phlegm, it is the duty of the Herbalist to encourage this very process, for it is essential in the restoration of healthy lungs.

To a lesser degree, Coltsfoot has been used in the treatment of giddiness and headaches, although in the latter case, these are more likely those headaches caused by pressure of the sinus passages filled with thick mucous, which can also be alleviated by Coltsfoot.

An idea of the effectiveness of this herb may be found in the custom, reported by Grieve, as seen in Paris, in which local apothecaries use the flower as a symbol of their craft.

- Tonic, demulcent, expectorant, pectoral, pulmonary.

COMFREY

The stalke of this Comfrey is cornered, thicke and hollow like that of Sow-thistle; it groweth two cubits or a yard high; the leaves that spring from the root, and those that grow upon the stalkes are long, broad, rough, and pricking withall, something hairie, and being handled make the hands itch . . .

— Gerard

Formerly country people cultivated Comfrey in their gardens for its virtue in wound healing, and the many local names of the plant testify to its long reputation as a vulnerary herb — in the Middle Ages it was a famous remedy for broken bones.

— Grieve

Comfrey will grow anywhere that doesn't expose it to excessively hot, drying sun, for its huge leaves hold a great deal of moisture. The flowers, a striking shade of soft purple, appear on tall, arched stalks, that hang down midst the deep green of the leaves. Care should be taken to allow a large enough space when growing it, for it is wont to take up much room and returns each year in greater abundance.

LORE

There is little lore attached to comfrey, although great delight can be found in reading Grieve's collection of names. It's only use today as a Magickal Herbe is to place a leaf in one's shoe to ensure a safe journey.

91

REMEDIAL

Comfrey contains even more mucilage than the famed marsh-mallow root. For those who wonder about its properties as a vulnerary, it also contains calcium, vitamin B12, iron, and silica, in addition to many other vitamins and nutrients. It is called more nutritional than soybeans, and is ranked as the highest in protein for the amount of fibre. It is one of the rare herbs which processes vitamin B12 out of the soil. It is edible as a green, steamed lightly, flavored with lemon and butter.

Comfrey is soothing to the stomach. The mucilage makes it an excellent choice of herb for those troubled with ulcers or with conditions leading to ulceration. It must be stressed, however, that the causes of the agitation must be dealt with. The only preventative cure for ulcers is relaxation and inner peace. The mucilage will also act within the lungs, and Comfrey is used in the treatment of rheumatism, arthritis, as its properties flow easily throughout the bloodstream to all parts of the body. The root is used to treat loose bowels.

Comfrey may be used in any chest infection or congestion of the lungs. It has also been used in the treatment of internal bleeding, but a skilled diagnostician is essential.

Externally, Comfrey is used in the treatment of a large variety of ills: injuries for bruises, burns, sprains, broken bones, ulcers, etc. It makes easily into a poultice, the fresh herb being the most desirable.

Comfrey is an herb worth learning well, for there are more uses to which it may be applied than space permits.

• Demulcent, vulnerary, mild astringent, expectorant, emollient, pectoral, pulmonary, tonic, nutrient.

——— CRAMP BARK ———

The 'Gaitre-Berries' of which Chaucer makes mention among the plants that 'shale be for your hele' . . . are the deep red clusters of berries of the Wild Guelder Rose . . . , a shrub growing 5 to 10 feet high.

— Grieve

Cramp Bark is known by many names and is a member of the elder family, looking somewhat like it in appearance. As Grieve says, it grows five to ten feet in height, and is plentiful throughout Britain

92

where it is planted in many places to denote the borders of property. It has a great clump of flowers, three-to five-inches across, which lead to the cluster of red berries found in late summer.

REMEDIAL

The bark of this small tree is most excellent in the treatment of convulsions, hysteria, and will also calm spasms caused by coughing spells. It may be used in the treatment of severe stomach cramps and all manner of nervous troubles. The bark contains valerianic acid, and will have a somewhat bitter flavor.

Apart from use as an antispasmodic, Cramp Bark has also been used in the treatment of rheumatism, arthritis, and heart disorders.

- Antispasmodic, nervine, sedative.

—— DANDELION ——

It is of an opening and cleansing quality, and therefore very effectual for the obstructions of the liver, gall, and spleen, and the diseases that arise from them, as the jaundice and hypochondriac . . .

— Culpeper

boyled in vinegar, it is good against the paine that troubles some in making of water; A decoction made of the whole plant helps the yellow jaundice.

— Gerard

Many little flies are to be found visiting the Dandelion to drink the lavishly-supplied nectar. By carefully watching, it has been ascertained that no less than ninety-three different kinds of insects are in the habit of frequenting it.

— Grieve

This is one of the few herbs for which it would seem no description is needed. It is helpful to know, however, that this is a nutrient herb, containing iron, copper, vitamins A and E, calcium, chloride, magnesium, silica, and potassium, and you can find it growing most likely within steps of your front door. They are excellent greens, made into an excellent salad or cooked, although it is wise to gather them when young, else the bitter juices permeate the leaf.

LORE

It is said that a dandelion in one's dream is a symbol of difficult times ahead. What they usually neglect to add is that these times are of advantage to the wise, for they are times of change, and can be understood and worked into a better situation.

Weather magick says that seeing the fluff blown free from the head of a dandelion is an indication of rain coming, should this happen when you feel no wind in the air. Although the planetary association is Jupiter, because of the juice and medicinal value of the herb, the Dandelion observes the sun, closing the flower when dark clouds are overhead.

REMEDIAL

Dandelions are excellent herbs for treating the internal organs of the body. Internally, they are a gentle and mild laxative, and clean the liver, kidneys, bladder and related organs and passages within the body.

Dandelions have been used externally, the gathered juice being excellent for the treatment of acne, boils, and similar skin disorders. The juice may be successfully used to clear eczema, although a decoction of the root may also be employed.

Dandelion is a good herb for urinary tract infections, and when it is necessary to restore health to the liver.

- Aperient, tonic, diuretic, nutrient.

——— DOCKS ———

All Docks are under Jupiter, of which the Red Dock, which is commonly called Bloodwort; cleanseth the blood and strengthens the liver; but the Yellow Dock root is best to be taken when either the blood or liver is affected by choler.

— Culpeper

The name Dock is applied to a widespread tribe of broad-leaved wayside weeds, having roots possessing astringent qualities united in some with a cathartic principle, rendering them valuable as substitutes for Rhubarb, a plant of the same family.

— Grieve

Gerard records many types of Docks and illustrates eight of them, which I mention as an example of the variety to be found. They are found nearly everywhere, but should not be confused with 'burdock', which is really not a Dock at all, but a member of the thistle family. The leaves and the young shoots of the Docks may be cooked and eaten, being quite nutritious, but less tasty, and could bring about loose stool if taken in quantity.

Some of the Docks grow to six feet in height, and all bear flowers on the tops of tall stems. They look much like the rhubarb when it has gone to seed.

95

REMEDIAL

Most of the Docks are generally astringent in property, with the root being primarily used medicinally. Herb Patience, one variety, is used in the treatment of jaundice, and can be helpful in the recovery of a person suffering from hepatitis. Gerard says that this variety may reach eight or nine feet in height, and recommends using the leaves as a garden green.

Yellow Dock contains rumicin, which makes it excellent in the treatment of liver disorders and skin ailments. It has also been used to calm an irritating cough, and is considered a useful herb in the treatment of cancer. The seeds of this variety are particularly astringent. Neither Culpeper nor Gerard record this particular variety.

Great Water Dock is recorded by both Grieve and Gerard. This is the largest of all the Docks, and has a very thick root of a yellow color, brown on the outside. As with others, the root is astringent, and with the Great Water variety the root is particularly strong. The root may be gathered, dried, and ground to a powder. This powder is excellent for many types of oral complaints, such as bleeding of the gums, and may be used for brushing one's teeth. The root may also be taken internally to alleviate severe cases of diarrhea.

- Astringent, hepatic, aperient, laxative.

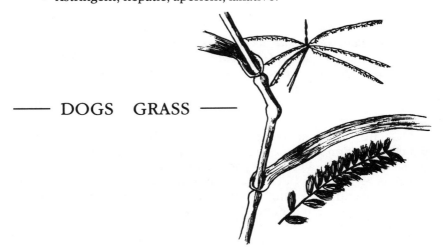

—— DOGS GRASS ——

It is well known that grass creepeth far about under ground, with long white jointed roots, and small fibres almost at every joint, very sweet in taste, as the rest of the herb is, and interlacing one another, from whence shoot forth

*many fair grassy leaves, small at the ends, and cutting or
sharp on the edges.*

— Culpeper

*. . . growes in gardens and arable lands, as an infirmitie
or plague of the fields, nothing pleasing to Husbandmen, for
after the field is plowed, they are constrained to gather the
roots together with harrowed and rakes . . .*

— Gerard

*Though commonly regarded in this country as a
worthless and troublesome weed, its roots are, however,
considered on the Continent to be wholesome food for cattle
and horses. In Italy, especially, they are carefully gathered by
the peasants and sold in the markets.*

— Grieve

Although you may not recognize the traditional name for this
prevalent herb in most areas, and if anyone wishes to grow it in an
herb garden, one merely needs to wait and it shall appear of its own
accord.

LORE

There is not much lore, although the first roots found in the
spring have been taken and tied in a knot to bind the promise of young
lovers and then buried in a field, thus insuring the longevity of their
troth.

REMEDIAL

The roots may be taken internally to alleviate kidney stones. It has
also been used for various urinary tract infections and afflictions of the
bladder. Culpeper recommends gathering the seed which makes a
strong diuretic. Gerard says that it is an excellent vulnerary for
wounds of a less-than-serious nature.

An expressed juice from the roots is excellent in the treatment of
liver disorders and jaundice. The roots are sometimes used as spring
tonic, which not only functions as a tonic, but also has cleansing
properties.

• Tonic, hepatic, vulnerary, diuretic.

97

ELDER

It mollifies the hardness of the mother, if women sit thereon, and opens their veins, and brings down their courses: the berries boiled in wine, perform the same effect: and the hair of the head washed therewith, is made black.
— Culpeper

The Elder, with its flat-topped masses of creamy-white, fragrant blossoms, followed by large drooping bunches of purplish-black, juicy berries, is a familiar object in English countryside and gardens. It has been said, with some truth, that our English summer is not here until the Elder is fully in flower, and that it ends when the berries are ripe.
— Grieve

Elder is a Queen among herbs. It is found throughout Europe and easily located in North America. Once identified and the fresh berries plucked and tasted, it is a plant always familiar as a friend. This herb is one deserving of a quest by the herbalist, for it not only entertains a complex and fascinating lore, but has a variety of medical uses as well. The berries, leaves, barks are all used, yet each differing somewhat from the other; the flowers having even a different application. From one herb comes many blessings.

The bark should be gathered in autumn from young shoots and trees. Great care must be taken that the amount taken is never enough to damage the Elder. The leaves should be collected around the time of Midsummer, taken in the morning when the dew is just left. The flowers and berries must of course be gathered in season, but those lovingly collected beneath a full moon are prime.

LORE

The lore and history of the Elder does much to give credence to those who study these arts. The same legends appear in diverse cultures, and one begins to believe truth to be the reason. Grieve tells us of legends that come from Northern Europe as far away as Russia, and devotes a lengthy section to exploring the magick of this herbe. There is said to be strong spiritual energy around a small growth of Elder which will manifest for the Herbalist as feminine. This 'Elder-tree-Mother', as she is sometimes called, is most protective of her grove, yet with the proper respect will pass on to the practitioner the more magical of her plants. Elder figures in many folklores and spells as protection against lightning, against disease and crippling ailments, in divination and serious magick. Elder enjoys current use as a Magickal Herbe, an Herbe of Protection, a Funereal Herbe, and the rich lore of this herb makes pleasant and interesting reading.

REMEDIAL

As stated before, each of the parts of the Elder should be treated differently, and understood separately. The flowers, first gathered in the season, are astringent and a stimulant in nature. They are primarily used externally, and have a long history for their work with the skin. Elder Flower Water is a well-known remedy for skin disorders and eye trouble. The recipe, from Grieve, is as follows:

> *Fill a large jar with Elder Blossoms, pressing them down, the stalks of course having been removed previously. Pour on them 2 quarts of boiling water and when slightly cooled, add 1 ½ oz of rectified spirits. Cover with a folded cloth, and stand the jar in a warm place for some hours. Then allow it to get quite cold and strain through muslin. Put into bottles and cork securely.*

Elder Flower Water has been used in the treatment of sunburn and acne, and was a favorite toilet water for ladies of the turn of the century.

The flowers are also useful in the treatment of fevers, for they induce perspiration and aid in comforting the person. A strong tea made of the dried flowers is always an excellent choice of remedy for severe colds and influenza.

The leaves of the Elder may be made into an ointment mixed with one part Elder to two parts fixative, either animal fat or vegetable shortening. This is an excellent ointment for treating bruises, wounds, and damages to the body which require soothing and healing. The leaves are considered cooling. If they are to be taken internally, great care should be taken with the amount. Some varieties of Elder have a toxic substance in the root which is poisonous, and this can be carried to the leaf. The leaves are also known for their property as a pesticide.

The berries are collected and dried slowly in a warm, dry, shaded place. These may be made into a strong tea useful in the treatment of diarrhea and are also used as a laxative.[7]

The bark is gathered and dried. It is a very strong purgative and must be used with great care. In large doses it provokes vomiting. The green bark may be made into an ointment similar to the leaf, and is also used in the treatment of severe asthma. In the later case it is used in diluted strength, and should not be employed as a common remedy.

- Flowers: astringent, stimulant, fixative, pectoral, aperient, febrifuge, anodyne, expectorant.
- Leaves: emollient, purgative, expectorant, diaphoretic.
- Berries: laxative, astringent.
- Bark: strong purgative, diuretic, emollient, pectoral.

─── ELECAMPAGNE ───

It is good for shortnesse of breath, and an old cough, and for such as cannot breathe unlesse they hold their necks upright. It is of great vertue both given in a looch, which is a medicine to be licked on, and likewise preserved, as also otherwise given to purge and void out thicke, tough, and clammie humours, which sticke in the chest and lungs.

— Gerard

This is a robust and stately plant; a perennial, with an upright handsome appearance. The leaves are of a dull faint green, and the root, which is long and large, contains the virtues of the plant.

Elecampagne was known to the ancient writers on agriculture and natural history, and evn the Roman poets were acquainted with it.

— Grieve

100

Elecampagne, also known as Elfwort, is a tall-standing herb, growing nearly five feet tall and bearing summer-yellow flowers throughout the hottest time of the season. From a distance it might appear to be a sunflower, but would not be mistaken up close. The leaves are softly furred with down, and it is said that you may find Elves living nearby.

LORE

Elecampagne has been used as a Religious Herbe by ancient Druids, and it is still an Herbe of Consecration today, being used much in rituals of initiation. It is said to have been given life upon earth from the Lady Helenium of Helena, who was happily married to Menelaus. Paris saw her, fell in love with her, and took her away. In her sadness she wept tears which fell to the earth and sprang forth as Elecampagne.

REMEDIAL

Elecampagne is one of the best herbs available to relieve the chest of congestion. It is excellent to clean the lungs from the ravages of smoking, and is useful in the treatment of colds, chronic coughing, bronchial infections, and other lung ailments. It not only makes breathing easier and freer but assists the body in coughing up phlegm and mucous. Not only is Elecampagne most effective, but it has a wonderful pungent flavor.

Elecampagne is used externally as a wash in the treatment of many skin disorders due to its antiseptic and astringent properties. External application should not be excessive, for it is a mild rubefacient.

• Diuretic, tonic, expectorant, alterative, diaphoretic, astringent, antiseptic, stimulant.

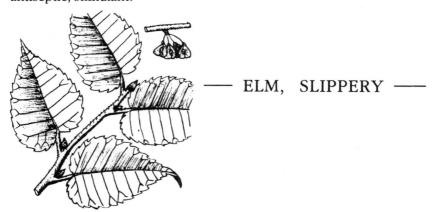

— ELM, SLIPPERY —

101

The branches are very rough, the leaves long, unequally
toothed, rough with hairs on both sides, the leaf-buds covered
with a dense yellow Wool. The flowers are stalkless.

— Grieve

This is one of the varieties of 'ulmus' to be found, much smaller
than the tall, stately elm we think of. This herb is found throughout
North America and Canada.

REMEDIAL

Grieve gives us a recipe called a Slippery Elm compound:

...excellent for coughs, it is made as follows: Cut
obliquely one or more ounces of bark into pieces about the
thickness of a match; add a pinch of Cayenne, flavour with a
slice of lemon and sweeten, infusing the whole in a pint of
boiling water and letting it stand for 25 minutes.

This mixture is used in the treatment of coughs, particularly when
they keep the person awake into the night. This same mixture has
been used to treat typhoid fever.

The bark is collected in Spring and has a variety of uses. As an
emollient it is one of the best, sometimes cooked into a mush and
flavored with herbs. As such, it is easy to digest, particularly for those
troubled with ulcers, inflammations of the stomach, or advanced
aging, being very high in nutrition. Taken as an infusion, it is a good
remedy for the same troubles, soothing the linings of the intestines
and stomach.

Many women use this herb to ease their menstral cycle and in
cases where the reproductive organs need a source of strength and
health.

- Demulcent, emollient, expectorant, diuretic, nutrient, pectoral.

——— EUCALYPTUS ———

The tree is indigenous with a few exceptions to Australia
and Tasmania. The genus contains about 300 species and is
one of the most characteristic genera of the Australian flora.

— Grieve

Eucalyptus is known for the tough pointed leaves, which contain an unusually high amount of volatile oil (Oil of Eucalyptus). The leaves have a most distinctive odor, easily distinguished, pungent and clean-smelling.

LORE

The tree is thought to be somewhat magickal, no doubt due to the extensive properties of healing to be found in the oil.

REMEDIAL

The oil of the leaf is one of the most powerful antiseptics the Herbalist can have available. It can be macerated at home, although it would seem far easier to purchase the oil already removed. The oil may be used as a disinfectant, killing bacteria and germs.

The leaves are of great value in the treatment of lung congestion, and a simple treatment may be had by boiling several of the leaves and inhaling the steam. This is an excellent herb to use in conjunction with a vaporizer.

A tea of the leaf is an excellent gargle, not only leaving the throat refreshed and strengthened, but working to kill off infections and inflammations. Eucalyptus also acts as a stimulant upon the heart, increasing the pulse and stimulating the action of the organ itself.

Externally, the oil may be applied as a local anesthetic. The oil is also applied to the throat or chest when those parts of the body are in need of treatment.

- Stimulant, cardiac, antiseptic, aromatic, pectoral.

——— EYEBRIGHT ———

Common Eyebright is a small low herb, rising up unusually but with one blackish green stalk a span high, or not much more, spread from the bottom into sundry branches, whereon are small and almost round, yet pointed, dark green leaves, finely snipped about the edges, two always set together, and very thick . . .

— Culpeper

It is very much commended for the eyes. Being taken it selfe alone, or any way else, it preserves the sight, and being feeble and lost it restores the same . . .

— Gerard

It is an elegant little plant, 2 to 8 inches high, an annual, common on heaths and other dry pastures, especially on a chalky soil, and flowering from July to September, with deeply-cut leaves and numerous, small, white or purplish flowers variegated with yellow.

— Grieve

The flowers of Eyebright grow in little spires and are often busy with bees. What is unusual about this herb is that it is parasitic, its roots sending out tendrils to explore the nearby roots of grasses and gather nourishment. Apparently there is no damage to the grass.

LORE

The healing power of Eyebright for the eyes is thought to extend to spiritual and psychic vision. In addition this is truly the herb of mirth and joy, its name 'Euphrasia' evolved from the Greek muse of joy and wonder. Eyebright is much used today as a Visionary Herbe, and in psychic balance for its ability to bring the practioner the ability to see life as joyous.

REMEDIAL

Eyebright is still much used in the treatment of poor eyesight. It is often combined with golden seal as a wash made to bathe the eyes. This is also an herb of the British Herbal Tobacco mixture, being particularly good for the lungs. It is sometimes taken as a morning tea for those troubled by hay fever.
- Tonic, astringent, pectoral.

———— FENNEL ————

Fennel is good to break wind, to provoke urine, and ease the pains of the stone, and helps to break it.

— Culpeper

The pouder of the seed of Fennell drunke for certaine days together fasting preservethe the eye-sight . . .

— Gerard

Fennel, a hardy, perrenial, umbelliferous herb, with yellow flowers and feathery leaves grows wild in most parts of temperate Europe, but is generally considered indigenous to the shores of the Mediterranean, whence it spreads eastwards to India.

— Grieve

Fennel is a close relative of dill, and they look much the same in appearance. Fennel can achieve a height of four to five feet, growing strong from deep, thick, white roots. The entire plant has a similar scent as that of its seed.

LORE

Fennel has been used as a Magickal Herbe, giving the user strength, vitality, and sexual virility and fertility. It has also been used as an Herbe of Protection, and has a very long history of magickal uses.

REMEDIAL

The primary use of Fennel among herbalists is as an aromatic, added to herbal mixtures to make them more palatable and pleasing for the digestion. When the seed is finely ground to a powder, it deters the presence of fleas and may be used as a pesticide for one's domestic pets.

Fennel is highly recommended for those who practise fasting, as it eases the process for the body, alleviating the pangs of hunger, and keeping the digestive system in a more content state.

• Aromatic, carminative, pesticide.

———— FENUGREEK ————

It is thought according to Galen in his book of the Faculties of nourishments, that it is one of those simples which do manifestly heat, and that men do use it for food, as they do Lupines, for it is taken with pickle to keep the body soluble . . .

— Gerard

The name comes from 'Foenum-graecum', meaning Greek Hay, the plant being used to scent inferior hay.

— Grieve

Fenugreek must be sown from seed each year, for it is an annual. It grows about two feet high, with many branches and leaves. The small white flowers are followed by pale, yellow seeds. Primarily the seeds are used in remedial work.

LORE

Fenugreek has been used as a Religious Herbe, and was held important in the temples of Apollo. It enjoys use as a Magickal Herbe yet today.

REMEDIAL

Fenugreek is very important to the Herbalist, for it is most effective in the prevention of fevers and is said to be as useful as quinine. Gerard suggests boiling the seed with dates, and drinking the decoction. Grieve reports of the Egyptian process of soaking the seeds in water until a thick paste results, which can then be taken.

Fenugreek is also used for cleansing the body and is thought to remove toxic substances from it. It has been used to treat ulcers and other disorders of the digestive tract. It is very high in mucilage, and useful for all types of inflammations of the stomach.

Externally, Fenugreek is used in the treatment of dandruff, and thicker preparations are useful poultices in the treatment of running sores, boils, and the like.

- Emollient, antipyretic, vulnerary, tonic.

—— FERNS ——

There be divers sorts of Ferne, differing as well in forme as place of growing; whereof there be two sorts according to the old writers, the male and the female; and these be properly called Ferne . . .

— Gerard

Ferns are herbs, with a perennial (rarely annual) short, tufted or creeping root-stock. The British genera comprise

106

about forty-five species, only one of which, a small Jersey species, is annual.

— Grieve

Gerard records numerous ferns in his herbal, as does Grieve. Culpeper discusses only the Bracken Fern and the Water Fern. Most Ferns are easily recognized with their large, leafy fronds, and graceful stature. The Fern may be found in nearly all parts of the world, although they may differ greatly from species to species.

LORE

Ferns have been used, as many other herbs, in forms of divination. Perhaps the most interesting lore is that when used magickally, Ferns will render you invisible.

REMEDIAL

Among the properties of Ferns are the ability to destroy intestinal worms and the excellent properties useful in the treatment of chest infections. Because of the many varieties, check your copy of Grieve before using.

- Anthelmintic, pectoral, demulcent, expectorant.

———— FEVERFEW ————

Common Feverfew has large, fresh, green leaves, much torn or cut on the edges. The stalks are hard and round, set with many such like leaves . . .

— Culpeper

It is a great remedie against the diseases of the matrix; it procureth womens sickness with speed; it bringeth forth the afterbirth and the dead childe, whether it bee drunke in a decoction or boiled in a bath, and the woman sit over it, . . .

— Gerard

Feverfew (a corruption of Febrifuge, from its tonic and fever-dispelling properties) is a composite plant growing in every hedgerow, with numerous, small, daisy-like heads of yellow flowers with outer white rays . . .

— Grieve

There are several varieties of Feverfew, well-described by the above commentaries. The leaves usually form a thick clump near the ground, and the flowers grow on stalks about knee-height.

REMEDIAL

Feverfew has been used for various difficulties with the menstrual cycle, particularly when the onset of the bleeding is preceded by much discomfort and delay. Culpeper says that "Venus commands this herb, and has commended it to succour her sisters (women) . . ." for it was widely used in his time as an emmenagogue.

Feverfew is also used for afflictions of the lungs, and is helpful for those suffering from congestion, asthma, and bronchial infections.

- Emmenagogue, pectoral, expectorant, aperient, carminative.

— FIREWEED —

This coarse, homely American weed is an annual and derives its name from its habit of growing freely in moist open woods and clearings, and in greatest luxuriance on newly-burnt fallows.

— Grieve

Fireweed is a striking plant to behold. It is slightly downy in texture, and can grow to remarkable heights. Some varieties grow taller than a person. It is a succulent, giving it an unusual appearance, and once it moves into an area, grows rampantly.

REMEDIAL

Fireweed was widely used among several tribes of North America. It has valuable use externally, being effective in the treatment of skin disorders such as psoriasis and eczema.

Internal use should be monitored carefully, for it has cathartic properties. It may be gargled for sore throat and laryngitis, but care should be taken to avoid ingesting large amounts. When used internally in controlled amounts, it is very helpful in the treatment of arthritis and rheumatism. It may be used internally or externally to inhibit bleeding.

- Astringent, carthartic, antispasmodic, emetic, alterative.

——— FOXGLOVE ———

The herb is familiarly and frequently used by the Italians to heal any fresh or green wound, the leaves being but bruised and bound thereon . . .

— Culpeper

The Foxglove is a favourite flower of the honey-bee, and is entirely developed by the visits of this insect. For that reason, its tall and stately spikes of flowers are at their best in those sunny, midsummer days when the bees are busiest.

— Grieve

The Foxglove is a truly beautiful herb. It is often found for sale in greenhouses, with its soft, downy leaves, awaiting a gardener who will love it for the flowers. Some of the common names will give you an idea of the the charm: Witches' Gloves, Fairy Glove, Fairy Caps, Fairy Thimbles, and so on. The leaves are collected from mature plants, usually in the second year when it has nearly finished flowering. The Foxglove usually lives about two years, but in some cases will propagate itself into many years of growth.

LORE

Foxglove is a plant which frequently is associated with fairies and the little people. Because of its poisonous nature, it is an herb of the underworld. The manner in which you work with the herb may make you kindred with the faery-folk or an enemy. It is best grown quietly in a garden for its beauty and natural magick, and not used.

REMEDIAL

Foxglove is a very potent herb. It goes by the name of 'Digitalis', for it is a powerful cardiac stimulant. Although it profoundly affects the muscle and tissue of the heart and major arteries, it also affects the rest of the muscular tissue within the body. It will bring about dramatic change within the circulatory system. As the body responds to the constituents of Foxglove, the muscles contract, which bring about a severe increase in the blood pressure.

Foxglove has been used to stimulate irregularities of the heart and circulation into a normal pulse. It also has an effect upon the kidneys, provoking them into working overtime. Foxglove is a powerful diuretic.

The poisonous constituent of Foxglove, notably digitoxin, is extremely poisonous, and is not easily passed through the body; rather building up and maintaining itself over time. Foxglove is known as an antidote for poisoning by aconite. Lily of the Valley is similar in effect to Foxglove, and has been used as a substitute.

Due to the nature of this herb, it should not be used in any manner other than as an herb in the garden collection.

• Cardiac, diuretic.

———— GARLIC ————

The whole plant, especially the root, is of a very strong and offensive smell.

— Culpeper

The bulbe or head of Garlicke is covered with most thinne skinnes or filmes of a very light white purple colour, consisting of many cloves severed one from another, under which in the ground below groweth a tassell of thready fibres . . .

— *Gerard*

The Common Garlic, a member of the same group of plants as the Onion, is of such antiquity as a cultivated plant, that it is difficult with any certainty to trace the country of its origin.

— Grieve

Perhaps one of the most widely used herbs in the kitchen, it is familiar by sight and smell both. Garlic is most beautiful when the dried leaves are braided, leaving a rope of the cloves.

LORE

A rope of garlic cloves brings health and protection to the kitchen. Garlic has been in use as a Religious Herbe among the ancient Egyptians, and Mohammedan legend says it sprang from the footsteps of Satan. It figures in many ancient legends.

REMEDIAL

Garlic is rich in sulphur, and this is an important element in its healing properties. As recently as World War I it was widely used as an antiseptic, the juice used to cleanse wounds and cuts and protect them from infection.

Garlic, as was Frankincense, was used by the Chinese to treat leprosy, and Garlic has held that use longer than other herbs. It has also been used to treat tuberculosis and other wasting diseases.

It is used externally for whooping cough, rubbed into the chest. It is also taken internally to relieve chest congestion. Taken regularly, internally, it is said to alleviate the distress of rheumatism and arthritis.

• Diaphoretic, diuretic, expectorant, antiseptic, stimulant.

— GOLDEN ROD —

This is a perennial, that grows by wood-sides, in copses, in moist as well as dry ground, and on heaths and among thickets.

— Culpeper

Golden Rod provoketh urine, washeth away the stones in the kidnies, and expelleth them, and withall bringeth downe tough and raw flegmatick humors stocking in the urine vessels, which now and then do hinder the comming away of the stones.

— Gerard

The plant contains tannin, with some bitter and astringent principles.

— Grieve

There are many varieties of Golden Rod, and they vary in height from about two feet to nearly four feet. It can be found easily throughout the summer by its golden-colored bower of flowers, coming to maturity particularly late in the season.

REMEDIAL

Golden Rod is one of the better herbs available for the passing of kidney stones. It has a long documented history of this practise. It also has a reputation as a vulnerary, useful in all types of wounds and bruises. Most of the varieties of Golden Rod work in a similar manner.

• Diuretic, astringent, vulnerary, stimulant, aromatic.

112

——— GOLDEN SEAL ———

The North American plant Golden Seal produces a drug which is considered of great value in modern medicine. The generic name of the plant, Hydrastis, is derived from two Greek words, signifying water and to accomplish, probably given it from its effects on the mucous membrane.

— Grieve

Smaller members of the Golden Seal grow barely higher than the ankle; the larger variety grows to about a foot in height. In gathering this herb in the wild, it can easily be overlooked due to it being shorter than most other herbs. It produces a single flower in the spring which leads to a bright, red cluster of berries. Golden Seal has been in popular use since the mid-nineteenth century, and used for a long time by the wise healers of the North Americans. It is easily located growing in the southeastern area of the United States.

LORE

Golden Seal has been used as a Religious Herbe among several tribes of the Appalachian areas, throughout the Carolinas, and in similar areas of the country.

REMEDIAL

Golden Seal is an important herb in treating wounds, promoting quick and easy healing. The root is powdered and applied directly, often as a poultice.

It aids in the removal of phlegm, both from the bronchial and sinus areas, and also from internal organs, giving them strength and health at the same time. It is considered an excellent remedy for the discomforts of pregnancy and the menstrual cycle. It is a comfortable remedy to use to correct constipation.

- Tonic, vulnerary, alterative, laxative.

GROUND IVY

Several countries give it several names, so that there is scarce an herb growing of that bigness, that has got so many. It is called Cat's Foot, Ground Ivy, Gill-go-by-ground, Gill-creep-by-ground, Turn hoof, Hay-Maids, and Alehoof.
— Culpeper

Although not a true ivy, Ground Ivy looks much like a member of the ivy family. It has lovely flowers in the spring, of a soft, blue-violet with white spotted edges. Often this flowering will continue throughout the summer, and aid in the identification of this herb. It was used by the Saxons in the making of their ales.

REMEDIAL

Ground Ivy is used primarily in the treatment of the kidneys and the urinary system. It is excellent in the treatment of bladder infections and urinary infections. It will stimulate a gentle bladder action and generally heal and tone the organ.

Ground Ivy may also be used for coughs, helping to break the cycle. It has also been used to stop a headache primarily caused by nerves and tension.

Ground Ivy has been considered a cure for a host of diseases over the years, and an Herbalist who intends to use this herb can explore it with great interest.

• Diuretic, vulnerary, stimulant, diaphoretic, astringent, tonic.

HAWTHORN

The seeds cleared of the down and bruised, being boiled in wine, are good for inward pains.

— Culpeper

Many country villagers believe that Hawthorn flowers still bear the smell of the Great Plague of London. The tree was formerly regarded as sacred, probably from a tradition that it furnished the Crown of Thorns.

— Grieve

The Hawthorn can grow to the height of 25-35 feet, and some of them are found which have seen many eras pass. They command respect, and can be easily identified later in the season, when they have born fruit. The small red berries are quite distinctive.

REMEDIAL

Hawthorn will ease the person who is suffering from most ailments of the heart. It is a cardiac tonic, bringing to the heart a sense of health and tone. It has been used in treating dropsy, and makes all cardiac subjects feel more vital.

The astringent properties of the berries and flowers have given them use in the treatment of sore throats and infections, and are also used for kidney inflammation and disorder.

• Astringent, cardiac, tonic, diuretic.

———— HEART'S EASE ————

The distilled water of the herbe or floures given to drinke for ten or more dayes together, three ounces in the morning, and the like quantitie at night, doth wonderfully ease the paines of the French disease, and cureth the same, if the Patient be caused to sweat sundry times . . .

— Gerard

The Heartsease is as variable as any of the other members of the genus, but whatever modifications of form it may present, it may always be readily distinguished from the other Violets by the general form of its foliage.

— Grieve

115

Although this is a member of the 'viola' or violet family, it is also known as the wild pansy, which is a good clue in identification of this herb. The stem of the plant grows close to the ground, reaching a maximum height of about seven inches, and the flowers are a combination of blue-violets and deep-yellows.

LORE

In times long past, the Heart's Ease was used in love charms, as may the pansy even today. This flower is even a part of the plot of the play "Midsummer Night's Dream."

REMEDIAL

Not only is Heart's Ease used magickally to attract love and romance, but the herb has a history of being a cure for those venereal diseases contracted from the joys and pleasures of love and romance! Culpeper recommends making a strong decoction of the flowers, stem, and leaves. It is interesting, however, that there is no reference to this in Grieve, perhaps due to the increasingly resistant strains of the infections which have evolved over the centuries.

Heart's Ease is used extensively in the treatment of skin conditions, being effective in the treatment of eczema (made into an ointment). It has also been used in the treatment of various itching irritations of the skin which lead to scabs.

Internally, Heart's Ease has been well-used to treat asthma, and epilepsy, and is thought to have a positive effect upon the health of the heart.

The root and the seeds of Heart's Ease may be used as cleansing agents, being somewhat emetic and purgative in nature.

- Roots and Seeds: emetic, purgative, expectorant.
- Herb: cardiac, expectorant, demulcent, emollient.

——— HOPS ———

The Hop doth live and flourish by embracing and taking hold of poles, pearches, and other things upon which it climeth.

— Gerard

116

The Hop is a native British plant, having affinities, botanically speaking, with the group of plants to which the Stinging Nettles belong.

— Grieve

Hops grow from a perennial root, and from the vines send forth heart-shaped leaves. Usually they grow in pairs on either side of the stem, and from this juncture come the flowers in bunches. The Hop is among those herbs giving forth both male and female flowers, and from this fruitfulness come the seeds. The seeds come forth in small bunches, and when dried are light and fluffy. The Hop fields throughout Britain are beautiful, with the green color reflecting the sunlight.

LORE

Hop figures in a minor way as a Religious Herbe, for it is used in the making of ritual beverages, such as the sacramental ales of the ancient tribes of the British Isles. Today its magickal use is primarily in inducing sleep when sewn into a dream pillow.

REMEDIAL

The oil contained within Hop has an effect upon the nervous system, relaxing it, and is one of the reasons that Hop has been used to bring about sleep. Whether or not this can be accomplished by inhaling the scent when sleeping upon a pillow of hop is open to debate, although those who pursue this practise feel it to be very effective. Hop may be taken internally for many nervous disorders, for its calming effect, and its soothing manner for ravaged nerves. Hop is excellent for those nights one lays in bed with an over-active thought process keeping the brain too alert to allow sleep.

The action upon the stomach when taken internally is stimulating to the appetite and makes Hop an effective remedy for those whose nervous conditions keep them from healthy eating habits.

The juice of the herb is very cleansing for the blood, and Hop has also been used to cleanse internal organs of the body. Culpeper reports the use of hop for cleansing the liver, spleen, digestive system, and the kidney.

Hop is also used externally, being good for disorders and afflictions of the skin such as boils and rashes, and is useful as a vulnerary in the treatment of bruises and pains. The sedative effect of the herb has given it use as a liniment in the treatment of rheumatism and arthritis.

• Sedative, nervine, tonic, diuretic, anodyne, stimulant, vulnerary.

117

——— HOREHOUND –———

*Common Horehound grows up with square hairy stalks,
half a yard or two feet high, set in the joints with two
crumpled rough leaves of a sullen hoary green colour, of a
good scent but a bitter taste.*

— Culpeper

*Boyled in water and drunke, openeth the liver and
spleene, cleanseth the brest and lungs, and prevales greatly
against an old cough . . .*

— Gerard

*The Egyptian Priests called this plant the 'Seed of Horus',
of the 'Bull's Blood', and thee 'Eye of the Star'. It was a
principal ingredient in the negro Caesar's antidote for
vegetable poisons.*

— Grieve

Although we frequently think of Horehound as a brown cough
lozenge, it is a very handsome herb to grow in the garden. It attracts
attention when it flowers, producing soft, white blossoms. The herb
grows somewhat compactly, but eventually will spread and grow into
a healthy bed.

LORE

Horehound was a Religious Herbe of Egypt. It was also a major
Religious Herbe of the Hebrew peoples, and still enjoys popular use
today. It is said to purge the person of those factors inhibiting
creativity and inspiration. It is a Visionary Herbe and a Magickal Herbe
throughout much of the world today.

REMEDIAL

Horehound is most widely used today for the treatment of coughs
and congestions of the lungs. Many people take it in strong doses as a
daily tonic, and their cough and cold are soon alleviated.
Horehound is an excellent herb to treat a smoker's cough, along

with other smoking herbs. A common mixture is Horehound, hyssop, coltsfoot, and the leaves of the marshmallow, which may either be smoked or made into an infusion.

Horehound is used today in fasts, when one wishes to cleanse the body of waste and unwanted matter. Horehound is a gentle purgative, and will not only cleanse but will be an excellent tonic for revitalization.

Externally, Horehound has been used in the treatment of eczema and psoriasis. A lotion may be applied, and a wash used to rinse the hair.

Horehound does have a particularly bitter taste, known to the Hebrews as one of the bitter herbs of Passover. It is usually flavored with honey or with licorice root.

- Pectoral, expectorant, tonic, astringent.

—— HORSETAILS ——

The great Horsetail at the first has heads resembling Asparagus, and afterwards grow to be hard, rough, hollow stalks, joined at sundry places at the top, a foot high, so made as if the lower parts were put into the upper, where grow on each side a bush of small long rush-like hard leaves. each part resembling a horse-tail.

— Culpeper

The Horsetails belong to a class of plants, the Equisetaceae, that has no direct affinity with any other group of British plants. They are nearest to the Ferns.

— Grieve

119

The Horsetails are considered remnants of plants from many ages past, and members of this family are found in fossils as a tribute to the many ages they have seen upon the Earth. They require the presence of water or adequate moisture, which determines their habitat. In appearance, they are quite unusual and unlike the majority of herbs sought by the Herbalist. They look quite primeval, and Culpeper's attempt to describe them, although accurate, shows the reaction this unusual herb provokes.

REMEDIAL

The stems are gathered from the plant and may be used for their properties as astringents and diuretics. They have been helpful in disorders of the kidneys and aid in the treatment of kidney stones. At one time they were used also in mild heart disorders. There are some who make a strong decoction for use as an emmenagogue.

- Diuretic, astringent, emmenagogue, styptic.

———— HYSSOP ————

Hyssop boiled with honey and rue, and drank, helps those that are troubled with coughs, shortness of breath, wheezing and rheumatic distillations upon the lungs.
— Culpeper

Hyssop is a name of Greek origin. The Hyssopos of Dioscorides was named from 'azob' (a holy herb), because it was used for cleaning sacred places. It is alluded to in the Scriptures: 'Purge me with Hyssop, and I shall be clean.'
— Grieve

Hyssop likes a pleasant climate and does not enjoy winter. It is thick, bushy, and appears as an evergreen. It flowers in profusion, and rarely grows above knee high.

LORE

Hyssop is used today as a Religious Herbe, as it has been since ancient days. Its ability to cleanse carries over into the sacred and spiritual. It is known as an Herbe of Protection.

REMEDIAL

Hyssop contains a volatile oil which is both sudorific in nature, and also stimulates the body. This combination makes Hyssop an excellent choice in the treatment of colds, and it is often mixed with preparations of horehound.

It may be used externally for the treatment of rheumatism and painful muscles.

- Stimulant, sudorific, expectorant, pectoral.

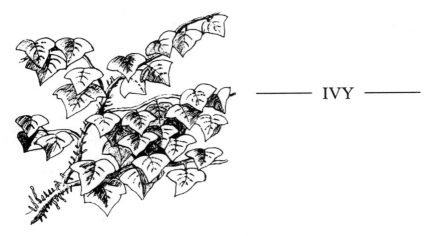

——— IVY ———

It is an enemy to the nerves and sinews, being much taken inwardly, but very helpful to them being outwardly applied.

— Culpeper

Ivy flourisheth in Autumne, the berries are ripe after the Winter-Solstice.

— Gerard

This well-known evergreen climber, with its dark-green, glossy, angular leaves is too familiar to need detailed description. It climbs by means of curious fibres resembling roots, which shoot out from every part of the stem, and are furnished with small disks at the end, which adapt themselves to the roughness or the bark or wall against which the plant grows and to which it clings firmly.

— Grieve

The nature of the clinging tendrils which furnish the support of the Ivy is such that they will, if in contact with soil, become roots. When Ivy grows upon a tree, they will grow into the tree itself, and seek nourishment, being somewhat parasitic in nature. There are many varieties of Ivy, the one most used herbally being Hedera Helix, or Common Ivy. This variety is capable of flowering, and may pass unnoticed if one does not look closely. The berries which will follow are dark in color, with a strong scent.

LORE

It is thought that Ivy leaves were the crown of Bacchus for their ability to prevent drunkenness when taking great quantities of alcohol. Ivy has also been used at times of celebration, those of athletic or political victory, and also at marriages and unions. There are a small few who associate Ivy with bad luck.

REMEDIAL

There is little use today of Ivy as a remedial herb although it is included because it is readily available to most persons. The berries are quite potent and disagreeable to the palate. They have been used in the treatment of the plague. As such, they are also strongly diuretic, and not recommended for popular use today.

Ivy may be made into liniment, particularly for athletes who overextend themselves. Culpeper also suggests combining the leaves with rose water and oil or rose, which, when massaged into the temples and stress points, is a remedy for headache.

• Diuretic, vulnerary, astringent, hepatic.

——— KAVA-KAVA ———

An indigenous shrub several feet high, leaves cordate, acuminate, with very short axillary spikes of flowers . . .
— Grieve

Kava-Kava is native to the South Sea Islands, particularly Polynesia. It comes to us as the chopped root, sort of gray-white in appearance, tough, and difficult to grind.

122

LORE

Kava-Kava is a Religious Herbe among many of the tropical islands, used before religious ceremonies. Taken as a fermented beverage, it induces visionary experiences. Current use of Kava-Kava is as a Visionary Herbe and an Aphrodisiac.

REMEDIAL

Kava-Kava works directly upon the nerves, first stimulating them, and then raising their pain threshold. It is useful in inflammation of joints and is used in the treatment of gout, rheumatism, arthritis, and many heart disorders. In extreme amounts, Kava-Kava will cause the respiratory system to greatly decrease its functions. It has been much used in the treatment of sexually-transmitted diseases, such as gonorrhea and vaginitis.

- Stimulant, anodyne, antiseptic.

— LADY'S SLIPPER —

American Valerian is one of the names given to the yellow Lady's Slipper....the roots of several varieties... are employed in histeria...

— Grieve

The Lady's Slipper is a delicate flower which, when in bloom, dominates the appearance of the plant. It does look similar enough to a slipper for one to easily see how it received its name. The roots are gathered, preferably when the plant is not in bloom. It can usually be found in wooded, shaded places.

REMEDIAL

The name American Valerian is given the herb, because of its effectiveness as a nervine, acting upon the nervous system in a similar manner to valerian. It is not always as quick as valerian, but is dependable and will relax the entire nervous system. It also alleviates pain, and can bring sleep when it is inhibited by pain. It has very much use as an emmenagogue. It is best used in combination with other herbs.

- Nervine, sedative, anodyne, diuretic, diaphoretic.

——— LAVENDER ———

Mercury owns this herb. It is of special use in pains of the head and brain which proceed from cold, apoplexy, falling-sickness, the dropsy, or sluggish malady, cramps, convulsions, palsies, and often faintings.

— Culpeper

Lavender Spike hath many stiffe branches of a wooddie substance, growing up in the manner of a shrubbe, set with many long hoarie leaves, by couples for the most part; of a strong smell, and yet pleasant enough to such as doe love strong flavours.

— Gerard

Lavender is a shrubby plant indigenous to the mountainous regions of the countries bordering the western half of the Mediterannean, and cultivated extensively for its aromatic flowers in various parts of France, in Italy and in England and even as far north as Norway. It is also now being grown as a perfume plant in Australia.

— Grieve

Lavender is a perennial, able to grow to solid strength, even though it has difficulty with winter in the more northern climates. The name is said to come from the Latin, 'lavare', which means "to wash". The flowers grow in small spikes, and are, of course, lavender in color. The herb is grown mainly for the flowers, from which the volatile oils are extracted.

124

LORE

Lavender as an herb was much in use in Pre-Christian Europe. It is known as a Magickal Herbe, a Religious Herbe, and has many other uses. It is still much used today.

REMEDIAL

Lavender tea is used to calm ravaged nerves, tendencies to hysteria and emotional outbursts, and also calms headaches caused from stress and fatigue. Lavender is made into a wash, and used externally, being excellent for acne and troubled skin.

Lavender is an excellent herb in the treatment of headaches. It may be taken internally, or the oil of the flowers rubbed into the temples.[8] It will calm and relieve pain. The anodyne properties of the oil also lend it to use as a liniment.

Large doses of the oil must be strictly avoided, for then Lavender may act as a narcotic poison.

- Aromatic, anodyne, carminative, nervine.

─────── LILY OF THE VALLEY ───────

The floures of the Valley Lillie distilled with wine, and drunke the quantitie of a spoonfull, restoreth speech unto those that have the dum palsie and that are falne into the Apoplexie, and is good against the gout, and comforteth the heart.

— Gerard

The Lily-of-the-Valley, with its broad leaves and fragrant little, nodding, white, bell-shaped flowers, is familiar to everyone.

— Grieve

Lily of the Valley contains a potent constituent called convallamarin, which is water soluble and may be extracted by infusion. This substance causes the same cardiac response as digitalis. Though milder than digitalis, doses of Lily of the Valley can still be quite harmful.

LORE

This lovely plant is said to have come to us from St. Leonard, who slew a mighty dragon, receiving wounds in the process. This cardiac herb sprouted from the places where his blood touched the Earth. Some consider this herb to be an Aphrodisiac, but current lore is more in the nature of Lily of the Valley being a favorite of faeries and herbe spirits.

REMEDIAL

Lily of the Valley may be used in the treatment of high blood pressure. It is much milder in action than digitalis or foxglove, the organic source of digitalis. It brings to the heart the ability to maintain a slow and steady pulse, without loss of strength.

During World War I, Lily of the Valley was used to restore strength in soldiers who had been attacked with gas. It is also used to treat various nervous disorders.

Some say that only the flowers should be used, for the root contains a stronger state of the constituents. This herb should be used with care.

- Stimulant, cardiac, tonic, diuretic.

——— LIQUORICE ———

Boiled in water, with some Maiden-head and figs, makes a good drink for those who have a dry cough or hoarseness, wheezing or shortness of breath, and for all the pains of the breasts and lungs . . .

— Culpeper

These plants do grow in sundry places of Germany wilde, and in France and Spaine, but they are planted in gardens in England, whereof I have plenty in my garden; the poore people of the North parts of England do manure it with great diligence, wherby they obtain great plenty thereof, replanting the same once in three or foure years.

— Gerard

The Liquorice of medicine and commerce is derived from the sweet root of various species of 'Glycrrhiza', a genus which contains about fourteen species, natives of warmer temperate countries of both the New and Old Worlds . . .

— Grieve

Liquorice also contains sugar, starch (nearly a third), protein, and glycyrrhizin, which provide the distinct flavor. It is a delicate plant with gentle leaves, feathery in nature, but remarkable for the roots, which extend deep into the soil. It grows for several years before the roots may be taken up and dried for commercial use.

LORE

Liquorice is one of the few herbs with little lore available, yet it has a history of use that dates back to the third century before Christ.

REMEDIAL

Liquorice is much-used in the treatment of congestion from colds, bronchitis, and all sorts of pulmonary complaints. It may be used in the treatment of sore throats, hoarseness, and laryngitis.

The natural ingredients in Liquorice make it ideal as a drink on hot summer days. A little of the finely ground root may be added to water and carried when hiking or at the beach. It not only quenches the thirst, but keeps the throat moist and a dry mouth at bay.

• Demulcent, emollient, pectoral, pulmonary.

——— MANDRAKE ———

The root formerly was supposed to have the human form, but it really resembles a carrot or parsnip.

— Culpeper

The male Mandrake hath great broad long smooth leaves of a darke green colour, flat spred upon the ground: among which come up the floures of a pale whitish colour, standing every one upon a single small and weake foot-stalke of a whitish greene colour: in their places grow round Apples of a yellowish colour, smooth, soft, and flittering . . .

— Gerard

The plant was fabled to grow under the gallows of murderers, and it was believed to be death to dig up the root, which was said to utter a shriek and terrible groans on being dug up, which none might hear and live. It was held, therefore, that he who would take up a plant of Mandrake should tie a dog to it for that purpose, who drawing it out would certainly perish, as the man would have done had he attempted to dig it up in the ordinary manner.

— Grieve

The root of the Mandrake may burrow itself into the Earth more than three feet, yet this is the part of the plant used by the Herbalist. The leaves are quite large, nearly a foot long and half as wide.

LORE

Perhaps few other herbs have attracted as much lore as the Mandrake, and that most likely due to the bizarre nature as quoted above by Grieve. Mandrakes have long been associated with all forms of Magick, for both white and black, and the root is said to be used in exorcisms, to drive out the spirits possessing the soul. It has often been carved into amulets and mixed into potions and magickal elixirs.

An idea of the extensiveness of the lore can be had from this list of properties: Fertility Herbe, Religious Herbe, Aphrodisiac, Funereal Herbe, Herbe of Protection, Magickal Herbe, Visionary Herbe, and Countermagicke Herbe.

REMEDIAL

The leaves are sometimes collected and made into ointments, poultices, and other external applications in the treatment of ulcerations of the skin, infected wounds, and the like. The root is dried, powdered, and taken internally. This process renders mandrake a very strong purgative and emetic, causing vomiting and evacuation of the bowels.

Large doses should be avoided, causing delirium and discomfort. In moderate doses it will ease pain.

For use as a laxative, it is recommended that Mandrake be mixed with liquorice.

• Purgative, emetic, anodyne, narcotic, sedative, nervine.

——— MARIGOLD ———

The yellow leaves of the floures are dried and kept throughout Dutchland against Winter, to put into broths, in physicall potions, and for divers other purposes, in such quantity, that in some Grocers or Spice-sellers houses are to be found barrels filled with them, and retailed by the penny more or lesse, insomuch that no broths are well made without dried Marigolds.

— Gerard

It promotes sweat and is frequently used to drive out small-pox and measles; it also helps the jaundice.

— Culpeper

It was not named after the Virgin, its name being a corruption of the Anglo-Saxon 'merso-mear-gealla', the Marsh Marigold. Old English authors called it Golds or Ruddes. It was, however, later associated with the Virgin Mary, and in the seventeenth century with Queen Mary.

— Grieve

Marigolds are a sturdy annual and quite familiar. They have been domesticated into a variety of sizes, some with tiny flowers, and others large and magnificent. Most have a golden color, but may range from bright yellow to deep, dark hues. The flowers may be gathered when in full bloom and hung upside down in a warm and dry place until the petals are completely dry.

LORE

Marigolds are used as Visionary Herbes, and are part of the lore of Mexico. In that country it is said that they have their origin in the blood of the native peoples slain by the invading Spaniards.

Marigolds are found in recipes for love divination, and it is also said that they give off bright sparks of light during a thunderstorm.

129

REMEDIAL

Marigolds are one of the most useful of herbs in the treatment of skin disorders. They are often included in herbal mixtures for the problems of eczema, psoriasis, insect bites, and wounds. They are given internally for various ailments, and are of particular note in easing the complications of measles and small-pox. They help stop the fever and quicken the process of the measle spots following their course.

Marigolds have also been used in the treatment of epilepsy, and are used internally in mild heart disease.

• Stimulant, diaphoretic, astringent, haemostat.

——— MARSHMALLOW ———

But the roots are of more special use for those purposes, as well for coughs, hoarseness, shortness of breath, and wheezings, being boiled in wine or honeyed water, and drunk.

— Culpeper

Marsh Mallow is also a certaine kinde of wilde Mallow: it hath broad leaves, small toward the point, soft, white and . . . cottoned, and sleightly nicked short the edges: the stalks be round and straight, three or foure foot high, of a whitish gray colour . . .

— Gerard

Dioscorides extols it as a remedy, and in ancient days it was not only valued as a medicine, but was used, especially the Musk Mallow, to decorate the graves of friends.

— Grieve

In common herbal practise, it is the root, an off-white color, that is most often used. It is dried, then chopped. The dried leaves and flowers may also be found, but are not as effective. It is perennial, but is not too happy with a rough winter season. Other members of the Mallow family are found wild throughout most of North America.

LORE

In ancient days, Marshmallow was a Funereal Herbe, and was also taken daily as a tonic to avoid all sorts of illness and disease. It has little magickal use today.

REMEDIAL

Due to the large amount of natural mucilage within the root, it is one of the most valuable herbs used in treating congestion. Marshmallow is excellent in relieving stuffed sinus passages, and also helps to remove phlegm from the bronchial passages and lungs.

A poultice may be made of ground root, and this used to draw out infection from insect bites or inflamed wounds. The same poultice may be used to treat burns, soothing and protecting the damaged area.

A wash may be made of either root or leaf and is an effective remedy in clearing up dandruff and itchy, flakey scalp. It may also be included in ointments used in the treatment of eczema and psoriasis.

The dried roots, boiled in milk and honey are considered most effective in the treatment of bronchitis and croup. A milder mixture may be taken by those with ulcers of the stomach, or with anemia, or those who have recently suffered loss of blood.

Marshmallow is sometimes taken by women following the bleeding of their menstrual cycle and is sometimes used as a wash, or a vaginal douche.

- Demulcent, emollient, pulmonary, expectorant, alterative.

———— MISTLETOE ————

Misseltoe is a cephalic and nervine medicine, useful for convulsive fits, palsy, and vertigo.

— Culpeper

The well-known Mistletoe is an evergreen parasitic plant, growing on the branches of trees, where it forms pendent bushes, 2 to 5 feet in diameter. It will grow and has been found on almost any deciduous tree, preferring those with soft bark, and being, perhaps, commonest on old Apple trees, though it is frequently found on the Ash, Hawthorn, Lime and other trees. On the Oak, it grows very seldom.

— Grieve

It has a somewhat woody stem, with small leaves growing in pairs. The flowers usually are found in threes, and have both male and female parts. The best Mistletoe may be purchased fresh at a greenhouse during the winter holiday season, brought home and dried thoroughly, care being taken to remove the berries and store them separately, for they are far more potent than the leaf.

LORE

Great lore has grown with the herb throughout many ages. It has figured in a few cultures as a highly revered Religious Herbe, particularly among the Druidic priesthood. It is both a Fertility Herbe and an Aphrodisiac, an Herbe of Protection, and a Visionary Herbe. There are few areas of magick where this herb is not used currently, or has a history of use.

REMEDIAL

Mistletoe is used in the treatment of high blood pressure and hardening of the arteries. It has been used to calm the convulsions of epilepsy and other nervous disorders. The berries are toxic to a degree, and commercially purchased Mistletoe usually has them removed. The berries are not recommended for remedial work, instead relegated to the use of the Practitioner.

Mistletoe is used to treat hemorrhage, severe headache, and difficulty with the menstrual cycle, particularly excessive bleeding and painful cramps.

The berries have been used to make a wash, useful in the treatment of oily skin, pimples, and acne.

Mistletoe is good for improving the circulation, making it healthy and keeping the arterial system toned up.

- Cardiac, haemostat, stimulant, nervine, emmenagogue.

——— MOTHERWORT ———

There is no better herb to take melancholy vapours from the heart, and to strengthen it.

— Culpeper

The pouder of the herbe given in wine, provoketh not

only urine, or the monthly course, but also is good for them that are in hard travell with childe.

— Gerard

It is often found in country gardens, where it was formerly grown for medicinal purposes, but it is rare to find it truly wild in England, and by some authorities it is not considered indigenous, but merely a garden escape.

— Grieve

Motherwort is a sturdy plant, and can grow as tall as three or four feet. It grows as a perennial and is many-leaved. It blossoms in late summer and then grows seed.

REMEDIAL

The first use of Motherwort is as a nervine tonic, given to those recovering from heart disorders, and who are plagued with chronic pain. Its primary use today is in the treatment of disorders with the menstrual cycle and in promoting a healthy birthing experience. It is not pleasant to taste in strong doses.

- Nervine, anodyne, emmenagogue, tonic.

 ——— MOUNTAIN GRAPE ———

The shrub was introduced into England from North America in 1823.

— Grieve

This variety of grape grows as a shrub, about the height of a tall

133

adult. It is filled with leaf, and grows small berries which appear as grapes. They grow purple later in the summer.

REMEDIAL

Although the berries may be used, they tend to leave a stain. There are some who use the leaves, and some who remove and use the bark. Mountain Grape is important in the treatment of psoriasis and eczema. It has also been used internally to treat syphilis, although the current strains of the disease are hardier than the treatment and require stronger medication.

Mild doses are taken as a tonic which increases the general health of the individual and improves the appetite.

• Tonic, alterative, stimulant.

——— MUGWORT ———

Its tops, leaves and flowers are full of virtue; they are aromatic, and most safe and excellent in female disorders.

— Culpeper

It cureth the shakings of the joynts, inclining to the palsie, and helpeth the contraction or drawing together of the nerves and sinewes.

— Gerard

Mugwort abounds on hedgebanks and waysides in most parts of England. It is a tall-growing plant, the stems, which are angular and often of a purplish hue, frequently rising 3 feet or more in height.

— Grieve

Mugwort is related to the wormwoods, the family called 'artemisia'. The bottom-sides of the leaves are soft, but the tops are shiny. It flowers in profusion, with masses of red or light yellow blossoms. It is thought to have received its name from once being a major flavoring for beverages.

134

LORE

Mugwort has both a large lore from past use as a Magickal Herbe, and enjoys great popularity even today. It is considered a Visionary Herbe, being much used by those practising prophecy and divination. It is used to protect homes, friends, and possessions, and to consecrate various implements of magick. It has a strong connection with the crystal ball.

REMEDIAL

Mugwort is primarily used by women today, for it has a strong value as an emmenagogue. It is used when the menstrual cycle is fraught with pain and difficulty, and having also nervine properties, it is excellent in this use. It is often recommended that it be mixed equally with pennyroyal. It is very useful in childbirth and is excellent to give as a tonic around the time of birth, restoring health to the mother and promoting an easier labor.

Mugwort has also been used in the treatment of feverish colds and has been a bathing herb for the same purpose. At one time it was used as a nervine in the treatment of epilepsy and other nervous disorders.

* Emmenagogue, nervine, diaphoretic, aromatic, diuretic, stimulant.

 MULLEIN

This has many fair, large, wooly white leaves, lying next the ground, somewhat larger than broad, pointed at the end, and dented about the edges.

— Culpeper

135

The leaves worne under the feet, day and night, in manner of a shoe sole or sock, bringeth down in yong maidens their desired sicknesse, being kept under their feet with some socks or other thing for falling away.

— Gerard

They are all tall, stout, biennials, with large leaves and flowers in long, terminal spikes.

— Grieve

The Mullein can reach extraordinary heights. It is not uncommon to find a plant which towers above a tall person. They are easy to distinguish, for the tall spike which reaches up is a definite characteristic of Mullein; they can even be spotted when driving along a country road. Generally preferring rural meadows, they are now found even along urban freeways. The leaves grow near the ground, and are nearly like coarse velvet to the touch.

LORE

Owing to the nature of its growth, it has been gathered and dried whole, the spike then dipped in tallow and used as a torch for outdoor religious festivities. There were some monasteries that grew it as a means of banishing the devil, and it is yet considered an Herbe of Protection.

REMEDIAL

Mullein is a valuable herb in the treatment of various complaints of the lungs such as chronic bronchitis and emphysema. They have also been used in the treatment of tuberculosis, and the leaves make an excellent smoking herb. As such, they can be mixed with any of the other smoking herbs for general consumption.

The leaves have sometimes been prepared as a thick poultice and used in the treatment of hemorrhoids, for they are emollient and astringent, both soothing the pain and tenderness and causing the swelling to diminish.

These same qualities, the astringency and emollient property, make Mullein an excellent treatment for diarrhea, and in severe cases of colitis may be taken at the strength of a decoction.

• Astringent, emollient, vulnerary.

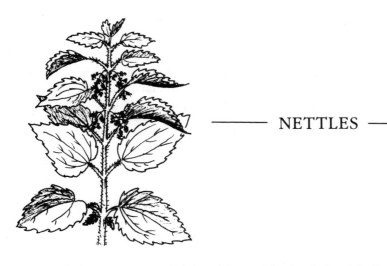

NETTLES

Being eaten, as Dioscorides saith, boyled with Pery-winkles, it maketh the body soluble, doing it by a kinds of cleansing qualities: it also provoketh urine, and expelleth stones out of the kidneys: being boyled with barley creame it bringeth up tough humours that sticke in the chest, as it is thought.

— Gerard

The Nettle tribe, Urticaceae, is widely spread over the world and contains about 500 species, mainly tropical, though several, like our common Stinging Nettle, occur widely in temperate climates. Many of the species have stinging hairs on their stems and leaves.

— Grieve

Nettles can grow easily to several feet or more in height. They have small, attractive, purple flowers, but are most offensive to the skin, causing itching and redness. They are rich in vitamins and iron, and very useful in maintaining nourishment and good health.

LORE

Albertus Magnus tells us that combining Nettles with houseleek and making an oil or infusion to bathe one's hand in is a certain way of attracting fish (the fish are said to swim eagerly to such a hand).

REMEDIAL

The high vitamin content makes Nettles one of the better tonics of the herb kingdom although care must be taken in the gathering. Nettles are also used as a haemostat, stopping bleeding. In past times they were ground to a fine powder and used as a snuff to stop nosebleed. Drinking a strong infusion is another means of stopping bleeding.

The irritant within the hairs and leaves made Nettles a useful aphrodisiac to the ancients, who used it to cause irritation to the sexual organs of domestic animals. Thus, the stimulation would increase their desire to mate and produce offspring for the herd.

Nettles are effective in treating a cold before it matures, catching it in the stage of chills, runny nose, and general discomfort. Taken as a tonic-tea, Nettles work wonders in restoring health.

The leaves are sometimes eaten as a cooked green, as this is said to improve one's complexion and circulation. A decoction of Nettles will cleanse the circulatory system.

The leaves may be used to clear the lungs and chest of phlegm. There are some who say the roots are more effective for this purpose.

- Tonic, rubefacient, astringent, haemostat, stimulant.

——— ONION ———

Onion bruised, with the addition of a little salt, and laid on fresh burns, draws out the fire, and prevents them blistering.

— Culpeper

There be, saith Theophrastus, divers sorts of Onions, which have their syr-names of the places where they grow: some also lesser, others greater; some be round, and divers others long; but none wilde, as Pliny writeth.

— Gerard

Onions are characterized by the white bulb, very succulent and containing much liquid and covered with a thin layer of paper-like skin. They send up tall, smooth green leaves, hollow within, and if left to grow long enough will flower and seed.

REMEDIAL

Onions are little used today in remedial treatment. They were once greatly used in the treatment of colds. They were also thought to make men more virile, to increase the appetite and cure the bites of venemous creatures.

- Vulnerary, antiseptic, diuretic.

——— PARSLEY ———

. . . it is very comforting to the stomach; helps to provoke urine and the courses, to break wind, both in the stomach and bowels, and opens the body, but the root much more.

— Culpeper

The leaves of garden Parsley are of a beautiful greene, consisting of many little ones fastened together, divided most commonly into three parts, and also snipt round about the edges . . .

— Gerard

There is an old superstition against transplanting parsley plants. The herb is said to have been dedicated to Persephone and to funeral rites by the Greeks. It was afterwards consecrated to St. Peter in his character of successor to Charon.

— Grieve

Although there are several varieties of Parsley commonly found growing in gardens, they are characterized by the fullness of the curly leaves. Left growing, Parsley will produce seed, and is thought best if grown from seed. It is possible for it to survive several years, but generally Parsley will need to be resown every other year or so.

LORE

There is quite a bit of lore attached to this herb. It represented honor to the Greeks, and was worn upon the head in wreaths. It is used today as a bathing herb, in order to commune with the Divine Mother aspect of Nature, and is thought to make horses more speedy.

REMEDIAL

The primary use of Parsley is for its action upon the kidneys. It has been used to cleanse them, helps to remove kidney stones, and as a diuretic aids in the removal of toxic substances from the kidneys. It also has some action upon the liver, and has been used in the treatment of jaundice.

As a remedial herb, it is best to plant the seed and nurture the grown plant through the winter, and at the end of the second year to dig up and preserve the root. It may be used to calm excitable conditions.

* Diuretic, nervine, sedative, carminative, aperient, tonic.

PENNYROYAL

If boiled and drank, it provokes women's courses, and expels the dead child and afterbirth, and stays the disposition to vomit, if taken in water and vinegar mingled together.
— Culpeper

This species of Mint, a native of most parts of Europe and parts of Asia, is the Pulegium of the Romans, so named by Pliny from its reputed power of driving away fleas . . .
— Grieve

Pennyroyal is a member of the mint family, but grows much smaller than the others. It has lovely purple flowers in the last half of the summer and a most distinctive scent. It may be found either growing native or as a domestic plant. It is easy to grow, but in severe winters may need special care to establish its domain.

LORE

The most curious of lore comes from A. Magnus, who says it will revive a drowned insect if the poor bug is placed in its warm ashes. Pennyroyal is used magickally today in rituals of consecration. It was once used as a Greene Herbe in the kitchen, but this is no longer the case.

140

REMEDIAL

Pennyroyal is primarily used externally in general practise. It is an antiseptic, and may be applied to cuts, wounds, and the like, to cleanse them and promote healing. It will calm itching skin, and may be used to quiet the discomfort of insect bites. Should it have been applied before the insect took control of your skin, it discourages them, and many swear that using it keeps them free from mosquitoes and other noxious insects. For this purpose, the oil is most effective.

As an emmenagogue, it should be used with great care. There is some disagreement among herbalists, and there are those who say it may endanger the user. It calms, and will also quiet spasms. As such, it is an excellent nervine, used in small quantities.

Pennyroyal will, as all of the mints, calm indigestion and a nervous stomach. It will assist greatly in the treatment of chills and the onset of a bad cold.

- Stimulant, emmenagogue, antiseptic, diaphoretic, nervine.

——— PEPPERMINT ———

The leaves of this Mint are broader and somewhat shorter than Spear-mint, growing on footstalks, half an inch long, sharpely serrated about the edges.

— Culpeper

It was only recognized here as a distinct species late in the seventeenth century, when the great botanist, Ray, published it in the second edition of his 'Synopsis stirpium britannicorum, in 1696. Its medicinal properties were speedily recognized, and it was admitted into the London Pharmacopoeia in 1721.

— Grieve

The Peppermint has, perhaps, the sweetest of scents of the mints. Spearmint is sharp, pennyroyal deep and pungent, but Peppermint reminds us of those pink candies so many of us received from our grandparents. The visible distinctions of the mints need be seen to be remembered, but learning to distinguish them by their scents is a certain way of easily identifying them.

141

LORE

Peppermint is found to have mythological associations, and enjoys current magickal use as a Visionary Herbe. It is said that drinking the tea in the evening makes for interesting dreams.

REMEDIAL

The presence of 'menthol' makes for Peppermint's use as a mild anodyne. It greatly anaesthetizes the nerve endings, calms them, and gives them a sensation of coolness. Used to quiet a nervous stomach, Peppermint makes for a contented person. It will quiet stomach cramps, and is not as intense in its action as penneyroyal.

Peppermint may also be used as a tonic. It contains magnesium, potassium, and other important constituents. It is most pleasant to the taste, and may safely be taken by all.

Peppermint is excellent in the treatment of nausea, and will help stimulate the appetite into a healthy state. A few herbalists recommend Peppermint for ease in childbirth, as it is safer than pennyroyal.

For aches, pains, and bruises, use the oil of peppermint, and gently work it into the flesh. Take care to not use an excessive amount, for it will create heat, and as many essential oils, could burn if used carelessly.

• Anodyne, carminative, tonic, emmenagogue, antiseptic, liniment, stimulant, stomachic, aromatic.

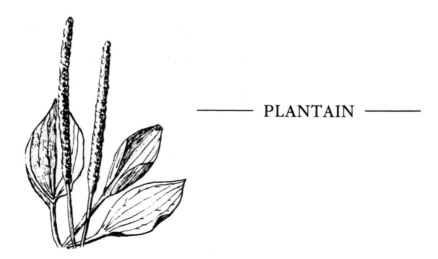

—— PLANTAIN ——

142

As the Greeks have called some kindes of Herbes Serpents tongue, Dogs tongue, and Oxe tongue, so have they termed a kind of Plantaine . . . Lambes tongue, very well knowne unto all, by reason of the great commoditie and plenty thereof growing everywhere . . .

— Gerard

The juice, clarified and drank for days together by itself, or with other drink, helps excoriations or pains in the bowels, the distillations of rheum from the head, and it stays all manner of fluxes, even womens' courses, when too abundant.

— Culpeper

The drug is without odour: the leaves are saline, bitterish and acrid to the taste; the root is saline in many species.

— Grieve

There is scarcely a large area of grass to be found without some Plantain growing about. It has the distinctive flat leaves which grow near the ground, and sends up a club-like flower on a thin stalk which supports both flower and following seeds.

REMEDIAL

Being readily available, Plantain is memorable for its use when freshly gathered, the leaves worked until moist with their own juices, and then being ideal to use in the treatment of burns, minor wounds, and rashes.

Plantain has been used in the treatment of malignant ulcers, both internal and external. However, its primary use today is found in its ability to reduce a fever, imparting a cooling sensation to the user.

• Astringent, diuretic, refrigerant.

——— POMEGRANATE ———

A strong infusion cures ulcers in the mouth and throat, and fastens teeth.

— Culpeper

The juicie grains of the Pomegranate are good to be eaten, having in them a meetly good juice; they are wholesome for the stomacke, but they all containe in them a thin and small nourishment, or none at all.

— Gerard

Having no close relations, the tree has been placed by various authorities in different orders, some giving it an order of its own, Granateae.

— Grieve

Pomegranates grow upon moderately sized trees, up to about thirteen feet in height. The flowers are large and striking, but we are most familiar with the fruit; the hard, red, round pods. Within the hard rind are numerous seeds and a runny, deep-red juice, which provides the delectable flavor.

LORE

Pomegranates have figured as Religious Herbes for many ages, remnants of this use being found by their inclusion into the design of religious artwork and construction. Today they are held sacred by many women.

REMEDIAL

The seeds are used for treatment of the kidneys, being somewhat diuretic, and the whole fruit, particularly the rind, is astringent in nature, and used to cure diarrhea and moderate fevers.

- Astringent, diuretic, antipyretic.

— RASPBERRY —

144

This cannot properly be called a fruit-tree, yet, as the fruit is valuable, something is expected of the shrub that produces it.

— Culpeper

An infusion of Raspberry leaves, taken cold, is a reliable remedy for extreme laxity of the bowels. The infusion alone, or as a component part of injections, never fails to give immediate relief. It is useful in stomach complaints of children.

— Grieve

As a member of the bramble, the Raspberry is characterized by the bramble-like quality of the stems which grow freely and are given to suckers. The small flowers lead to the distinctive red fruits which are abundantly gathered.

REMEDIAL

One of the primary uses is the leaf for its astringent property. It is nearly as effective as the blackberry which is a close relative and friend of the Raspberry. It has less use externally, but may be used as a vulnerary which cleanses.

Raspberry Tea, made of the leaves, is highly recommended by many Herbalists as a tonic to be taken by the mother during childbirth, beginning with the labor and continuing until after the child has been brought forth.

- Astringent, stimulant, tonic, vulnerary.

——— RED CLOVER ———

145

If the herb be made into a poultice, and applied to inflammations, it will ease them.

— Culpeper

Oxen and other cattell do feed of the herbe, and also calves and young lambs. The floures are acceptable to Bees.

— Gerard

The fluid extract of Trifolium is used as an alterative and antispasmodic. An infusion made by 1 oz. to 1 pint of boiling water may with advantage be used in cases of bronchial and whooping-cough.

— Grieve

Red Clover is a legume, its roots extracting nitrogen from the soil. It is found readily along roadsides, in fields, and even along sidewalks in urban areas. It is usually a biennial or perennial, and has wonderful pink-to-lavendar-colored blossoms. The flowers are used gathered and dried.

LORE

This was a Religious Herbe among the Celts, and aside from the good luck of a four-leafed Clover, has figured widely as a Magickal Herbe.

REMEDIAL

Red Clover is excellent for cleansing and restoring health to the blood. It has also been explored as a remedy for cancer, although there is still medical doubt today, yet there are those who say regular infusions work in the treatment of the disease.

Red Clover is an excellent herb to add to healing ointments and works well with comfrey. It may be used to treat wounds, cuts, sores, and infected areas.

It has long been used to treat bronchial infections, particularly those which produce severe coughing. It not only works against the condition, but Red Clover has been known for its calming effects also. It has been combined with hops and lettuce as a tonic which aids in gaining sleep.

- Nervine, pectoral, tonic.

——— ROSEMARY ———

It helps a weak memory, and quickens the senses. It is very comfortable to the stomach in all the cold maladies thereof; helps both the retention of meat, and digestion, the decoction of the powder being taken in wine.

— Culpeper

Rosemarie is a wooddie shrub, growing often times to the height of three or four cubits, especially when it is set by a wall.

— Gerard

The evergreen leaves of this shrubby herb are about 1 inch long, linear, revolute, dark green above and paler and glandular beneath, with an odour pungently aromatic and somewhat camphoraceous.

— Grieve

A healthy Rosemary plant looks very much like an evergreen with thick dark needles. Yet it is not very fond of the winter, and in northern climates is usually brought in, potted, and kept warm through the winter.

LORE

Rosemary is an herb that has lore dating back to the ancients. It has been used in both weddings and funerals, and is a favorite among the Greene Herbes. The strong-scented volatile oil has led to Rosemary's inclusion in many recipes for incense, both among Christian and Pagan religions.

REMEDIAL

Not only is Rosemary said to improve the memory, but it is an excellent herb to take in the event of headache, even of a migraine. It is also soothing to all the nervous system, and is used in stomach disorders caused by tension. At least one Herbalist says that the constituents of Rosemary are most beneficial to the brain, giving it vitality and health.

147

Rosemary tea is highly recommended for those who have trouble falling asleep, particularly when they are bothered with troublesome thoughts. A wash may be made of the herb which is strengthening to the roots of the hair and is considered effective in the treatment of dandruff.

Some take Rosemary daily as a tonic, for it is also good for the heart, toning it and keeping it in good working order.

- Stomachic, tonic, astringent, diaphoretic, nervine, rubefacient.

RUE

It helps disorders in the head, nerves, and womb, convulsions and hysteric fits, the colic, and weakness of the stomach and bowels; it resists poison, and cures venemous bites.

— Culpeper

Garden Rue or planted Rue, is a shrub full of branches, now and then a yard high, or higher . . .

— Gerard

Rue is first mentioned by Turner, 1562, in his Herbal, and has since become one of the best known and most widely grown simples for medicinal and homely uses.

— Grieve

Rue is quite branched, with small leaves and it blossoms throughout the summer. Although it has a tendency to seed itself, it has been cultivated for many centuries. It is known for its strong, disagreeable odor, and is preferred to the wild varieties of Rue.

LORE

Rue has been long considered an Herbe of Protection, and is found in various herbal amulet recipes made to protect one's home and family. It is said also to banish all evil and negative energy. Today it is also used to consecrate religious and magickal tools.

REMEDIAL

Rue is a strong antispasmodic, and this is one of its chief uses for the herbalist. It is popular today as an emmenagogue, but in large doses is not safe and may cause vomiting. It is not recommended following a meal, as it may provoke the stomach into distress. It will calm many of the distresses of the menstrual period.

As a nervine, it is used to treat many nervous afflictions and may also be used to dispel violent coughing, such as may accompany the croup or severe bronchitis.

Rue is not recommended for external use, one exception being its use in a liniment for the chest in the treatment of bronchitis and the like.

- Antispasmodic, stimulant, nervine, rubefacient, stomachic.

SAGE

A decoction of the leaves and branches made and drank provokes urine, expels the dead child, brings down womens' courses, and causes the hair to become black. It stays the bleeding of wounds, and cleanses foul ulcers or sores.
— Culpeper

Sage is singular good for the head and braine, it quickenth the senses and strengthneth the sinews, restoreth health to those that have the palsie upon a moist cause, takes away shaking or trembling of the members, and being put up into the nostrils, it draweth thin flegme out of the head.
— Gerard

When wild it is much like the common garden Sage, though more shrubby in appearance and has a more penetrating odour, being more spicy and astringent than the cultivated plant.
— Grieve

Sage is a shrubby plant, found growing wild throughout much of the world. It is indigenous to the Mediterranean from which it spread throughout Europe, becoming an important household and medicinal herb. It is found throughout our western mountains, where it was well known by the native Indians for its healing and religious properties. It is a tough plant, with the oblong leaves, a singular light green color, and can always be distinguished by its scent. One of its constituents, thujone, is a potent antibacterial, one of the best among herbs, which is contained as a volatile oil.

LORE

Sage is much used to cleanse the thinking process, to rid the mind of negative thoughts. It is a significant Religious Herbe among the tribes of North America. Among its properties, it brings one in touch with common sense, a much-needed virtue in the world today. Sage is used as a Greene Herbe, being well used in various kitchen recipes.

REMEDIAL

Sage is one of the best styptics available. A few fresh leaves, lightly worked (chewing is best) and applied to a cut or wound will quickly stop the bleeding. The same effect may be had with dried Sage, but it is more difficult to create a natural poultice with it other than immersion in hot water, both awkward and time consuming, for bleeding needs immediate attention. Sage is an essential herb to grow in one's garden. An ointment of Sage may be kept at hand and, like comfrey, should be in any working area, such as kitchen, construction areas, etc.

Sage is taken internally, being good for the stomach, calming indigestion, and also used to discourage constipation. Sage works well in the treatment of ulcerated stomachs, helping to tone the tissue; the astringent working against the ulcer itself.

Sage may be used externally as a liniment, being good for sore muscles, arthritis, and the like. It should be kept handy for athletes, and for those old of joint, prone to stiffness, and likely to ache.

A wash made of Sage may be used as a gargle, one of the most effective in the treatment of oral infections. This gargle can also be used in treating throat infections, and preventing the germs of colds and viruses from spreading. Sage is also used in early treatment of colds and chills, and may be added to any remedy for the lungs and respiratory system. Sage will reduce fever, and also works as an expectorant.

• Aromatic, astringent, styptic, tonic, febrifuge, antiseptic, emmenagogue, stomachic, expectorant.

SAINT JOHN'S WORT

A tincture of the flowers in spirit of wine, is commended against melancholy and madness. Outwardly, it is of great service in bruises, contusions, and wounds, especially in the nervous parts.

— Culpeper

The leaves stamped are good to be layed upon burnings, scaldings and all wounds; and also forgotten and filthy ulcers.

— Gerard

A herbaceous perennial growing freely wild to a height of 1 to 3 feet in uncultivated ground, woods, hedges, roadsides, and meadows.

— Grieve

Saint John's Wort is a light-green in color, with drop-shaped leaves. The flowers are bright yellow, and an indication of the healthy virtues of this herb. They may be found blooming throughout the summer.

LORE

Saint John's Wort is considered an Herbe of Protection, which history dates back to the early Greeks. It attracted an amount of superstition during the Middle Ages.

REMEDIAL

The astringent properties of this herb have led to its use in the treatment of a variety of conditions. It has been used to control bleeding and diarrhea. Internally, it also works upon the liver, and is helpful in clearing jaundiced conditions.

It works also upon the nervous system and calms extreme emotional states, either hysteria or depression. It has been used extensively in various complaints of the lungs, being an effective pectoral in chronic bronchitis, and in removing excessive phlegm.

An interesting use is found in the treatment of chronic bedwetting with the recommendation that a glass of Saint John's Wort tea be given a child before bedtime.

- Astringent, expectorant, nervine, haemostat, hepatic.

—— SELF HEAL ——

Prunell or Brunel hath square hairy stalks of a foot high, beset with long, hairy and sharpe pointed leaves, & at top of the stalks grow floures thicke set together, like an eare or spiky knap . . .

— Gerard

Self Heal is one of those common wildflowers that have found their way to North America, tending even to oust the native flowers. It is known there as 'Heart of the Earth' and 'Blue Curls'.

— Grieve

Grieve talks of this herb as one which can be confused with no other herb due to the appearance of the flower. When finished flowering, and the seed is ripe, it looks like a small ear of corn.

REMEDIAL

Self Heal may be used internally or externally in any case requiring the use of an astringent. It may be used for all manner of wounds, internal disorders, and skin conditions.
- Astringent, vulnerary, styptic, tonic.

──── SHEPHERD'S PURSE ────

The root is small, white, and perishes yearly. The leaves are small and long, of a pale green colour, and deeply cut in on both sides . . .
— Culpeper

Shepheards purse stayeth bleeding in any part of the body, whether the juice or the decoction thereof be drunke . .
— Gerard

A native of Europe, the plant has accompanied Europeans in all their migrations and established itself wherever they have settled to till the soil. In John Josselyn's Herbal it is one of the plants named as unknown to the New World before the Pilgrim Fathers settled there.
— Grieve

This herb is so called because of the small containers for the seed of the plant resembling a small, flat, leather purse. It may, in good conditions, reach knee height. The flowers are small, white, and, in time, are followed by seed pods.

REMEDIAL

Shepherd's Purse is one of the most effective herbs in the treatment of bleeding. It may be used internally or externally. It has been used for haemmorhages, and its excellent properties as an astringent render it useful for the treatment of diarrhea.
- Styptic, haemostat, astringent, diuretic.

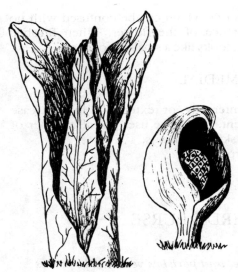

SKUNK CABBAGE

The plant grows in abundance in moist places of the northern and middle United States.

— Grieve

One of the means of identifying this herb is by the odor, which is considered foul to most people other than herbalists. The leaves grow from a rhizome, which is the part used in remedial work. These should be gathered either early in the spring or late in the fall, and due to the quick deterioration of the constituents, are useful for only a year. The seeds may also be gathered and used, and have a longer shelf life.

REMEDIAL

Skunk Cabbage must be used with care, for large doses are narcotic and have very unpleasant side effects. In cautious doses, Skunk Cabbage may be used in the treatment of asthma, arthritis, and rheumatism. It has also been used to treat some heart conditions, and is currently used by some women during difficult labor, when the spasms are too intense to allow for comfortable delivery. It may be used externally as a liniment for many types of pain.

• Anodyne, antiseptic, antispasmodic, diaphoretic, narcotic, expectorant.

154

───── SPURGE ─────

(Garden Spurge) grows with a thick reddish stalk, beset with long and narrow blueish green leaves, and so continues, without running into branches, till the next year.

— Culpeper

These herbes by mine advice would not be received into the bodie, considering that there be so many other good and wholesome potions to be made with other herbes, that may be taken without peril.

— Gerard

Resembling a cactus in appearance, this leafless perennial plant has a stem about 4 feet in height, and many branches . . .

— Grieve

If the paradox between the passages from Grieve and Culpeper seem at odds, it might be noted that Gerard records over twenty varieties of Spurges, all of them encompassing a wide range of appearance. Due to the toxic nature of this herb, it is included merely for reference, and should not be taken internally. It is native to Morocco.

REMEDIAL

Grieve says that "the internal use of the drug has been abandoned, owing to the severity of its action." Spurge is very severe, and causes uncomfortable vomiting and evacuation of the bowels. It also is a dangerous irritant of the internal passages. It has been used in the treatment of ulcers, syphilis, and cancers, but even in these severe diseases, it has led to the loss of the person from the treatment rather than from the disease. It has been used with great caution in the treatment of warts and corns, but if the application contacts the surrounding skin, great damage may result.

- Emetic, cathartic.

155

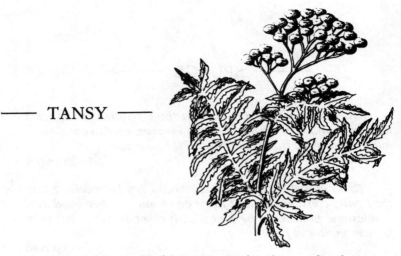

—— TANSY ——

It is an agreeable bitter, a carminative, and a destroyer of worms, for which a powder of the flowers should be taken from six to twelve grains at night and morning.

— Culpeper

The plant is conspicuous in August and September by its heads of round, flat, dull yellow flowers, growing in clusters, which earn it the name of 'Buttons'. It has a very curious, and not altogether disagreeable odour, somewhat like camphor.

— Grieve

When in flower, Tansy may be recognized by the yellow buttons surrounded by very small, white petals. The leaves are fine and feathery. It may be found growing wild in many areas of North America, particularly in waste areas.

LORE

In esoteric use, Tansy is known as an Herbe of Immortality. It is in current use as a Magickal Herbe, and is of particular value to women. Tansy was once used for embalming.

REMEDIAL

Tansy is highly recommended for those with heart trouble. The root should be gathered, dried, and may be roasted in an oven. When ground, it may be used instead of coffee, particularly for those with high blood pressure. It is used as a coffee substitute among those who desire to avoid the effects of caffeine.

Tansy is helpful for those suffering from hysteria, depression, and extreme states of emotion. It may be used for most nervous afflictions, having a tonic and calming effect. It will help to stimulate the appetite, when used in moderate amounts, and helps to regain health.

Tansy may be used externally, being employed in the treatment of sprains, bruises, gout, rheumatism, arthritis, and injuries resulting in swelling. It may be applied as a poultice, or a thick decoction made and the area wrapped with gauze soaked in the solution.

Tansy may also be used to bring a fever down to normalcy. It contains diaphoretic properties and the nervine constituents make it excellent for many feverish conditions.

Before modern times, many people were afflicted with worms and there are still areas of the world in which worms are most troublesome. Tansy is excellent in causing the worms to be dispelled from the body.

- Anthelmintic, tonic, diaphoretic, carminative, cardiac, hepatic.

——— THYME ———

It is a strengthener of the lungs, a good remedy for the chin-cough in children. It purges the body of phlegm, and is an excellent remedy for shortness of breath.

— Culpeper

Of his native propertie, it relieveth them which be melancholicke.

— Gerard

The Garden Thyme is an 'improved' cultivated form of the Wild Thyme of the mountains of Spain and other European countries bordering on the Mediterranean.

— Grieve

Thyme has many branches growing from a single root stalk, set with small leaves, and flowers which usually grow at the end of the branches. The flowers are a pale blue or purple, and look similar to marjoram in appearance. The scent of this herb is most distinctive.

LORE

Thyme is a delightful herb, and it is said that it may be used to bring the fairies and wee folk into one's life. It has been used to ward off evil, and in rituals of burial.

REMEDIAL

In the treatment of wounds, Thyme is an excellent herb although its properties are best taken when the herb is fresh. It will cleanse the wound, for it is an antiseptic. It has been used in a number of other external uses, even for that of leprosy, although its reputation in that disease comes most likely from the antiseptic property.

Thyme may also be used internally, and its primary reputation in this manner is for upset stomachs and the treatment of the lungs. Due to the nature of one of its essential oils, it calms coughing spasms, and is somewhat relaxing in its application. In the treatment of colds, it is thought to be most effective if taken at the onset.

The extracted oil may also be used to treat the pain of arthritis, rheumatism, and bruised muscles. Care must be taken, for too much oil or too vigorous an application will irritate the skin. The pure oil is a rubefacient.

• Tonic, antispasmodic, expectorant, antiseptic, carminative.

———— UVA URSI ————

The dried leaves are the only part of the plant used in medicine. The British Pharmacopoeia directs that the leaves should be obtained only from indigenous plants. They should be collected in September and October, only green leaves being selected and dried by exposure to gentle heat.

— Grieve

Uva Ursi, also known as Bearberry, is a shrub with tough, shiny green leaves. They are small, about an inch long. The flowers are lovely, waxen in nature, and followed by the berry, bright red and distictive. Uva Ursi is usually found in small thickets and tends to grow along hilly areas. Generally it prefers the more northern areas — the upper Midwest of North America and Canada.

LORE

Uva Ursi was a Religious Herbe among a number of Native American tribes. It was included in the herbal mixture which was smoked in the sacred pipe. It is currently used as a Visionary Herbe among those who seek increased psychic ability.

REMEDIAL

Uva Ursi is one of the most effective astringents available to the Herbalist. It is widely used in infections of the kidney and urinary tract. Taken internally it will give tone to those organs and promote kidney action. It works to destroy the bacteria and cleanse those parts of the body. Uva Ursi is an excellent remedy in the treatment of urethritis.

- Astringent, diuretic, tonic.

——— VALERIAN ———

This has a thick, short, greyish root, lying above ground, shooting forth small pieces of roots, which have all of them many long green strings and fibres under them in the ground, whereby it draws nourishment.

— Culpeper

The drie root, as Dioscorides teacheth, provoketh urine, bringeth downe the desired sicknesse, helpeth the paine in the sides, and is put into counter-poisons and medicines preservative against the pestilence . . .

— Gerard

It is supposed to be the 'Phu' of Dioscorides and Galen, by whom it is extolled as an aromatic and diuretic. It was afterwards found to be useful in certain kinds of epilpsy. The plant was in such esteem in medieval times as a remedy, that it received the name of All Heal, which is still given it in some parts of the country.

— Grieve

159

The plant grows on a singular stem, sometimes surpassing waist height. Paired leaves form on branches and pink flowerlettes at the top. The roots are most unusual, as described above by Culpeper.

LORE

Although Valerian was once known as an 'herb of witches', its use today is primarily medicinal. It is still used in purification rituals.

REMEDIAL

Today Valerian is primarily used as a nervine for it calms the nerves, and when the root is ground and taken in gelatin capsules, is certain to relax the body in order to sleep restfully.

Valerian is useful in the treatment of all spasmodic and nervous conditions. To a degree it will alleviate pain and is best employed when pain is caused by muscular tension, spasms, or a knotted muscle.

In inducing sleep, the proper amount of Valerian is excellent. There are no narcotic effects, although an excessive dose will have the opposite reaction causing distracted thinking, possible headaches, and a definite inability to sleep.

Other diuretics have replaced Valerian in that use. It is also useful mixed into expectorant mixtures.

• Anodyne, antispasmodic, carminative.

—— VERBENA or VERVAIN ——

It helps the yellow jaundice, the dropsy and the gout, kills and expels worms in the belly, and causes a good colour in the face and body . . .

— Culpeper

They report, saith Pliny, that if the dining roome be sprinckled with water in which the herbe hath beene steeped, the guests will be the merrier, which also Dioscorides mentioneth.

— Gerard

The name Verbena was the classical Roman name for 'altar-plants' in general, and for this species in particular.

160

The druids included it in their lustral water, and magicians and sorcerers employed it largely. It was used in various rites and incantations, and by ambassadors in making leagues.

— Grieve

Vervena, or Vervain is found in several species. It grows about knee-high, and has, at its tip, a stalk of pale lavendar-colored flowers. It is more fully leafed nearer the ground.

LORE

There is a great deal of lore attached to Verbena, as it has fascinated gardener and Herbalist minds since early times. It has been said to have many properties of magick and has been used to bless, to protect, and to purify. It is currently a Magickal Herbe, and has many many magickal attributes.

REMEDIAL

Among its constituents is found tannic acid, making Verbena excellent for toning the liver, kidney, and other internal organs. It calms irregularities in digestion and at the same time relieves nervous and mental strain. In stronger doses it has been used to calm spasms and convulsions.

Verbena has been used to comfort habitual bronchial coughing, and is a great aid in the treatment of asthma. It is sometimes employed as an emmenagogue in irregular and difficult menstrual cycles.

Verbena is useful in lowering fevers, and is used particularly in those fevers caused by an infectious condition.

Verbena tea will calm the nerves and promote a comfortable night's rest.

• Hepatic, nervine, antispasmodic, tonic, emmenagogue, febrifuge.

——— WILLOW, WHITE ———

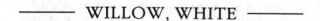

The leaves, bark, and seed are used to staunch the bleeding of wounds, and at mouth and nose, spitting of blood, and other fluxes of blood in man or woman, to stay

vomiting, and the provocation thereto . . .

— Culpeper

The leaves, floures, and barke of Willowes are cold and dry in the second degree and astringent.

— Gerard

The bark contains up to 13 per cent of tannin as its chief constituent, also a small quantity of salicin.

— Grieve

Beautiful to behold, the graceful Willow is found growing in places where there is enough ground moisture to be had, frequently near rivers and small bodies of water. The long, draped branches carry narrow, green leaves.

LORE

A Religious Herbe among the Chinese, the Willow is seen in European mythology as an herbe of eloquence. It is used magickally today by many as the source for the wood of a magickal wand.

REMEDIAL

A strong tea made from the bark may be taken internally in nearly all cases which require an astringent. It is also most useful in cases where the person is low on strength and in need of restoration of health. It has less use today as a haemostat, but the presence of salicin makes it an excellent remedy for treating headaches.

- Anodyne, astringent, tonic.

——— WINTERGREEN ———

A small indigenous shrubby, creeping, evergreen plant, growing about 5 to 6 inches high under trees and shrubs, particularly under evergreens such as Kalmias and Rhododendrons.

— Grieve

The leaves are glossy and very green, although not as bright beneath. Wintergreen will have flowers along the branches earlier in the summer, and these are followed by bright berries. The scent of this herb is most distinctive, much like a mint, but also with a certain sweetness about it.

REMEDIAL

This is one of the best herbs in the treatment of rheumatism, and also for pains caused by chills. It is warming and stimulating to the system. In no circumstances should wintergreen be taken in large doses, however, for the oil is strong and potent, and has the ability of harming the stomach, similar to the way its rubefacient properties would irritate the skin. This property is so serious that Grieve even recommends using the synthetic oil externally, to avoid burning the skin. It is possible to macerate the herb in a fixative, such as sunflower oil, so that it is not nearly as potent.

Other uses of this herb include as a liniment, for which it is considered most valuable. It has also been used to ease the pains and cramps of a difficult menstrual cycle.

- Tonic, rubefacient, stimulant, astringent, emmenagogue.

—— WITCH HAZEL ——

The name 'Hamamelis' was adopted from a Greek word to indicate its resemblance to an apple-tree.

— Grieve

This herb is most often found as a large shrub, although it can attain easily over ten feet in height. It is a fascinating tree to observe, for it flowers only after the leaves have fallen in early autumn. The flowers are yellow, and are followed by black nuts, which may be gathered and eaten.

163

REMEDIAL

Both the leaves and the bark may be used remedially, as they are very similar in properties. They are excellent in the treatment of pain, and an oil may be used to soothe most minor pains.

Made into a tea or infusion, Witch Hazel is good for complications of both stomach and bowels such as ulcers or colitis. Witch Hazel has also been used for internal bleeding.

Witch Hazel is one of the few herbs used in the treatment of varicose veins, applied with a gauze bandage, which should be kept moist regularly. The astringent properties have also been useful in the treatment of swellings and external tumors.

- Astringent, anodyne, sedative, styptic, tonic.

——— WORMWOOD ———

This useful plant grows about a yard high; the stalk is pale green, tough, upright, and divided wildly into many branches; the leaves are of a pale green on both sides, divided into many parts, soft to the touch, but make the fingers bitter. The flowers are numerous, small, chaffy, hang down, and of a pale olive colour at first; but, after standing a while, they grow brownish.

— Culpeper

The Wormwoods are members of the great family of Compositae and belong to the genus Artemisia, a group consisting of 180 species . . .

— Grieve

Wormwood contains, among its constituents, thujone, phellandrine, and purine. It was named for the Greek Goddess, Artemis, and has been in use at least since its earliest recorded history, by the Assyrians, in 600 B.C.

LORE

Wormwood has been a Religious Herbe among both Hebrew and Greek cultures. It is a patron herb among Herbalists, and is said to have been handed down from the Gods to the Herbalists through Chiron, a centurian.

REMEDIAL

This herb is excellent to use but is best in small amounts. It is likely that its bitter flavor will keep the dosage proportionate. It is excellent for treatment of stomach disorders. For this, the tops of the plant when in flower should be used.

Wormwood may also be used in pains associated with nervous disorders, but the quantity should be carefully regulated. In large doses, Wormwood is unpleasant, producing disagreeable side effects. Wormwood may be used in cases of colitis.

- Tonic, stomachic, stimulant, antipyretic, anthelmintic, febrifuge.

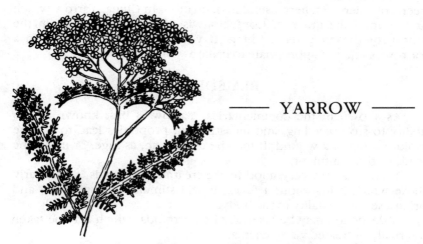

—— YARROW ——

An ointment of the leaves cures wounds, and is good for inflammations, ulcers, fistulas, and all such running as abound with moisture.

— Culpeper

The leaves of Yarrow doe close up wounds, and keepe them from inflammation, or fiery swelling; it stancheth blood in any part of the body, and it is likewise put into bathes for women to sit in . . .

— Gerard

Yarrow was formerly much esteemed as a vulnerary, and its old names of Soldier's Woundwort and Knight's

165

Milfoil testify to this. The Highlanders still make an ointment from it, which they apply to wounds, and Milfoil tea is held in much repute in the Orkneys for dispelling melancholy.

— Grieve

Yarrow grows on tall, proud stalks, with irregular leaves attached to them. The leaves are fine, nearly like little ferns, very delicate in appearance. At the top appears a large, flat head of many small flowers. Most of the Yarrow indigenous to the United States will have white flowers, but there are other varieties, even deep purple, grown for their appearance.

LORE

Yarrow has been used in the celebration of marriages, and has been considered an herb useful in divination. In China, Yarrow which grows upon the grave of Confucious is considered the best in the world for throwing the I Ching. If you see the first blossom in a Yarrow patch, it is appropriate to make a wish.

REMEDIAL

As shown in the commentaries, Yarrow is best known for its ability to stop bleeding, and its astringent properties lead to a more rapid healing of a wound. It may be used fresh, as sage, or it may be made into an ointment.

Yarrow is also very good in the treatment of colds, particularly those which bring about a fever. It will stimulate perspiration, and bring a sense of vitality to the body.

A decoction may be taken for hemorrhoids, which may be taken internally or treated via an enema.

Its ability to stop bleeding has been long known, and at one time it was dried, ground finely into a powder, and snuffed to stop a nosebleed.

• Astringent, diaphoretic, tonic, stimulant.

DOSAGE GUIDE
FOR THE REMEDIAL HERBAL

DOSAGE GUIDE
FOR THE REMEDIAL HERBAL

his section of the herbal is to serve mainly as a guideline for the beginning herbalist. Standard proportions are given which will indicate the mixture of various herbal preparations. Any herbs which deviate from these standards are noted.

The purpose of this guide is to protect the user from excessive doses of herbs which could be harmful. It is also recommended that one avoid using the same herb for extended periods of time. If the condition has not abated, seek consultation and change the remedy to a different herb.

In the addition of aromatics to the formulae, the total herbal weight should not exceed the guideline. In the case of mixtures, the same rule of thumb is to be followed.

Please take into consideration the mass weight of the user, their age and condition, for these are the true indications with which the dosages should be administered. All of the following are conservative. If you have any question in preparing your remedy and feel uncertain, stop at once. Never attempt to replace a doctor.

INFUSION

- Strong:
1 ounce herbs
1 pint water
steep 20 minutes

- Moderate:
⅔ ounce herbs
1 pint water
steep 20 minutes

- Weak (Tea):
½ ounce herbs
1 pint water
steep 15 minutes

DECOCTION

- Strong:
1 ounce herbs
2 pints water
simmer 10 minutes
steep 15 minutes

- Moderate:
⅔ ounce herbs
2 pints water
simmer 10 minutes
steep15 minutes

- Weak (Tea):
⅓ ounce herbs
2 pints water
simmer 8 minutes
steep 15 minutes

POULTICE

½ ounce herbs
½ cup boiling water
steep 20 minutes

OINTMENT

1 ounce herbs
16 ounces fixative
heat off & on 24 hours

WASH

- Strong:
½ ounce herb
1 pint water
steep until lukewarm

- Moderate:
⅓ ounce herb
1 pint water
steep until lukewarm

ACONITE
- Internal use, in extreme emergency only: moderate infusion. Administer no more than ½ cup while awaiting emergency medical assistance and report herbal dosage to medics.
- External use: decrease amount of herb to ½ ounce and macerate into ointment. Apply once or twice daily.

AGRIMONY
- Internal use, for colds, sore throats, etc: moderate infusion. Taken as a tonic, may be used three times a day, ½ cup amounts. Internal use for hepatitis, jaundice and other serious conditions: strong infusion, administer in like amounts.
- External use, for eyes, skin, etc: moderate wash. Apply no more than twice daily for eyes, as needed for skin.

ALOE
- Internal use, for ulcers: use commercial preparation of powder, and administer according to directions.
- External use: use fresh gel, apply as needed.

ANGELICA • Internal use, for all conditions: moderate to strong infusion, depending upon taste. Take as much as one pint daily for no more than three days.

ANISE • Internal use, all conditions: moderate infusion, as needed.
• External use, antiseptic: use commercial oil, dilute in three parts fixative oil, use as needed. To clean fresh wound, use pure oil.

AVENS • Internal, as strong astringent: strong infusion, no more than one pint per day for no more than two days. Internal for other use: moderate infusion as needed.
• External use, styptic: use fresh herb, apply as needed.

BALM • Internal: moderate infusion, as needed, not to exceed one pint per day.

BARLEY • Internal use: cook and serve, take as needed.

BASIL • Internal, for rheumatism and pain: strong infusion, one pint per day. Internal, other conditions, moderate infusion, same administration.
• External: using the fresh herb is ideal; if dried herb, use as poultice or ointment.

BAYBERRY • Internal, for severe conditions only: moderate infusion, no more than ⅔ cup a day for no more than three days. Internal, other conditions: weak infusion, no more than ¼ cup three times a day for no more than four days.
• External: use commercial oil, to four parts fixative oil. Use as needed.

BAY LAUREL • Internal: weak infusion, administer no more than ¼ cup three times a day; strong infusion, no more than ¼ cup once a day. Continue no more than three days.
• External: use commercial oil, mix one-to-one with fixative, as needed.

BENZOIN • Internal: use commercial tincture, administer as needed via vaporizer.
• External: use one part tincture to two parts sterile water, use as needed. If you must use the herb, make a weak decoction.

173

BETONY, WOOD • Internal use: moderate infusion, as needed.

BLACKBERRY • Internal for diarrhea and influenza: strong infusion, as needed. For gargle and sore throat: moderate infusion, as needed.
• External: use either an ointment or strong wash, as needed.

BLESSED THISTLE • Internal: weak infusion, administer no more than ¼ cup twice a day; as emmenagogue: moderate infusion, no more than ¼ cup twice a day.

BLOODROOT • Internal use not recommended.
• External use: strong decoction, used externally twice a day.

BONESET • Internal, for severe influenza, etc: strong infusion, no more than ¼ cup three times a day. Internal, as a tonic: weak infusion, take ¼ cup three times a day.

BURDOCK • Internal, for blood and kidneys, etc: moderate decoction of the root or moderate infusion of the leaves and burrs. As needed.
• External, for skin: strong wash, use as needed.

CARAWAY • Internal use: moderate infusion, take as needed.

CATNIP • Internal use, for all conditions: moderate to strong infusion, depending upon taste. Take as needed.

CAYENNE • Internal use: one rounded teaspoon per cup of boiling water, steep and drink. May be taken twice daily.
• External use not recommended.

CELANDINE, GREATER • Internal use for stones, etc: strong infusion, no more than ¼ cup doses in severe cases only. Not to exceed three doses per day.
• External, for warts: use the fresh juice, apply directly. For other external use, either ointment or strong wash, use as needed.

CELANDINE, LESSER • Internal use, for hemorrhoids: use ointment or suppositories, and apply as needed. Moderate infusion may be taken, ⅓ cup three times daily.

CHAMOMILE • Internal, for pain: strong infusion, no more than one pint per day. Internal for other purposes: moderate infusion, as needed.
• External: steep 1 ounce herb in 2 cups fixative oil, heated for 12 hours, apply as needed. Use strong wash as needed.

CHICKWEED • Internal: moderate infusion, take as tonic.
• External: fresh juice of the herb is best. If not possible, use a strong wash as needed.

CINNAMON • Internal uses: a weak infusion, taken as needed.
• External: use commercial oil, dilute in three parts fixative oil, as needed.

CINQUEFOIL • Internal use: moderate infusion, take no more than one pint per day.
• External use: moderate wash, apply as needed.

CLEAVERS • Internal use should be avoided by all diabetics. For kidney stones, use a strong infusion, take no more than one cup per day. For other uses, moderate infusion, taken carefully. Large amounts are strongly diuretic.
• External use: strong wash, as needed. To stop bleeding, use the fresh juice of the herb.

CLOVER • Internal use: moderate to strong infusion, depending upon the taste. Take as needed.

CLOVES • Internal, for the stomach, etc: weak infusion, as needed.
• External, for toothaches, pain: apply commercial oil being careful to avoid skin.

COHOSH, BLACK • Internal: moderate infusion. Take no more than three ⅓ cup doses per day.

COHOSH, BLUE • Internal: a moderate infusion may be taken, ⅓ cup per day. If more than one day, monitor reaction closely.

COLTSFOOT • Internal use: a strong decoction may be used sparingly, or a strong infusion may be taken as needed.

COMFREY • Internal use: either a strong infusion of the leaves, or a moderate decoction of the roots may be taken as needed.

175

- External: a strong wash, poultice, or ointment may be used as needed.

CRAMP BARK • Internal: a moderate decoction, ¼ cup three times a day for no more than three days.

DANDELION • Internal: moderate infusion of leaves, or moderate decoction of roots. Take ¼ cup three times daily, and monitor condition for aperient effects.
• External: fresh juice applied as needed is best; strong wash may also be used as needed.

DOCKS • Internally for diarrhea, etc: moderate decoction of root. Internally for liver, etc., weak infusion of ground root. Take no more than ⅓ cup three times a day.

DOG'S GRASS • Internally, for stones: strong decoction of roots, ½ cup twice daily. Internally for infections: moderate decoction of root (or seed), ⅓ cup twice daily.

ELDER • Internally, for all conditions: moderate to strong infusion of either leaves or flowers, as needed. Moderate decoction of bark or berries, in ¼ cup doses no more than four times daily.

ELECAMPAGNE • Internal: moderate to strong decoction of chopped root, depending upon condition. Take ½ cup four times daily.
• Externally: strong wash, as needed.

ELM, SLIPPERY • Internally: strong decoction, use as needed.
• Externally: strong decoction or poultice, as needed.

EUCALYPTUS • Internally, for throat: weak infusion. Gargle three times daily. For chest conditions, inhale via vaporizer as needed. For heart conditions, take weak infusion, ⅓ cup three times daily.
• Externally, use direct, or one-to-one with sterile fixative oil, and apply as needed.

EYEBRIGHT • Internally: moderate to strong infusion, taken as needed. Do not continue for more than four days.

FENNEL • Internally: weak to moderate infusion, as needed.

FENUGREEK • Internally: moderate to strong decoction of the seeds, ⅓ cup four times daily.
• Externally: strong wash, or poultice, as needed.

FERNS • Internally: may vary greatly depending upon variety. As a rule, take a moderate infusion, ⅓ cup three times daily.

FEVERFEW • Internally: moderate to strong infusion. Take as needed, but monitor for aperient effects.

FIREWEED • Internal use very dangerous. For rheumatism and severe conditions, moderate doses only, monitored extremely closely. As a gargle, weak infusion.
• Externally for bleeding, poultice or fresh herb.

FOXGLOVE • Internal use discouraged. For emergency, administer ¼ cup while awaiting medical assistance. Inform medics of dosage.

GARLIC • Internally: moderate infusion, as needed.
• Externally: use fresh juice as needed.

GOLDEN ROD • Internally: moderate infusion as needed. Monitor for aperient effect.
• Externally, poultice, ointment, or fresh herb as needed.

GOLDEN SEAL • Internally, moderate infusion, as needed. Monitor as needed.
• Externally, poultice, ointment, or fresh herb as needed.

GROUND IVY • Internal use for all conditions: moderate to strong infusion, taken as needed, for four days.
• External use: poultice, ointment as needed.

HAWTHORN • Internal use for all conditions: moderate infusion, ⅓ cup three times daily.

HEART'S EASE • Internally: moderate to strong infusion of leaves and flowers may be taken as needed. Moderate decoction of root and seeds may be taken, ⅓ cup three times daily, monitoring for effects.

• Externally: strong wash, as needed; ointment, poultice, as needed.

HOPS
• Internally: moderate to strong infusion, may be taken as needed.
• Externally: strong wash, poultice, ointment, liniment, as needed.

HOREHOUND
• Internally: moderate to strong infusion, ¼ to ½ cup three times daily. Discontinue after four days.
• Externally: poultice, ointment, strong wash, as needed.

HORSETAILS
• Internal use, emmenagogue: strong decoction, ¼ cup four times daily, not to exceed three days. Internal use, other conditions: moderate decoction, same administration.

HYSSOP
• Internal use, all conditions: moderate to strong infusion, taken as needed.

IVY
• Internal use, avoid berries: moderate infusion, ⅓ cup daily, not to exceed three days.
• External use: make liniment at same strength as ointment strength, and use as needed.

KAVA KAVA
• Internal use: decoction at moderate strength, take ½ cup three times daily, and monitor system for effects. Lower dose if necessary. Discontinue after three days.

LADY'S SLIPPER
• Internal use: moderate decoction of root, ¼ cup three to four times daily. Not to be used for more than three days.

LAVENDER
• Internal use: weak to moderate infusions may be taken as needed.
• External use: the commercial oil may be diluted with two to three parts fixative oil and used as needed. Do not take oil internally.

LILY OF THE VALLEY
• Internal use discouraged. Weak infusion may be taken, ¼ cup four times daily, not to exceed two days. For emergencies only, use strong infusion, give ⅓ cup, awaiting emergency medical treatment. Notify medics of dosage.

LIQUORICE[9] • Internal use: primarily mixed with other herbs. May be used as needed. For gargle, use moderate infusion.

MANDRAKE • Internal use not recommended.

MARIGOLD • Internal use: moderate to strong infusion, may be taken as needed, not to exceed one pint per day.
• External use: strong wash, strong decoction, ointment, poultice, as needed.

MARSHMALLOW • Internal use: strong decoction for ulcers, moderate decoction for other conditions. May be taken as needed.
• External: moderate to strong poultice, as needed.

MISTLETOE • Internal use (leaves only): moderate infusion, ⅓ cup taken twice daily. Not to be taken more than four days.
• External use (berries): strong wash, used cautiously.

MOTHERWORT • Internal use: moderate infusion, may be taken as needed. For birthing, use strong infusion, and administer in ½ cup doses.

MULLEIN • Internal, for most conditions: moderate to strong infusion, taken as needed.
• External use, as vulnerary: fresh leaves, best; poultice, as needed.

NETTLES • Internally as tonic: moderate infusion, ⅓ cup taken twice daily. May be continued as needed. Internally for bleeding: strong infusion, ½ cup doses. Eaten as a green, on occasion only.

MOUNTAIN GRAPE • Internal use for tonic: moderate infusion of leaves. Internal use for severe disease: moderate to strong decoction of bark, ⅓ cup three times daily.

MUGWORT • Internal use, usually in equal portions with pennyroyal: together, moderate to strong infusion, ½ cup three times daily, not to exceed four days.

ONION • Internally: ingest one fresh onion.
• Externally: apply fresh juice as needed.

179

PARSLEY • Internally for stones and jaundice: strong infusion, ⅓ cup taken four times daily. As tonic, etc: moderate infusion, as needed.

PENNYROYAL • Internally, must be monitored with care. Take with mugwort, and follow directions under mugwort.
• Externally: commercial oil primarily used. For wounds, apply direct. For skin, etc., mix with two parts fixative oil.

PEPPERMINT • Internally, may be taken in moderate to strong infusion, as needed. Take no more than one pint per day.
• Externally, use the commercial oil, which must be diluted with fixative oil, in two parts fixative to five parts fixative, dependent upon purpose.

PLANTAIN • Internal use, ulcers and fevers: moderate infusion, monitoring diuretic properties.
• External, fresh juice is the best. Poultice.

POMEGRANATE • Internal, seeds: moderate decoction, as needed. Rind, use moderate decoction, in ⅓ cup doses every two hours, not to exceed eight hours.

RASPBERRY • Internal use, moderate infusion, may be taken as needed.
• External use: strong wash.

RED CLOVER • Internal use: moderate to strong infusion, depending upon the taste. Use as needed.
• External use: ointment, poultice, fresh herb.

ROSEMARY • Internal use, moderate to strong infusion, taken in ⅓ cup doses. As needed, but not to excess.
• Externally: strong wash.

RUE • Internal use, on empty stomach: moderate infusion, ⅓ cup doses, not to exceed four per day for three days.

SAGE • Internal use: moderate infusion, as needed.
• Externally, fresh herb best for bleeding. Moderate infusion for gargle.

SAINT JOHN'S WORT • Internally: moderate to strong infusion, ¼ cup doses taken four times daily. Take for no more than four days.

SELF HEAL • Internally: strong infusion for bleeding, taken as needed. Moderate infusion for other conditions, as needed.
• Externally, fresh herb best for bleeding. Poultice.

SHEPHERD'S PURSE • Internally: strong infusion for bleeding, taken as needed. Moderate infusions for other conditions, as needed.
• Externally, fresh herb best for bleeding. Poultice.

SKUNK CABBAGE • Internal use discouraged. For labor, moderate infusion, administered in ⅓ cup doses. Monitor closely.
• Externally: mix ½ ounce herb with 1 pint oil for liniment.

SPURGE • Internal use dangerous, discouraged.
• External use: fresh juice of herb on warts and corns, avoid contact with other parts of surface skin.

TANSY • Internal use: moderate infusion (stronger too unpleasant to palate). Taken in ¼ cup doses four times daily, for four days.
• Externally: ointment, liniment (same proportions).

THYME • Internally, as stomachic, etc: moderate infusion, ½ cup doses, as needed.
• Externally: fresh herb or commercial oil to three parts fixative oil.

UVA URSI • Internal: moderate infusion, ⅓ cup four times daily. Use for four days.

VALERIAN • Internal use requires caution. Preferred method: take three capsules. Moderate decoction of root, take ¼ cup dose for sleep, etc. Wait at least 1½ hours before taking another dose. No more than three daily. Discontinue after three days. If taken for sleep, do not use two days consecutively.

VERBENA or VERVAIN • Internal use: moderate to strong infusion, taken as needed. Not to exceed one pint daily. Discontinue after five days.

WILLOW, WHITE • Internal: moderate to strong infusion, ½ cup for pain. Do not repeat dose for two hours. Take no more than three doses per day.

WITCH HAZEL • Internal use: moderate infusion for most conditions. Strong infusion for ulcers and colitis. Take as needed, not to exceed one pint moderate or four ⅓ cup doses strong.
• External: commercial oil is excellent. Use also poultice.

WORMWOOD • Internal use for nervous conditions, etc: moderate infusion, ¼ cup doses, four times daily. Discontinue after third day.

YARROW • Internal use as tonic: weak infusion, taken as needed.
• External use: fresh herb best, poultice, for bleeding.

THE HERBALIST
AS MAGICKAL PRACTITIONER

THE HERBALIST
AS MAGICKAL PRACTITIONER

ctually, I believe that the phrase Magickal Practitioner is something of a misnomer, for the appropriate word would be either Priest or Priestess, for at some time in the training and growth of an Herbalist comes the awareness that your inner spirit is flowing with the rhythms of the Universe. One cannot watch the rising and setting of the Sun, Moon, and other planets and stars without becoming involved in those potent tidal rhythms. One cannot observe the beauty of the seasonal cycles without responding to them. One cannot daily observe the birth, life, and death of the world of nature without also receiving wisdom about life. For most of human history, the realm of the healer was also that of religion.

Some of these traditions are yet preserved, but in our complex and technological age, religion has become technology, and those who observe the quiet passings of time are considered antiquated. Yet, in discussing the Magickal Practitioner, I should also like to return to times past, and discuss a most fascinating figure in the history of the healing profession. His name was variously Philipp Theophrastus Bombastus von Hohenheim, and he was born one year after Columbus landed in the Americas, in 1493. He studied traditional medicine at the University of Basle, and was outstanding enough to be given a chair of medicine. A radical to the core, his inaugural lecture was marked by the burning of the most respected medical text of the time. This action, and also his views, led to his forced resignation two years later.

Von Hohenheim took the name of Paracelsus as he later wandered around the country, studying from famous magicians and mystics. He examined mysteries in many cultures, and his later writings, in an attempt to reform the field of healing, included principles from India and other remote (in those days) countries.

Paracelsus believed that a physician should be also a philosopher, capable of seeing universal truths even by the observance of nature. He felt it essential to have a solid training in astrology in order to perceive the links between the spiritual and physical health of the patient. He also felt that alchemy was a necessary study for the physician in order that one be able to heal using herbes, mineral salts, even colored rays and energy. He felt that Witchcraft and Magic were pure, positive, and respectable forms of healing, and in describing the attributes one should attain in becoming a physician, said that:

> ". . . a true physician is much the same as a priest, ordained by God, and should be working Christlike in demeanor. A physician must be worthy of trust, capable of restoring energy even by physical presence, living life with such morals as to maintain a pure aura and inspirational being."

These are goals of the Herbalist even today, and the study of herbal magick is recommended, for then one learns self control, and the potent powers of the mind. The study of Magick for the Herbalist is not to wield power, but to understand the flow of the Universe, growing in ability to recognize when illness is a result of resisting the ways of nature. There are many role models in the history of herbecraft; one frequently brought to mind being the village wiseperson, also known as the medicine man, wise woman, shaman, or priest. There are many cultures and many names, but the function was nearly always the same. The healer was responsible for knowing the patterns of nature, for knowing how to change our personal energies and our social energies in order that the village would flow with the Earth. The healer knew the local herbes, and as civilization advanced became responsible also for those imported. Greatly respected and admired, this lore also came to encompass the energy of the herbes, for one cannot work with herbes continuously, day upon day, without also learning of their power, which is in itself a form of magick. Often the healer was also the priest(ess), for in those days there was no organized religion.

Religion then was communication with nature. If one wished to communicate with the trees, the means of focusing the energy was by 'naming' a tree spirit. Then, one could relate to it on a personal level, and call upon the energy by more direct means.

When the people wanted to reach out to the Universe, to directly feel the Divine presence of its wonder, ritual evolved. The healer would often cast a circle, for it represented the seasons, the passing overhead of the Sun, Moon, and stars, and the eternalness of life. This space was representative of infinity, and rituals evolved which were attempts to duplicate nature and her eternal cycles. Thus, by duplicating the ways of nature, was a religion of nature made ritualistic.

From our 'modern' perspective, there is much to be learned from the ancient healers and wise people. It strikes me as most curious that various cultures, without even knowing of each other's existence, all 'named' an herbe the same, by giving it the same lore. Is it not interesting to find cultures separated by oceans and thousands of miles, all using the same herbes in their rituals for the dead? The Herbalist has a responsibility to study this lore, for it is a part of the name of an herbe, and we must know our herbes intimately, by all their names.

In many traditions of folk magick there is a principle of "knowing" the name of something, which process is said to give you its inner energy and power. For the Herbalist, it means that you must know its scent, its flavor, the names it is known by (both scientific and Latin), and you must also know the folklore associated with the herbe. This lore has not grown by accident, and it is a wealth of information. It is not to be taken literally, but represents a series of keys, capable of unlocking the mysteries of the Herbalist's art.

The Traditional Herbalist has among required skills, those of ritual ability, skill at meditation, and the knowledge to channel forms of energy. In the process of learning these skills, magick is seen as a skill to be used in healing. Magick is magick, meaning that the same magick which is used to acquire a new car, or coerce someone to fall madly in love with you is the same magick which is used to harm another or place a deadly curse. Yet, this is the same magick which turns loaves and fishes into a feast, or parts the waters, and it is the intent of the practitioner which defines the magick of a person.

Magick does work, but for the serious Herbalist, there is no time to play with spells, for the study of magick is merely a tool, and used only to gain wisdom, never goods or control over people. It teaches one how the Universe moves. The wise practitioner would never use magick to avoid difficulty, for it must be known that this is part of karma, and must be experienced. The wise practitioner would not even use magick to heal someone who has made themself sick, using the herbes instead to promote understanding within the person of the true cause, so they can make changes and learn a healthier way. Magick used to avoid trouble usually means the learning experience is merely delayed, and the extra waiting can often make the new experience even more intense.

When one draws healing from the Earth as does the Herbalist, it is no longer possible to ignore Her rhythms, for it is the way we live,the way we think, and the means by which we relate to our Divinity, which some would call God, some would call Goddess, some would call both, and some would use no name at all. For the Herbalist, power and understanding lie with the Earth. It will be with joy that our bodies are returned to Her.

I must caution you that the magickal lore of herbes does indeed work. There have been students in the past who did not respect this fact. One used herbes to invoke the Crone, the ancient aspect of the Goddess who is old, wise, and deals with death. It was a fairly

189

traumatic process for the student, having to experience death, and death-defying dreams. Another, reading that herbes could be used in spells, used that lore to attract a job, and another, and another. Timing is always curious with magick, and suddenly there were many phone calls and the student went through a few weeks of terrible distress with too many job offers, and a worse quandry than before. The wise practioner would only use herbal magick to receive patience, understanding, and the ability to have the right job occur at the right time. Working with herbes to make an employer hire you or a person love you is manipulation, and it will lead to unhappy events in your life.

The law of Karma states that everything you do will come back to you three-fold; it is this law which dominates the Magickal Herbalist. Should you impose your will on another, be prepared to be imposed upon three-fold. Should you steal from another, you will lose many of your own goods. Should you wish unhappiness upon another, that will be your own reward. In my study and exploration of all aspects of Herbecraft, I have come in contact with many people. Among them have been some who work with magick to manipulate and do harm to others. I give you my word that not one person I have seen do 'black' magick is happy.

Yet, many who study the art in order to better know the universe· are happy. They sing, dance, and feel joyous when nature is manifest. Yet, they do not lead uncomplicated lives. They still experience sadness and death, but know that this is the way of the Earth. All things will pass, and only change and growth are life.

Read on, and enjoy this lore.

HERB GATHERING

There are a number of ways in which one may gather herbes for magickal use. It should always involve some form of ritual, and the balance of the laws of conservation must be maintained. Herbes used for adding positive energy to the working should be gathered beneath the waxing moon, and herbes used to exorcise or banish negative energy should be gathered beneath the waning moon. Religious herbes may be taken with either new or full moon, which may well vary according to the ritual or deity appropriate for their use. If the herbes will be used to begin a project, definitely take them with the new moon.

Herbes should be collected with the magickal working blade, often called a boline, a single-edged, white-handled knife. However, those of us who are more practical have one or more hand spades, which are reserved only for the magickal collection of herbes.

There can be great delight in packing yourself to go off gathering, with a bottle of purified water (ritually consecrated and blessed with the black-handled knife and sea-salt), some incense, preferably the stick-kind, which you can easily insert into a bare patch of ground, and containers to carry the herbes in. A basket of woven material lined with cloth is the best, but don't be afraid to make do if need be. Remember to take along gifts to reward the Earth and thank Her for Her bounty.

Herbes may be gathered with either hand, although lore says to use the left hand. There are also herbal magicians who use the right hand if the herbe is feminine in nature (herbes of the Moon, Venus, Neptune), or left hand if the herbe is masculine (Sun, Mars, Jupiter, Pluto). Herbes of Mercury or Saturn may be considered with either, for Mercury is androgenous, and Saturn is both Crone and old man. The lore which says you should speak to the herbe is based upon the principal of focusing your attention completely upon the work at hand. If your concentration is totally within the herbe, your mind is at work keeping the magickal energy of the herbe intact. Actually, singing as you work is one of the best ways to go about your work.

Gather your herbes as a solitaire, unless you have perfect love and perfect trust with those who would accompany you. Under no circumstances would you wish to have anyone involve their feelings of doubt into your work. The most appropriate dress would to be as nature would have you, wearing only your happiness. Sometimes the presence of mosquitoes and the like will discourage this practise, but there is a delightful sense of the child to be found in playing naked among the herbes of the Earth. For those who gather herbes for magick as Priest and Priestess, and who also share the Great Rite in their work, it is most appropriate to celebrate this powerful ritual at or near the place where you have gathered your herbes, ensuring the fertility of the land.

POTIONS & LOTIONS

A potion is not much different than either an infusion or a decoction, excepting that its purpose is for magickal use. The same holds for a lotion. A potion is to be taken internally, and a lotion is for external use.

The primary difference is that they are made in a ritual setting, timed with lunar (or other planetary) aspects and changes. Ideally, one would even bring the water to boil within a ritual circle, and for most this means casting a simple circle in one's kitchen.

Potions may be used to invoke spiritual energy. If one has a need for strength, select herbes which will bring this energy. It may then, once completed, be taken as a daily magickal tonic. A potion might also be made to use for a ritual beverage. If one is calling upon divine energies to come and fill the self, choosing herbes associated with one or more deities is an excellent means. It is important to do a little research into mythology, to better understand the personalities and attributes of the various Gods and Goddesses of the many religions.

Lotions are used externally, and may be used to bathe chakras and other psychic portals, to enhance intuitive vision, to increase clairvoyance and so forth. Magickally, potions and lotions work in similar manner, bringing the person in direct communion with the herbal energy. Sometimes the word 'wash' is used to denote a lotion. The strength of the solution is dependent upon personal desire, and is only a serious consideration when irritants and toxic substances are used. Either potion or lotion may be as weak as a tea, still being very effective, or as strong as a decoction.

ELIXIR

This is an alchemical preparation of the Traditional Herbalist, and comes from the studies of the Alchemist. In the science of transmutation, an elixir is a mixture of three elements: salt, sulphur, and mercury. Salt is seen to represent the body, the tangible, the mundane. Sulphur is seen as a mixture of God (dess) and human, or soul. Mercury is that of divine spirit.

The presence of salt is given by making an ash of the herbe. It is burned alchemically to produce calcined ash, which yields the salts and metallic salts produced by the herbe in the natural state. The sulphur may be made by extracting the volatile oils, in a pure state, from the herbe(s), and using those to represent the element of sulphur. Mercury may be used by fermenting the herbe, and this will yield an alcohol solution.

It is believed that these three ingredients are essential for any alchemical preparation, first broken down into the basic parts of salt, sulphur, and spirit by the alchemist, and then united again to produce a transmuted, potent elixir.

FLUID CONDENSERS

These are sometimes called the elixir of life, or also known as Universal Condensers. This form of herbal solution is a fluid which can be used magickally as a lotion. It can be used in rituals of evocation, and is said to improve psychic vision, clairaudience and clairvoyance.

192

The manner in which it works is to focus concentration and energy flow through the portals of your personal psychic self. A traditional recipe is to take two measures each of chamomile and eyebright, in a pint of water. Make an infusion of this mixture over an open fire, steeping for fifteen minutes.

At this point, seven sticks of willow are ignited from the fire, and then plunged, burning, into the infusion, mixing alchemically, all the ingredients together. Then, the mixture is poured through a philtre of four layers of purified (boiled and sun-dried) linen, one layer for each of the four elements. It should be cooled, and stored in tightly sealed bottles. If it is to be kept for a period of time, store it ·in the refrigerator.

There are other herbes which lend their use to fluid condensers, which may be found in the magickal herbal of this book.

INCENSE

The main ingredients of incense are the aromatic herbs. These may be leaf, flowers, root, resin, or powdered wood, scented with essential oils, either naturally, or added to the mixture. There are no herbes which may not be used, but it is wise to first experiment with a piece of burning charcoal. Drop them on, and assess the smoke with your sense of smell. There are some herbes which smell wonderful but distasteful if burnt, and other which have little smell at all, but smolder into a heavenly fragrance.

There are also incense gums which are essential ingredients for heady, rich-smelling incenses including benzoin, camphor, galbanum, frankincense, myrrh, mastic, and storax. These, generally, are resins from coniferous trees, and others such as pine may easily be used. Balsams and dragons's blood resin may also be used. These are the herbaceous substances which produce a large amount of fragrant smoke. Not only are they dramatic, but they inevitably have much history as Religious Herbes.

The use of incense has a long history with religion and magick. It may have been first used as a form of sacrifice to appease the spirits of nature, which must have seemed capricious and whimsical to the first humans. It is likely that this happened as fire was being domesticated, and among the woods gathered for fuel were aromatic trees such as bay, sandalwood and cedar, which when burned, produced a rising smoke to the heavens, thick and scented. One may not partake of the scent without it producing emotional or psychological effects, and early humans were most likely quick to mark these as different from other fuels; worthy of saving for sacred occasions.

Even when sacrifice was no longer needed, the practise of

communing with the spiritual side of nature over aromatic smoke continued. In time, it was learned that certain herbes produced visions when the smoke was inhaled. As civilization developed, priestly incenses evolved, usually including frankincense and myrrh. Many magickal recipes come from the grimoires of Ceremonial Magick, but there are also religious recipes from Christians, Hebrews, and nearly all religions. Incense is a truly universal means of communicating with the spiritual and divine.

The simplest recipes for incense involve choosing whichever herbes you wish, grinding them in your mortar and pestle, and placing a measure upon a burning block of charcoal. Nothing could be simpler. Herbes are chosen by scent and/or corresponding magickal virtues.

If you wish to make stick incense, go to a nearby artist supply store and purchase some gum arabic or acacia gum. This is a very sticky bonding agent which you may mix into the finely-ground mixture and adhere to a broomstraw, making sticks, or work with your fingers into little cones. Give it time to dry, and then you have wonderful, handmade, incense for use in your own work, or as a most wonderful gift.

The making of incense is of a very personal nature, and I am resisting the inclination to include several recipes, for there is nothing difficult, and I encourage you to follow your own curiosity. You now have all you need to know, and to this add your imagination.

OIL

There are several approaches to creating a magickal herbal oil. One, the most difficult, is to use an extractor and extract the pure essential oils yourself. It involves complex equipment, but is rewarding for the serious practitioner. The results are pure, essential oils which can be used in a variety of ways.

Pure oils of an essential, volatile nature may also be purchased commercially. It is important to know that many of these are too strong to use directly upon the skin, but make excellent incense by merely placing a couple of drops upon a burning piece of charcoal. These oils may also be used with a fixative, or carrier, such as olive, sunflower, or other oils.

The simplest means of making your own oil is to begin with a fixative oil. This is placed in a sturdy pan, and to it are added herbaceous parts which have a high content of natural oil within the cellular structure. You may wish to use the flowering parts, or leaves, and in some cases the root. Gently bring this to warmth, stirring carefully. Never allow it to boil, and you may accomplish excellent results by avoiding even a 'hot' temperature. This process may be repeated several times over a day or more. Thus, the natural oils within the herbe are released into solution with the fixative, as they are soluble in oil.

There are many recipes for oils. The herbes are chosen according to their meaning and attributes. A personal mixture may be made by combining equal parts of three herbes: one for the Sun sign, one for the Moon sign, and one for the ascendant, or rising sign. One might also make a protective oil, by combining several herbes known for their ability to give protection, the individual choices made by preference of scent.

It is important to experiment. One means of trial and error for finding compatible scents is to take small amounts of the dried herbes and grind them together. Smell deeply of the aroma, and feel how it suits you.

BALM

The actual process for the making of an herbal balm is basically the same as for an ointment. Of course, there is the element of magick brought into the procedure. It should be done in a magickally prepared space, with attention given to appropriate timing with the moon.

In using a balm for meditation, it may lightly be applied to the chakra associated with the third eye, somewhat in the middle of the forehead. Use a small amount, for it is not the quantity that counts. Herbes appropriate for a balm are those associated with peace and vision, specifically many of the Visionary Herbes.

Find a comfortable position, one in which you can remain for a period of time. Dry the palms of your hands upon your jeans or clothing, and use them as covers for the eye sockets. They should not be allowed to touch the eyelid. This creates a warm, dry, and dark cover for the eyes which is most conducive to relaxing those muscles.

Begin by visualizing a large number five. Some have an easier time than others in perceiving an image with the mind, or the mind's eye. The reason for this first step is to focus the attention. Do not attempt to 'see' the image with your eyes but with the mind, much as you would if you were dreaming. In time this skill will improve, so do not allow yourself to become distracted by judging the quality of your image.

Then, imagine a bell sound, and visualize a large number four. This image is to clear your mind. Imagine that a fresh, spring breeze blows through your mind and clears it of all clutter, leaving it clean, free, and capable of focusing. Practise clarifying the image. Develop the image, making it more distinct in time. Then, when you feel satisfied with your attention and concentration, again imagine the tone of a bell.

Visualize now a large red number three. This is a warm, physical color, and its purpose is to bring a thorough sense of physical relaxation. When the image is clear, bring your attention to the very top of your head, where the psychic area known as the 'crown chakra' is located. Become aware of your scalp, and place your mental concentration there. Relax it, taking time to explore each muscle, and then let go of all tension. Bring this sensation down over your forehead, slowly, feeling the calm, warm, energy slowly moving downward. Relax your eyebrows, carefully and thoroughly, then your temples.

Become totally familiar with each muscle, next moving into your eyes. Continue this process through your face, neck, chest, down to the very tips of your toes. Take your time, and even though this is most relaxing, maintain mental alertness. When the sensation reaches your toes, then draw it back up to your head. At this point, again imagine you hear the tone of a bell, and visualize a large, green number two.

This is the number and color of tranquility, calm, and serenity. Green is the color of nature, and once this image is clear in your mind, take yourself away to a magickal place in nature, one you will visit in your mind, alone, and in peace. This is your place, for here you are magickal and special. There should be several elements in this mental construction such as some water, be it a pond, river, or lake. Some take this opportunity to visit the ocean. There should also be one major tree, larger than all others, and also a flat, grassy area where you may come to meditate, or perform healing rituals for yourself or for others. It is important to be constant in this mental scene, for this is where you will come alone, time and time again to refresh yourself, to relax and restore yourself. Enjoy this place, feel the oneness with nature, and feel its energy flow thoroughly through your body. The more vivid this experience, the more effective the meditation.

From this place, this nature scene, you may explore a variety of visionary and magickal experiences. You may bathe your afflictions in the healing waters, you may visualize a friend or relative upon the water's surface, seeing them healthy, happy, and vibrant with life, which is a potent form of psychic healing. You may practise flying, with the joy of a child in dreams.

The deepest level of this form of meditation is to next hear the tone of the bell, and visualize a large, white image of a number one against a violet or lavender background. At this point, allow the images and pictures to flow through your mind. Take note of them, and remember them, for they are much like the images and symbols of dreams, tarot, and other divinatory works. They are important clues to your inner creativity and intuition.

When you are done with your meditative work, slowly reverse the process, visualizing the numbers back to the five and open your eyes, feeling filled with joy and health.

ACONITE

Aconite may be used to invoke the presence of Hecate, for it is said to have been used by her, and created by her from the foaming mouth of the triple-headed dog which guards the gates of hell. It may be burnt as an offering or may, with great danger be taken as an elixir of Hecate. Know that such psychic work is very serious, and should not be attempted unless the seeker has been properly prepared, for Hecate is the aspect of the Goddess who knows all of the secrets of death.

This herbe also has a reputation as an ingredient of 'flying ointment' which is an indication that it has a history of use for the visionary experience the poison provokes in one's body.

The primary use it has today is in the consecration of magickal blades. It is used both to wash them and to cleanse them as an incense. This brings the power of protection and the magickal watchfulness needed to guard the ritual against any negative energies.

ACORNS

Acorns fall into the realm of the Herbalist as a product of the Oak. Because they are small and easily gathered, these small and beautifully formed Oak seeds can be gathered simply, by collecting them whenever you see them. They are traditionally symbols of fertility and as such, can be brought into magickal use whenever you are desirous of your Work being more fertile. Apart from the obvious fertility magick, that of desiring the conception of a child, the Acorn may be used to bring creativity to fruition. Acorns also represent the continuity of life, and thus may be incorporated into temple decoration or amulets. They are very appropriate for the Hallow's Eve celebrations.

AGRIMONY

Agrimony is very useful for persons who are unable to fall asleep due to emotional troubles, particularly when that inner, nagging voice keeps going and going into the night. Stuffing it into a dream pillow is the traditional approach, but other magickal uses may be employed. Agrimony has been used in combination with mugwort for varied forms of psychic healing, such as ritual healing and in aura cleansings. It is an herbe with a history of being used in countermagick, for it is known to repel all forms of negative energies.

ALFALFA

Alfalfa is said to remove money anxieties. One tradition has it that you carry ashes in an amulet with you, which has been constructed ritually. Alfalfa also enjoys a reputation as an Herbe of Protection.

ALMOND

Almond has a deep history as a Religious Herbe. It has been offered as incense and in sacrificial fires to invoke the deities of Artemis, Hecate, and Zeus. Almond was the tree which Aaron, high priest of the Hebrew people, selected as the source for his magickal wand. This heritage keeps Almond within contemporary Hebrew rites, the blossoms used to decorate the temples. Grieve reports a Greek myth in which Phyllis is transformed into the Almond. It might appear that the gods could not bear her grieving over having been abandoned by her lover, Domophoon. However, he does come back, and unable to find her, finds instead the Almond. It is only when he feels appropriately guilty for having left her and embraces the tree that it bursts into leaf and bloom. Almond may be used today to capture the essence of a love which will survive all trouble.

Almond is an excellent choice for a magickal wand, particularly when employed as a tool to be shared by both Priest and Priestess who are lovers beyond the Temple of their art. It may well enhance their potential for again sharing both love and magick in lives to come. Perhaps the most curious element of lore attached to Almond is that it will prevent one from becoming drunk. As the wand is a tool of control, perhaps Almond does have that power.

ANEMONE (WOOD)

The magickal lore of the Wood Anemone has some curious references. The Chinese associate it as a ''Flower of Death'' and the Egyptians see it as a symbol of sickness. It is perhaps that it touches a little understood form of magick which has led to its mixed understanding.

The Greeks held that this lovely plant was a gift from the God of the Wind, Anemos, and it has certain magickal use today in working with the spiritual wonders of the element Air. It may be used to commune with the sylphs, the mythological creatures which inhabit the air, and they may be invoked into the temple by offering some Wood Anemone as incense.

The Greeks also thought that this herbe had come from the tears of Venus, who was mourning the death of Adonis; it was offered in rites in their honor. It is best used when both God and Goddess are invoked as personified by Venus and Adonis. This herbe should not be taken internally. It is mildly poisonous, and in any case, tastes terrible.

ANGELICA

Angelica has many interesting magickal properties. It is one of the most valuable Herbes of Protection, with a long history of use in work against spells, enchantments, and all forms of evil. Not only does it grant protection from negative energies, but use also brings good energy into one's life, manifest as good fortune. Use of Angelica through bathing brings a most healthy aura, and a radiance of joyful, positive energy to the psychic self.

Angelica is said to be an herbe of Atlantis, and current use in meditation as incense and ritual drink has put practitioners in touch with Atlantean energies, visions, and understandings. Whether or not Atlantis existed in the mundane world is irrelevant to the value of touching into its legends.

Use of Angelica may take many forms. It gives off a pungent aroma when included in incense, may be ingested as tea or elixer, may be used in ritual bathing, burnt as offering, or kept intact as an amulet. Some of the values of Angelica are a deeper understanding of inner light, insight and inspiration in the purpose that the self may hold for bettering the world, and the wisdom of being in touch with that part of the inner self which is truly immortal. Angelica has also been used as a Visionary Herbe, used to increase one's ability to see into other realities and times.

Ritually, Angelica may be used to commune with the Archangel Michael.

ANISE

Anise is most helpful in treating those who feel most unfulfilled, and are of the conviction that romance would cure the trouble. The word 'enchantments' is sometimes associated with Anise, and it can be used to work gentle spells to aid a person in finding happiness.

Anise is much used in the making of amulets to protect against disturbing dreams, and to protect the person who travels in the astral realms while in the dream state.

There are rare references to Anise as an Aphrodisiac Herbe, perhaps from its history of use in the wedding cake. It is certainly an herbe to include in the ritual cake for a handfasting, and finds itself often added to the dough for moon cakes.

Anise may be used to invoke Mercury and Apollo, and may be incorporated with meditation upon the Chariot Card of the Tarot for a better understanding of its symbols. Anise stored for magickal use should be stored with a piece of amber, and may also be used to consecrate amber which will be used for psychic work. Anise is used to allow our physical awareness to be in communion with the spiritual, immortal elements of our being.

Anise is easily added to amulets, may be worn in a decorative sachet about the neck, included in incense, or delightfully taken as elixir.

ANISE, STAR

The Japanese hold this herbe to be very sacred. Its use as a Religious Herbe includes its plantings around temples and holy burial sites, where it will bring sacred energies of protection and beneficence. It is also collected from the tree as bark, and ground into powder to use as temple incense to drive away negative spirits and invoke the gods.

APPLE

Apples are considered sacred to Aphrodite, and may be offered in rites of her honor. The juice of the apple may be shared in those rituals, and the seeds or bark of the apple may be used as incense. In some places there is a custom of planting an apple as a gift for this lovely Goddess.

Among Earth Religions, the Apple is sometimes eaten for good luck at the celebration of Hallow's Eve, when it is felt that the circle of seasons makes a dramatic turn. Thus, one can bring about deep internal change.

The Greeks held the Apple as a source of wisdom, said to grow on a tree of life in the garden as Hesperides.

ASAFOETIDA

Due to the terribly bitter taste of this herbe, its use is primarily external. It is often mixed into incense, especially for rituals of a sombre, ceremonial nature. It is used to banish all negative energy, evil spirits and demons.

For the student of Tarot, Asafoetida may be used as incense to learn the mysteries of the Devil Card, and to learn to what earthly desires the self has become chained.

One of the names of Asafoetida is 'Food of the Gods' and it is also used to invoke male Gods, particularly of a phallic nature. There is some mythology suggesting that Asafoetida grew from semen of a god of fertility when it soaked into the Earth.

For the student of initiatory paths and rituals, Asafoetida is used to gain insight and to enhance the magickal work of any ritual.

This is the herbe to use to consecrate a black diamond, and if possible, one should be stored with the herb.

ASH

Ash is useful in removing unwanted energies. Historically it has been used to remove spells and hexes. Superstition says that it will cure warts, when a pin has been inserted into an Ash Tree, and then stuck into the wart, removed and returned to the tree. Grieve gives the following charm for this:

"Ashen tree, ashen tree, Pray buy these warts of me."

Another practise says that placing an Ash leaf in your automobile or upon a motorcycle, etc., will keep you protected from accident while traveling, and bring you safely home.

ASPHODEL

This is an important herbe when doing magickal work for those who have passed to the underworld. It is said that planting Asphodel near the grave will provide sustenance and energy for the soul as it passes into the other realm.

Another use of Asphodel is in the consecration of the magickal wand. It may be used in the incense, or in the wash for the cleansing.

BALM OF GILEAD

This is used ritually as an oil, thoroughly coating a candle which will be used in psychic healing. The proper procedure for dressing a candle is to first rinse it in cold water, to which a bit of sea-salt has been added. This is to rid the candle of any unwanted energy. Next, beginning at the center, anoint the candle working outwards towards both ends. When it is completely coated, it is ready for use.

BASIL

Basil has strong associations with the dragon-like Basilisk, which accounts for its contemporary association with salamanders and dragons. It is used today to invoke the presence of these astral and mythological creatures. Indeed, Basil is a favorite of herbes among the many friends I have who keep a few Dragons around their homes and temples for advice, inspiration, and protection. It may be burnt as an incense to invoke them, or may be taken as ritual drink to commune with these spirits.

Basil is used widely today for those who desire further courage when preparing to experience Initiation. It provides the novice with the strength to pursue positive expansion to the most desirable limit. There is no specific means of use, but any approach will put you in touch with its energy.

Basil has been planted upon graves, and used in Rituals of the Dead as an incense. It must have been with serious thought that Solomon chose it when making his ritual tool to aspurge his temple.

Basil is also a Fertility Herbe, it may be used to invoke Krishna and Vishnu, and releases us from the fears of having a psychic vision. Basil protects against the unknown, and from fears associated with spiritual growth.

BAY LAUREL

Bay may be used to attract love. There are several approaches; one in which the leaves are offered in a fire, another in which the oil is used to anoint a candle which is then lit during meditation.

Those who have a large garden may desire to plant a Bay Laurel, for it will bring protection to the home and all who reside within it.

Bay Laurel is a Visionary Herbe, as used by the Delphic

priestesses, although extreme caution must be used. They were a most intensely trained group of women, trained through initiation, with years of preparation before they would chew the leaves to enhance their mediumship of the Oracle. Under no circumstances can this be recommended.

A current practise is to make a wish box, decorated and constructed with three Bay leaves inside, and given to a friend. The friend may then make a wish during the course of the waxing moon.

It is said that the tree will protect you from thunderstorms. This may be due to its association with Apollo, in his aspect as player of the lute. Bay may also be ritually used to invoke this God-form.

For the student of Tarot, Bay will aid in the understanding of the Sun Card. You may also wish to make a crown of the leaves, and present them to the one who initiates you, as a symbol of love and esteem.

BENZOIN

Benzoin is an excellent herbal substance for those who pursue spiritual journeys. It is most excellent for the mind, assisting the mind to focus and concentrate on the subject matter. Used in meditation, it gives one a sense of harmony and internal peace and calm.

Benzoin is brought into ritual to guarantee success of the magickal project, and is used by many adepts for easing the transition into the spiritual realms to explore the joys of astral travel.

In self-growth it is used to cure selfishness, to allow the individual to see the delicate balances between give and take, and to see the nature of giving as a tool to bring harmony to one's life.

Sacred to Venus, Aphrodite, and Mut, Benzoin may be burnt in their honor, its fumes filling the temple space to aid in the invocation of any of those deities. For the student of the Cards, Benzoin aids in learning about the mystique of the Seven of Cups.

BIRCH

Birch is sometimes known as 'Lady of the Woods', and may be used to commune with the Goddess of the Woodlands. To touch the heart of the Earth Mother, it is only necessary to do a simple ritual and follow that with a deep meditation within a small grove of Birch. Legend says that the Lady of the Woods will become most angry should you malign one of her trees by taking its bark. Birch is also held to be an honored tree of the God Thor. Should one desire to have some of the bark, wait until Thor has singled a Birch tree and stricken

203

it with lightening. Then you have access to the paper-like bark, which
will be a very potent magickal parchment.

BITTERSWEET

Bittersweet is an Herbe of Protection. It is most often hung within
the dwelling, to protect family and friends alike from all negative
energy. It differs from other herbes in that it should be hung in secret,
for its power will wane if any other than you (or the practitioner) is to
know the place of its charm.

BLESSED THISTLE

Blessed Thistle may be used today in rituals to invoke the God
principal, particularly as embodied by Pan. It may be offered as an
incense, or may be an herbe for the ritual cup, taken as an elixir of the
God.

The astrological associations would provide one with ability to
motivate the self, or to take a brilliant idea out of 'cranial-storage' and
bring it joyfully manifest into reality.

Blessed Thistle is an herbe of great value. It has been used for
protection among peoples who have 'hexing' in their culture, said to
remove from the self unwanted influences, particularly of malevolent
intent. Therefore, should someone you know be wishing you harm,
this is an excellent herbe to bring into use.

BLUEBELLS

These are flowers used in Rituals of the Dead. They are associated
with hyacinths in mythology, and have strong connections with
mourning.

BORAGE

Borage was one of the Magickal Herbes of the Celts. It is believed
that the name, Borage, is evolved from a Celtic word meaning a person
of strong courage and bravery.

Current magickal use of Borage is to fortify the inner self. Borage
may be used daily in a ritual bath, taken internally as a tonic, or burnt
with incense in daily meditation. The results will be most gratifying,
for Borage enables one to feel happiness and joy, even during the most
difficult of crises.

BROOM

Broom has a mixed reputation. In some cases it is seen as very lucky, magickal, and prized, yet there are legends which call it an herbe to avoid, one which has been cursed. Should you have Broom growing on your property, the amount of flowers is said to be a sign of your fortune . . . many flowers mean abundant luck. It is said that Broom should not be disturbed, that a curse will follow one who picks the blossoms for mere decoration. Yet, it is also said that the blossoms, picked for sacred use, are a good and powerful source of magick.

Grieve tells us of Christian legend, in which the Virgin Mary cursed the plant because it made noise as they passed it by fleeing the soldiers of Herod. This may be an attempt to put the common magickal uses of the plant in negative light, to turn the people in a Christian direction, and to encourage them to discard their Pagan practises.

Broom is a chosen herbe for temple purification. This may be due to its name, for many will gather it, bunch it together, and use it to sweep away all negative energies. It is sometimes used to dip into holy waters, and to purge the temple or ritual space.

Broom has been used at weddings and handfastings, tied brightly with ribbons as a symbol of joy and survival of the union. It has been used as a Religious Herbe to invoke Blodewwedd.

BURNETT

Aside from the mundane use in vinegars for salad, there are some valuable uses for this simple plant. Not only does it drive away the problems of despair and depression, but the wise magician uses this herbe in the preparation of most magickal tools. It is used to both purify the tool and to focus and concentrate strong vibrations and currents of power within, which will only be released within a consecrated space.

CAMPHOR

Camphor may be used to purify and cleanse a home or Temple of all negative energies, to leave the space pure and clean so that it will absorb joy and health, and contain these positive energies for those who pass within. In crystalline form, it has been used as an incense in the evening meditation to produce dreams of prophecy and divination, and may also be used in similar fashion to study the Chariot Card of Tarot.

CARAWAY

Caraway is used to consecrate magickal and ritual tools, but may also be used to consecrate any of your personal possessions. The property that this brings is that of retention. Once consecrated, they will remain in your possession. It should be pointed out that if this is done out of selfishness you are then more likely to lose that which you selfishly desire to possess.

Caraway is sometimes thrown at weddings and handfastings and sometimes added to the wedding cake or food being served, for it is thought to help the lovers remain faithful and avoid breaking apart.

CATNIP

Catnip was, at one time, recommended as a treatment for barrenness. It also appeared as a fertility charm in folklore. Currently, Catnip is used as a Religious Herbe, particularly with two Egyptian Goddesses: Bast, who often manifests as a cat; and Sekhmet, who manifests as a lion. It must be certain that either of these Divine Felines would love the scent of this herb.

For self-growth, Catnip may be mixed with the resin of Dragon's Blood, and this burnt in order to exorcise the self of a particular bad habit.

There is also some use of Catnip for those who practise shape-shifting, and desire to prowl about the night transformed into cats. The connection between Catnip and cats is so strong that this is an herbe sure to be effective in any magic or healing associated with the feline kingdom.

CEDAR

Cedar has much value beyond its use in the construction of closets and chests for clothing storage. In ancient times Cedar was a major incense ingredient. It is still used in incense, most often in the form of sawdust. The resin within is pungent, and easily released as smoke in this manner.

The incense of the cedar is highly recommended in the consecration of a magickal wand, and may be used to study any of the 'wand' Cards of Tarot. Specific study in Tarot with Cedar would be the Four Cards (all four suits).

Folklore holds that carrying a small piece of Cedar in one's billfold or wallet will attract money. It certainly will keep the moths away.

As a Religious Herbe, it is used to invoke Wotan, either as an incense, as a sacrificial herbe, or by using a wand or staff of its wood. Cedar is the appropriate herbe for using amethysts and sapphires. Should you have these gems, they should be stored in a small box made of Cedar. Incidentally, it is said that Unicorns absolutely love to have little Cedar boxes around in which to store their treasures.

CELANDINE

Celandine the Lesser is used today as a Religious Herbe among those peoples who celebrate the growing of the sun in their late Winter and Springtime rituals. It is sometimes tossed into the fire in celebration of the days of growing sunshine, and sometimes included in the ritual drink.

It is said that boiling Lesser Celandine with white wine and then drinking this pleasant drink with honey before going to bed is a sure way of inducing pleasant dreams. Lesser Celandine is a Visionary Herbe, used widely to increase one's psychic abilities, and is used as a wash in some forms of divination, either to consecrate a divinatory tool, or to bathe various portals of psychic experience within the body.

CELERY SEED

This herbal seed, found in most kitchens, is used as a Visionary Herbe. There are forms of divination which recommend drinking a tea of the seed as it opens the mind and allows for better concentration. It should be mentioned that this is the garden celery under the rulership of Mercury, rather than wild celery, which is under the dominion of Venus.

CENTAURY

This herbe is named after the famous Centaur Chiron, who holds a place of great importance to the Herbalist. Chiron was wounded by the poisonous hydra, according to Grieve, and cured himself with the use of herbes. Chiron is one of the mythological heroes of the Herbalist; a patron of the Craft. Centaury may be used as a tonic, completely safe and complete with healthy qualities, which may be

207

taken by one learning the crafts of the Herbalist.

Folklore puts this herbe as one used by witches of the medieval era, who were said to mix it into their incenses, increasing their psychic powers and taking them into trance-like states. It was also used as a Countermagicke Herbe, and these properties may be found within Centaury today.

CHAMOMILE

Chamomile may be planted in a magickal herbe garden to function as a guardian herbe spirit for the energy of the space. It will bring magickal and mundane protection.

The inclusion of Chamomile into an amulet or magickal working is said to guarantee the success of the endeavor. It is used to invoke various Sun Gods, particularly Karnayna. This may be done by way of incense or through ritual drink.

CHASTE TREE

This is an herbe of particular interest to women. It has appeared in two of the three aspects of the Goddess. The seeds of the herbe are seen as symbols of virginity, and appropriate for the maiden aspect. The women of Greece, anciently, used the leaves, wearing them when doing rituals to invoke the Goddess Ceres. Chaste Tree has been used to exemplify the Goddess as Maiden, and is also used in incense for rituals for the Crone.

CHERVIL

Chervil is an Herbe of Immortality. An elixir of the herbe, or its use as incense in a ritual will bring the user a greater sense of those parts of the self which will exist beyond life. Communion with Chervil as it grows in one's garden will bring about the same wisdom. Chervil may be added to amulets for magickal workings, and makes an excellent ingredient for regular use in rituals. It is of great value for those who work with the religious principle of the Goddess, and for those who choose to study the mysteries of the Cauldron of Cerridwen.

CINNAMON

Although Cinnamon has been assigned to the rulership of Mars most likely due to its stimulant property, it currently is given to Uranus, for the main work it brings about is for the mind.

Cinnamon may be burnt as incense or taken as tea in order to increase one's ability to concentrate and focus the mind, and to communicate with greater ease with others. It is also sometimes used in prophecy, and may be employed internally or externally.

As was done in ancient China, Cinnamon is still used to purify the space of a temple, and is an excellent ingredient for ritual incense. It is said to bring peaceful energy, so that the rite may be conducted with no distraction and with full concentration.

The more mundane magickal properties of Cinnamon find its use in love magick, where it is mixed with other herbes to create a love potion, and added to amulets so that it will bring the practitioner good luck.

For the adept, Cinnamon will bring a keener understanding of the properties of immortality. It is said that it may also aid a person to be in touch with that aspect of the self. Cinnamon may be used in meditating upon the Tarot, and is in vibration with the Lovers card. Magickal Cinnamon should be stored with a small tourmaline, and is the appropriate herbe for the consecration of that stone.

CINQUEFOIL

The best Cinquefoil to be had for the Practitioner would be that gathered beneath the full moon. It is also said that you should gather it at midnight, as the night turns from Wednesday to Thursday, beneath a waxing moon.

Religious use of this herbe says that it brings a sense of communication and awareness with the maternal aspect of all nature. It is this property which has Cinquefoil included as an ingredient in countless magickal recipes. It brings a natural balance to the energy, and allows the intent to manifest.

Cinquefoil is sometimes burnt as incense, said to bring dreams of one's perfect partner. It is also given among close friends, a full, five-fingered leaf pressed and dried, sent between the pages of a personal book. Such a gift is said to guarantee a protected and joyful journey for the recipient.

The association of Cinquefoil with 'flying ointment' is very likely a result of its quality as a Magickal Herbe, rather than any distinctive constituent of the Cinquefoil. It has no narcotic properties.

CLARY

Clary has strong association with the eyes and the ability to see. It is used to enhance the visions found within the state of meditation. It may be used within the Universal Condenser, in which the herbes are alchemically prepared to give forth a powerful healing energy.

Clary is an Herbe of Protection, and it is said that it will specifically protect one's ability to see. This is usually interpreted as the eyes, although Magick has its own sense of humor.

It is best used by making a lotion, this being applied directly to either eyes or chakras.

CLOVER

Clover is well known for the luck associated with finding a four-leafed variety, said to bring good fortune because it represents a perfect balance of the four elements. The four-leaf Clover has also been used to dissolve the spells caused by those fairies which tend to be a bit mischievious.

The four-leaf Clover has been used to divine one's perfect soulmate, some versions calling for placing it under your pillow to bring the image in your dreams, carrying it with you, and knowing that the first person you meet will be your intended, and the like. Did you know, however, that the five-leaf Clover is said to be unlucky? This is due to the energy associated with the magick of the number of five, which is joyful to the adept, but very difficult for the amateur.

Clover has been a Magickal Herbe for many cultures, among them the Druids, the Celts, Romans, and the Greeks. Red Clover, presented to a loved one, asks for a pledge of fidelity. When the White Clover is given, it is seen as a promise that the giver will maintain fidelity. The best Clover is that gathered beneath a full moon.

Clover should be used in the consecration of Magickal tools made of copper, and is of great value in consecrating a ritual pentacle. The procedure is irrelevant as long as the energies of the pentacle and of the clover are mingled.

CLOVES

Cloves are included in one of the most popular of love philtres. It is an herb of the New Age, and possibly one of the reasons for the reappearance of this recipe. Cloves bring Aquarian Magick to the kitchen, conveying to all who share the repast a sense of kinship and amiability.

Ground Cloves may be mixed into incense. They carry the ability to enhance one's psychic ability and are sometimes used for those who work to perceive astral visions.

Although most psychic endeavors use Cloves in the form of incense, there are some who drink teas and elixirs made of Clove to achieve the same goals.

COFFEE

Coffee has a history of use as a Religious Herbe. It has been used for the sacred drink in rituals among the Aztec, Mayan, and Inca peoples. It may be used in a similar manner today, but it is effective primarily for those who do not include Coffee as a daily or regular beverage. If this herbe is used for ritual drink, it should be held in esteem in that household, and used solely for that purpose. It will bring greater insight and clarity of purpose to the ritual.

CORIANDER

When Coriander is grown in a garden it will protect the gardener and all who reside in the gardener's household. It may be gathered at the harvest season, and a bunch of it hung within the home as an Herbe of Protection, decorated with ribbon to bring peace and security to the house.

Coriander is associated with peace, and may be used in rituals performed to reach that end. It may be used in the ritual drink, or burnt as incense. The seed is generally used for the incense.

Coriander has been used in spells of love magick, but also is known as an Herbe of Immortality. It is therefore an excellent herbe in unions of two persons who desire to share their love beyond this life.

CORNFLOWER

Cornflower is an herbe which can be used in the making of a Fluid Condenser as it is a Visionary Herbe. Filtered through three layers of blue linen and then ritually consecrated beneath the full moon with a Moonstone, it may be used to bathe the eyes, bringing an increased sense of clairvoyance, enabling one to see aspects of the creative forces of the Universe.

Cornflower has mythological associations with the Goddess Flora, and enjoys current use as an herbe used to invoke the Creative Mother forces of nature. The brilliant, Goddess-blue flowers are most appropriate to decorate an altar with their five-pointed stars, and may be worn by a woman who seeks to embody the Goddess of Nature.

COWSLIP

This herbe was chosen by the Norse peoples, who felt it embodied the qualities of the Goddess Freya. They dedicated it to her, and used it as a Religious Herbe in rites in Her honor. It is thought to bring a sense of direction to the practitioner, one which would take the spirit of the source of Freya's Goddess energy, and bestow mysteries which would keep the practitioner in Freya's graces. Some believed that following the path of the mysteries to Freya would grant earth-plane treasures and abundance.

Later this herbe became associated with the Virgin Mary, as have many herbes once the domain of the Goddess. Its properties remained unchanged, and the country people knew that it still reached out for the Maternal.

Cowslips have been used in spells performed to increase one's physical charm and attractiveness. They have also been hung over the main entrances to a home, used as an Herbe of Protection. Thus could only good and benevolent energies enter the home.

CUBEB BERRIES

Cubeb Berries have a history of sexual association. They have been used as an Aphrodisiac, ground and mixed with honey. Taking a regular dose of the mixture has been said to prolong erection, increase passion, and greatly increase the physical activity of lovemaking and sex. It appears to be used primarily for men. Cubeb Berries are used remedially in the treatment of gonorrhea, urethritis, and other painful afflictions of those whose passions love to wander.

CUCUMBER

Cucumbers are known as Visionary Herbes, said to bring peace to the soul, a sense of calm to one's well-being, and increased psychic ability. Generally they are used in the fresh state. Pieces of the green rind, placed across the closed eyelids during meditation, are said to put one in closer touch with the subconscious and all the wisdom we can reach through our intuition.

CUMIN

Cumin has been used as an herbe to add to amulets and charms made to protect a family and bring them good luck and prosperity. Recipes usually call for a pinch of ground Cumin. The same measure is found included in recipes which are said to increase the sexual drive. Some say that taking a pinch of Cumin daily will guarantee vigorous sexual ability throughout one's life.

DAFFODIL

For yellow Daffodils, collect the root on Tuesday beneath the waxing moon. The other colors are ruled by Venus, and may be gathered on a waxing Friday, or beneath any full moon. The root should be dried, finely ground, and this powder worked into magickal balms, ointments and unguents.

DAISIES

Daisies have been planted in gardens which are grown to attract various fairies and spirits. It is said that the Dryads are attracted to those places where Daisies grow, and sitting among them is a means of learning to communicate with the Devas of the herbes.

Daisies are used as a Religious Herbe in rituals of honor to Freya. They are strewn about the Circle, may be placed upon the altar, and the Priestess who will symbolize the Goddess wears either a strand about the neck or a garland in her hair.

Daisies have more than one folk custom associating them with love divination. Aside from counting the petals to see if your intended loves you, one custom would lead you to a clump and the number of flowers you touch with your hand represent the number of years you must wait to meet your partner. It might be better to keep your hands in your pockets!

DAISY (OX-EYE)

This Daisy has religious uses which differ from the rest of the family. It has been dedicated to Zeus, Jupiter, and various names for the

213

Thunder God. It is said that grown in one's garden it will protect the home from lightning, and has been used to decorate the altar in rituals to those deities.

It was once dedicated to Artemis, and enjoys current use in rituals by groups of all-women. After Artemis waned in popularity the Ox-eye Daisy became associated with Mary Magdelen. There are also cases in which it has been dedicated to St. John.

DAMIANA

Damiana is found growing in the western hemisphere. It is a small, bushy plant which grows as far north as Texas, and also upon the West Indies Islands. Because it directly affects the sexual organs with its stimulant properties, it has a growing reputation as an Aphrodisiac. It is found used in potions to increase the arousal of a partner, but also has a reputation as a Magickal Herbe.

It is currently used in a variety of ways, some choosing to drink or smoke it prior to a ritual. It is said to magickly increase the amount of energy generated, making it more intense. It is also used in sacred rituals which will explore sex magick. It is taken as a tea by those who study the sexual forms of yoga, and is said also to increase psychic ability and clairvoyance.

Damiana should ideally be stored with a piece of quartz, and an oil of this herbe is said to be the best for the protection of the crystal.

DILL

Other than for relieving stomach gas, Dill is used primarily for its aromatic properties, in flavoring pickles and the like. The green, ground, is excellent in salads, but it has a more interesting history as a Magickal Herbe. As such, it is a good choice for kitchen magick, to bring an air of well-being to your guests.

Dill is an Herbe of Protection. It has been used to repel negative energies and black magic. It keeps one's mind clear, and gives strength to reason. It has been used to protect the user from falling prey to the results of the belief in superstition.

Dill is also an herbe used in blessings, particularly those for the home and the kitchen.

DITTANY OF CRETE

This herb may be used ritually to seek wisdom from those who live between lives. It is best used on the occasion of All Hallow's Eve, when mystics and practitioners of ancient workings do their rituals to communicate with their teachers and their kin, all passed through death into another existence. In this manner will the practitioner be given insight and wisdom to help them through this life.

As a Religious Herbe, Dittany of Crete has been used to invoke the presences of both Persephone and Osiris, two deities of different cultures who hold the mystical keys to the Otherworld. In the study of Tarot, Dittany of Crete is used to better understand the Ten cards, bringing a better ability to translate their meaning.

Sometimes this herbe is associated with the Sphinx.

DOGWOOD

Not only is this plant beautiful as a symbol of the voluptuousness of Spring, but it has a somewhat unique historical aspect to it. It is said to invoke Consus, who is best present when an important meeting is to be held. Consus aids in keeping the proceedings of the meeting secret, and aids all in attendance to hold their tongues. If you have a secret, Dogwood will help you to keep it that way. This herbe is excellent for guarding sacred books, private journals, and the like.

DRAGON'S BLOOD

Although this herb is an ingredient for a remedy found in Grieve for severe syphilis, it is primarily in use today as a Magickal Herbe. Two forms of the herbe are found, one in which it is ground into a fine, reddish powder, and the other in long reeds, looking a bit like cinnamon sticks.

It is said that the energy of Dragon's Blood is such that it will increase the power of any ritual energy. It is also well known as an Herbe of Protection. As such, many magickal rites are sealed and protected by writing in ink made of Dragon's Blood. It is also used to seal sacred documents, oaths and vows.

Dragon's Blood enjoys use as an Herbe of Consecration, and may be used to consecrate tools of ritual, magick, or divination.

One of the more interesting associations with Dragon's Blood is involved with the art of shape-shifting, in which it is said that the practitioner may take on another shape and travel both astrally and disguised upon the earth. Such a skill also takes many years of strict discipline and diligent practise.

Dragon's Blood may be used to study the Emperor card of Tarot, primarily as an incense. It works well with rubies, and may have one stored within its container. It is also associated with the Sword of

Truth, and is of great value in the ritual preparation of this magickal weapon.

Dragon's Blood invokes Shiva, and rituals to Shiva have this herbe burnt in his honor.

ELDER

Elder is an herbe for those attuned to the countryside. It may be used to protect the livestock, most commonly by tying two small pieces with red yarn to the barn or stable. A farm which has Elder to be found within its reaches is considered blessed, and the Elder growth should be considered a sacred place, free from being despoiled. Allowing one's livestock to wander amid the Elder-growth is a means of bringing them protection.

The magickal power of Elder is most potent, and as a result much of the lore treats Elder with warning. It was once thought that using a rod of Elder to punish a child would cease the child's growth, for magickally the rod represents control, and the spiritual energy of Elder would amplify this desire to control until it would be out of hand. Elder will bring magick to even the slightest wish; no wonder then it has a mixed reputation.

There are various approaches to gathering Elder, all of which would appear to require appeasement of the Goddess as She manifests through this tree or shrub. Grieve tells an ancient verse, "Lady Ellhorn, give me some of thy wood, and I will give thee some of mine when it grows in the forest." This is an herbe never to be gathered out of selfishness, for it is said that the spirit of the Elder will follow and plague one who does so.

Elder Blossoms are gathered and used magickally as a fixative in dry incense mixtures, for they easily attract and hold oils which are added to the incense, releasing them with their own when burnt upon glowing charcoal. They will increase the power of a ritual, but require clear goals and pure ethics.

There are so many stories which associate the Elder with sadness and grief, going so far as to say Elder was that wood upon which the traitor Judas was hung. These are believed, in large part, due to the natural magick of the herbe. Magick in the hands of those with questionable motive, or in the lives of those who understand it not and fear it, becomes confusing, disorienting, and leads to life-shaking events. Although the cause is within one's own heart, Elder has become the scapegoat.

Those who wish to see the spirits of the wood, known as Dryads among magickal folk, would do well to spend the full moon night in a small grove of Elder, making certain that there is no evil in the heart, and that proper fasting and ritual preparation has been made.

Elder may be used in incense or oil to keep one safe and protected. It finds occasional use in the blessings of babies, both Christian and pagan. As a Funereal Herbe, it has been used as the wood for the pyre, and is sometimes buried with the departed to give protection.

Its use is a growing trend among people who study magick, and it is said to coincide with a renaissance in the proliferation of the Fairy-Folk of old, coming back to dance with the Earth into the New Age. Elder is the herbe which gives one sight of these delightful and fanciful beings, and Midsummer Night is the time to see them. Take yourself to the grove, and wait in belief and patience.

The customs Grieve includes in her section on Elder are worth reading.

ELECAMPAGNE

This herbe is widely known for its association with Elven magick. This type of energy has been brought into love spells, but caution should be given, for Elven magick is capricious.

Elecampagne should be ground and this substance offered upon glowing blocks of charcoal in rituals of sacred magick. The smoke from the incense may be used to purify candidates for initiation, and they would be wise to have come prepared by taking Elecampagne daily as a gentle cleansing tonic, so that they will freely breathe of the sacredness of the rite. Elecampagne makes an excellent ritual drink, and may be taken safely as an elixir of magick.

ELM

The stately Elm which one might think a common tree has some interesting lore of its own. Meditation with this tree will aid one in developing communication with the spirits of herbes and with the little people. One is said to be able to develop a rapport when choosing one particular Elm, consecrating it in ritual, and then spending frequent times beneath its protection, meditating upon the plant kingdom, and doing rituals to open communication with the Devas.

The leaf of the Elm has been used in several forms of folk divination, such as pricking it with a pin and dreaming upon it.

ENDIVE

An oil made of this herbe is used to find fulfillment, particularly for those who feel left out of social events, who seek the comfort of friendship and companionship but feel too unworthy to attract such people into their lives. Using the oil in the bath, or after the bath, or in ritual fashion will build self-confidence, and leave the practitioner more desirable to the surrounding society.

EYEBRIGHT

This is the best herbe to choose when working to change the energy of one's attitude to a more positive state. In times of difficulty, Eyebright allows one to see where the growth and stress can lead, and to carry within the joy of perceiving growth and better times ahead. It brings to the mind a sense of perspective, that makes even hard trials fall into the perspective of minor difficulties in the whole of time.

Eyebright is often included in magickal tonics, or during periods of fasting and study, for it makes the work pleasant and the time enjoyable. It is said to aid the memory, and to bring clear thinking.

This is an herbe of which fluid condensers are made, as a lotion for the eyes and psychic channels of the body, clarifying visualization and assisting the practitioner in gaining visionary experiences.

Eyebright is a primary choice when working magickal ritual to help another, for it will allow the user to have the necessary change of attitude, thus able to help the self.

FENNEL

Fennel is often relegated by the practitioner as a kitchen herbe, used to flavor fish, and occasionally brought into remedies in conjunction with purgatives to make them easier on the stomach, but Fennel has a most interesting history as a Magickal Herbe. Taking Fennel as a magickal tonic will bring the ability to have a long life, filled with ability to face danger, and be strong in the face of adversity. It is also said to help maintain fertility and virility.

Fennel has the ability to protect one's home and kin, and for this purpose it should be gathered on Midsummer's Eve, and hung over the portals. As the wise magician Solomon chose this herbe when making his ritual tool to aspurge his sacred Circle, it might be considered appropriate to use a bunch of fennel to sprinkle water about the house, doors, and windows, before it is to be hung as a protective amulet.

Fennel, also used by the Saxons in herbe magick, is an herbe of value for those who practise meditation. For the Kabbalist, it is important in learning about the Sphere of Hod, and for those who fast, Fennel will aid the stomach in enjoying the prospect.

Grieve quotes Longfellow in a verse which attributes to Fennel the property of restoring lost eyesight.

FENUGREEK

The seed of this herbe may be steeped into an elixir, which will bring the wisdom of Apollo into one's heart. It is used by priests who wish to invoke this Sun Deity, and is also burnt as incense in rituals of His honor.

FERNS

The most fascinating aspect of working magickally with Ferns is that carrying the seed will make the practitioner invisible. Although this is seemingly impossible, many have found that collecting the spore and ritually encasing it in an amulet gives one the ability to go about one's business in privacy, and without attracting the attention of others.

The spore is also useful in seeing one's future. Within a properly prepared ritual Circle, cast the spore upon a basin of water, and watch your image as it begins to shift and pass through the potentials of the future.

FLAX

Flax is of interest, beyond linen and the seed, often found in health food stores. The flowers should be gathered just after morning's dew passes. They may be dried, and used as incense for protection, to banish any evil or negative magick, or to bring blessings and good health.

Grieve tells of a Bohemian custom which sends the children dancing in the fields of Flax. This is done when they are seven years old, and will keep them handsome and beautiful as they move into maturity.

Those who sew, weave, or otherwise work at those arts, might consider Flax as a 'patron herb'. It is said that Flax may be used to invoke the Goddess Hulda. This is the Goddess who taught the human race how to spin thread and create cloth. A small vase filled with the beautiful blue blossoms would make a wonderful gift for a weaver or sewer.

FOXGLOVE

The 'Fairy' legends associated with this herbe make it of value to those who, as part of the art, communicate with the little people of the garden world. For those who wish to see the Fairies, it is said that you should prepare a fully cast circle, and taking a chalice of the fresh juice of the Foxglove, draw an unbroken line from East to West, and then from South to North. Although the Circle is taken down when the ritual is complete, the crossed lines remain, as an invitation to the little people that the practitioner is of good intent, and invites them to visit.

Foxglove is an herbe of the underworld, and has been used by those with intense initiatory training to commune with those who live there. This is a dangerous practise for the untrained, for Foxglove is also capricious, and the unwise or foolhardy could easily find the communion with the underworld permanent and too vivid.

FRANKINCENSE

Frankincense is a staple of the practitioner. It was once used medicinally as a stimulant, and according to Pliny as an antidote for the poisoning of hemlock, but now is an essential ingredient of incense. It has a long history as a Religious Herbe. Frankincense comes to us as a beautiful golden resin, dried into small gravel, and is gathered by cutting into a tree and gathering the dried sap.

The Hebrew religion regards Frankincense highly, using it often in their rites, and it is part of the Roman Catholic tradition, according to Grieve, used ten parts to four of benzoin and one of storax. Its color, scent, and the spiritual energy which permeates it have long made it an herbe used to invoke the male aspect of the Universe. It was much used by Balthazar, King of the Chaldeans, as an herbe of their priesthood. The Babylonians used it to honor their Sun God, Bel. It has also been used to invoke Apollo, Adonis, and the Golden-Haired Sun God of modern Pagans. Frankincense is also used to invoke the feminine principle of the Universe, notably Demeter and various of the Moon Goddesses, said to call upon Her heart and bring Her compassion.

In magick, Frankincense is used to bring the practitioner success in both the spiritual world and the mundane, or practical world. Its fragrance in incense aids in the focus of concentration, and keeps the mind aware of that which is going on within the ritual.

Frankincense is an Herbe of Protection, cleansing and purifying the soul and spirit, and keeping one safe when wandering in the astral realms. It is useful for Leos, for it will help them remain in balance, and not go too far off with pride and self-indulgence. It has within it an element of seeing the value of discipline, particularly for those who study spiritual paths.

Frankincense should be used to consecrate Topaz, magickal wands, and tools of control. Placing some pieces of Frankincense upon glowing charcoal, and watching the melting resin turn to smoke will enable the student of Tarot to better understand the four Sixes.

FUMITORY

Fumitory is an Herbe of Consecration and of Protection. It also, as Frankincense, has associations with the underworld; indeed, legend says that it sprang from the vapors and gases of the earth, born of the Earth's inner spirit rather than from seed upon the soil. As an incense, it purifies, and may be used in the purification of any ritual tools before their consecration.

It may be used to purify a ritual space, and cleanse it of distraction and of negative energy. It is also used in rituals of exorcism.

GARLIC

Garlic has been used in rituals of purification and is often seen as an Herbe of Protection, even in modern legend, against vampires. The Greeks used it to invoke Hecate, placing a clove upon a small pile of stones at a crossings of roads or paths.

Garlic is seen as a powerful amulet against all forms of negative energy and evil. It contains the power of strength, no doubt, in part to the odor.

Garlic is also sacred to Cybele, although reserved for Her alone. Those who worship the Goddess in that aspect are recommended to avoid use of this herbe.

GINGER

Ginger is known for its ability to improve the state of health. A piece of the dried root may be worn within an amulet, or Ginger may be taken as a daily tonic, in order to strengthen health and protect the wearer. Ginger may also be grown in a garden, and the manner in which it flourishes is said to govern the health of the gardener.

GUM MASTIC

Gum Mastic is known as an herbe which will purify. As such, it is most valuable as an Herbe of Consecration, cleansing all tools of divination and magick of previous energy before they are ritually consecrated. It may be used as an incense, allowing the smoke to bathe the instrument and leave it free of any influence. The incense may also be used to purify a person of negative energy, or of the influence of another.

Gum Mastic is also known as an Herbe of Protection. It will banish any negative energy and work to keep the space pure. It is commonly added to ritual incense, for it will enhance and intensify ritual energy.

It is said to vibrate in like manner as Hod on the Tree of Life.

HEATHER

Heather is an Herbe of Immortality. Partaking of it as a daily tonic, or wearing an amulet of the wood will bring a long physical life, and will enable one to perceive the truly immortal soul and remain in touch with the everlasting elements of the Universe. It is a valuable herbe for those who pursue initiatory paths, as they work to unfold the inner self.

Bathing in heather is said to bring increased beauty. For this purpose, using the blossoms in a bath of water, lit by candlelight, once each full moon for a year, would be an advisable method. Keep in mind that in receiving the magickal gift of increased physical attractiveness there will be a price extracted in order to keep the karmic balance.

HELLEBORE, BLACK

Magickally, Hellebore is related to the fern, for it is used in order to render oneself less visible to others. It is used for those who seek discretion, and the ability to pass through a crowd undetected.

Black Hellebore is also used in the blessing of farm animals and domestic pets. When it is used for either this purpose or that of invisibility, it should be collected by the practitioner in the live state, with the specific intent in mind.

HEMLOCK

Hemlock is an Herbe of Consecration. Under no circumstances should this herbe be taken internally. Its use is for the preparation of magickal tools and ritual instruments. It was one of the sacred herbes chosen by King Solomon to consecrate his ritual knife.

HEMP

Magickally, both the seed and the leaf are used. The seed figures in several old love spells, most notably the delightful one in which a young woman sows the seed in a large circle around a church on Midsummer's Eve. Any maiden capable of doing this, without notice, surely deserves her beloved.

The fresh juice may be extracted from the plant and saved for the purpose of divination. The Hemp juice should be used to anoint the tool of divination before entering a trance-state to seek the answer.

The leaf has been dried or cured, and then used as a smoking herbe, producing an altered state. Although 'pot-smoking' has become socially popular and is illegal in most areas of the country, its magickal heritage is worthy of note. The Herbalist who chooses to smoke Hemp for Religious or Ritual use would find the herbe works when treated as sacred, and used only for those purposes, and not for social pleasure.

HENBANE

Henbane is one of the herbes of the underworld. As is true with most of them, it is toxic, and dangerous to ingest. It is used ritually to summon spirits, relatives who have passed into other lives, and beings who live in the astral realms. These are most serious workings of magick, and should not be undertaken by any but the adept.

Common usage of Henbane is in working with increased psychic perception and clairvoyancy. Due to the toxic nature of the herbe, it is best used as an incense, or as a lotion for the tools of the work.

When ingested, Henbane can cause spasms and serious problems. The root is safer to use, being gathered, dried, and worn as an amulet. In this fashion can the above workings also be achieved.

HENNA

Henna is used primarily in sexual magick. The Arabian custom is to make an ointment of Henna and thick olive oil. This is rubbed onto the male organ at sunrise and sunset for two weeks, or preferably for the period of the waxing moon. Doing this will bring potency and virility. It is also likely to leave the penis brightly-colored as a result. Henna may also be macerated in vegetable shortening, and this used as a lubricant before entering sacred sexual rites.

HOLLY

Holly was a sacred herbe of the Druids. When winter would come, they would keep Holly in their homes, and thus would all of the little people and woodland spirits have a safe refuge against the cold and snow.

Holly may be sent with a gift to a friend, as the Romans did during the festival of Saturnalia. It is also an ideal herbe to fashion into a wreath, to celebrate the welcome of a new Priestess or Priest into the community.

HOLLYHOCK

Hollyhocks are related to the mallow family of herbes. Their bright flowers are a delight to see towering outside a window. The seed pods that form later may be used in magick to bring material success, money or possessions wanted to fulfill a need. When the flower is grown by a home, it is said to bring the family the ability to flourish.

Hollyhocks are also known for their ability to attract Devas and to often give shelter to the little people.

HONEYSUCKLE

Honeysuckle is an Herbe of Immortality. No doubt it gained this reputation from its ability to grow in nearly any condition and to flourish even when severely cut back. It is most easily used by the practitioner as an oil, the commercial varieties which are pure being the best, for they have the scent. Worn as an oil, it will aid in understanding non-physical realities. It may also be added to rituals being performed to pass through the mysteries of the Cauldron of Cerridwen.

HOP

Hop is most known for being used in dream pillows, said to bring peaceful and restful sleep. It is also used by many who practise religion honoring the Gods and Goddesses who brought ale and beer to humans.

HOREHOUND

Horehound is an herbe considered sacred to Horus. It is used either as incense or as ritual beverage in rituals performed to worship Horus, or to share in those virtues. Horehound may also be used in rituals working with Isis or Osiris.

Magickally, Horehound will help you 'keep it all together' when performing a ritual. It protects you from outside influence, and also gives the ability to perform ritual with a clear mind and a trust of inner intuition. It is said to bring forth those parts of the self which are creative and free, and to stimulate inspiration and new ideas. Many who pursue the arts of divination drink Horehound tea regularly, as it enhances their work.

When flowering, Horehound may be gathered and dried, tied with a ribbon and hung in the home. It will aid in balancing personal energies and keep the home free from negative energy.

Horehound may be macerated and the oil used in psychic healing, aura cleansing, and magickal healings. It vibrates with the energy of Hod.

HOUSELEEK

This onion family member was grown by the Romans in small pots. These kept at the portals of their homes were said to please the God Jupiter who would protect them from fires and destruction by lightning.

It was also used in Wales as a protection against the violence of storm, and it has this virtue today. It is also said that you must be wary of anyone else taking your pot of Houseleeks, for it will carry a curse to plague the thief. Some choose to grow them in a flower bed, and others sink the pot into the earth.

HYACINTH

Hyacinth is a beautiful flower which figures interestingly in ancient legend. It's origin was not from Earth, but as a young man, very attractive, who was fought over by the Sun God Apollo, and the Wind God Zephrus. When Hyacinthus fell to the handsome Apollo, Zephrus was overcome with jealousy and wounded ego, and blew one of Apollo's arrows off course and into Hyacinthus. Apollo, rather than restore the lad, followed the course of mythology and turned the dying Hyacinthus into this flower, as a token of his love and grief. Hyacinthus and Apollo are sometimes invoked with this herbe, although it should be pointed out that their affair did not have a happy ending.

Hyacinths are sometimes used as a patron herbe for male homosexuals.

HYSSOP

Hyssop is an Herbe of Protection. It may be gathered, dried, and hung in small bunches at all windows and doors, to keep out all negative energies, burglars, and unwanted intruders.

When the plagues visited Egypt, the Hebrew people made brushes of dried bunches of Hyssop. These were used to paint the portals with blood, which protected their children until the Priest Moses would lead them away.

Hyssop is said to have gone into the making of Solomon's Sprinkler, and is the best choice of herbe today to make a sprinkler for holy water. Gather Hyssop beneath the New Moon in Cancer, and dry it through the Full Moon (although it may take longer than this). The handle may be fashioned of wood, or a binding of leather wrapped around it. As such, it will cleanse your temple and make it sacred for ritual.

Hyssop makes an excellent oil for cleansing auras and for healing by the laying on of hands. It is an herbe excellent for consecrating magickal tools which are of tin and is the herbe for amythyst and lapis lazuli.

IRIS (ORRIS ROOT)

Irises have a long reputation as Religious Herbes. They are named for the deity who leads the souls to the Elysian Fields, and may be used

226

as Funereal Herbes to bring peace to the departed and hope for a happy reincarnation. Iris was the Goddess of the rainbow, representing hope and the symbol of the eternal spirit.

Irises have also been associated with Juno, Isis, and Hera, and may be used in rituals in their honor. In Egyptian lore, the Iris is seen as representing the sceptre of the pharoah, and is sometimes seen carved upon the head of the magickal wand. They thought the three petals to represent the three virtues of faith, wisdom, and valor.

Irises are considered Herbes of Protection, the tuberous root gathered, dried, and ground. In this form, the Iris is more commonly called Orris Root, and may be added to incense, or amulets, in order to bring protection for both physical and spiritual aspects. Magickally, Iris has been used to bring love, romance, companionship, and the ability to have a close and loving mate.

The Iris has been a symbol of France for many years.

IVY

Ivy brings to mind the ancient Greek custom of making wreaths, and crowning victors and newly-marrieds. Its ability to hold on through all weather and seasons is seen as similar to its virtue of fidelity.

Ivy is also associated, as a Religious Herbe, with Dionysus and Bacchus, both Gods of great revelry, drink, and late-night parties. Magickally, Ivy is said to prevent drunkenness. In the study of Tarot, Ivy may be used to better understand the suit of pentacles.

JASMINE

This very delicate, flowering herbe is often associated with Goddesses. It is an herbe sacred to Diana of Ephesus, and in later years became one of the herbes dedicated to the Virgin Mary. It is also sacred to Quan Yin.

Jasmine oil is considered one of the best for dressing a candle, and burning a candle with this oil gives psychic protection and brings health to one's aura.

Jasmine is seen as similar to the number nine in numerology, which is often described as feminine, and related to the manifestation ability of the Maternal aspect of the Universe.

Jasmine is an excellent herbe for charging a quartz crystal, and dried Jasmine should be stored with a small chip of quartz in the bottom of the container.

Jasmine will stimulate the creative aspect of the mind, and will bring an influx of original ideas, independent of others.

JUNIPER

There are several methods of working with Juniper. As an evergreen, the resin may be collected, dried, and used in incense. The berries are also gathered, dried, and may be used in amulets, ground, or made into a tea. The needles are sometimes taken, and may be burnt upon charcoal as incense, even when fresh.

Juniper is an excellent herbe to use in rituals for good health. It has the energy necessary to keep banished all those things which are injurious to one's health. Juniper will also attract good, healthy energies.

KAVA-KAVA

Kava-Kava is used as a sacramental drink, first fermented into a potent beverage, and taken before important rituals. It then induces visions and altered states of perception. The root is also made into a potion, and this also used as a Visionary Herbe.

Due to the physical action of the herbe upon the sexual organs, they are stimulated and yet the sensation is dulled, making Kava-Kava one of the most effective of Aphrodisiacs. It is most used in ritual today, when sex is being explored as a sacred tool of the Gods.

Kava-Kava is used among practitioners of the Huna religion when they are working out in the astral realms.

LADY'S MANTLE

This herbe has very ancient lore attached to it. It was earlier considered sacred to various Earth Goddesses, and later became an herbe of the Virgin Mary.

Lady's Mantle is primarily used as a Magickal Herbe, and adding it to any magickal mixture will make the nature of the work more effective. It will increase the power and focus the energy. Considered an herbe of alchemists, Lady's Mantle is said to contain the ability to transmute the formulae of an alchemist.

The dew is also collected early in the morning, and this is added to any potion of magick to seal the power within it.

228

LAVENDER

Lavender is used as a Religious Herbe in the celebration of the beginning of summer. It is a primary ingredient in the incense used by many on Midsummer's Eve. Lavender is also used in rituals of a mystical nature throughout the year, and is capable of invoking the more severe deities of Hecate and Saturn.

Lavender is used as a magickal tonic to bring a sense of stability into one's life, or to make the magickal work of a permanent nature. It was one of the herbes chosen by Solomon when he was constructing his sacred sprinkler for holy water, and may be used to spurge sacred circles and temples.

Lavender attracts energy of a high vibrational nature. It is thus brought into meditation where increased awareness is sought. It is said to bring great inner calm, peace of mind, and freedom from emotional and mental stress. In magickal spells it is used to attract money, to bless homes, and to attract possessions.

Interesting practises involving the use of Lavender include its being burnt in birthing rooms, the scent of its smoke filling the room, keeping it pure, and welcoming the new life into the world. It has also been woven into small wreaths to crown a newly-married couple, and is often used in handfasting rituals today. It was thrown into fires on St. John's Day, to gain protection from the many wild and terrifying spirits roaming the land. It is said to be an herbe which will protect snakes, and has been used in the worship of Goddesses who are associated with serpents.

LEMON

Lemon is often used in rituals of love. Usually the rind is collected, dried, and ground into a powder, which may be added to any incense. The oil may also be extracted, which may be made into a lubricant for rituals which will involve sacred sexual activities.

Some lore says that the peel should be taken and a small heart-shaped piece cut from it, dried, and carried in one's purse or pocket to attract a mate. Another lore involves cutting the peel from a lemon in a single piece, without breaking it. This is said to attract a new love within the period of a Moon.

LEMON BALM

Lemon Balm is primarily used in the pursuit of romance. It is an herbe which attracts, and is sometimes made into a charm and worn to bring a lover into one's life. It may also be used as a bathing herbe, some of the delightfully scented leaves scattered over the water, or an infusion poured to mix with the bath. This is also said to attract romance.

LIFE-EVERLASTING

This is an Herbe of Immortality. Grown in one's garden it is said to help carry the soul of the gardener far into the spiritual realms upon death. Ritually, Life-Everlasting may be used to invoke the spirits of both Earth and Water. The dried flowers are often placed upon altars, and some of the compact, white blossoms given into a sacred fire when calling upon these elementals.

LINSEED

The oil of the Linseed may be used to consecrate magickal tools of divination, particularly crystals and the like. The outer surface should be lightly coated with the oil beneath a full moon.

LOTUS

The Lotus is an herbe with a long history as a Religious Herbe. It has been used to invoke Isis, Osiris, and Hermes. The pod, an attractive pocketed brown woody thing, has been used as an incense burner in temples, and in sacred rituals. The oil of the Lotus, or a wash made of the flowers, may be used to dress a candle, carefully coating it from the center, outwards, and burning a candle thus prepared will keep one's spiritual energy safe from all harm, and cleanse the psychic energy at the same time.

In Tarot, Lotus may be used to enhance understanding of the Hanged Man card, learning how to translate inaction into action. Lotus is associated with two stones, both amber and aquamarine, and may be used to charge them, or the two stored together for a better attunement of vibration and energy.

LOVAGE

Lovage is often used as a bathing herbe, cast into the bath, the pleasant scent filling the room and delicately scenting the bather. In this manner, particularly when combined with a candle and poems of a romantic nature, is one able to attract romance. Lovage is one of the most dependable herbes for drawing romance into one's life.

Not only will it bring you love, but regular bathing with this herbe will enhance your beauty, physically, and will also allow the inner radiance to shine forth more brightly.

MALE FERN

This is one of the most potent of magickal Aphrodisiacs. The root is taken and burnt, and the ash added to oils which may be kept as lubricants for sexual activity. It stimulates potency, and keeps sexuality vibrant and alive.

A very powerful amulet may be made out of the root. On Midsummer's Eve, one of the most traditional nights for the Herbalist to be about the Work, the root should be dug whole, and slowly dried over the ritual fire. This is sometimes called "The Hand of the Gods," or a "Lucky Hand," and is a powerful amulet, directing magick and energy as is willed by the practitioner.

MANDRAKE

As a Religious Herbe, reference to Mandrake can be found in the book of Genesis, for its magickal use and medical properties have long been used by mankind. Mandrake has been used to invoke Circe, who is today somewhat of a minor deity to some sects of Witchcraft, and also may be used to invoke Diana, the God Saturn, and other Gods and Goddesses.

Mandrake is an herbe of creativity, setting free the visions of the mind, the works of art hidden within the inner person, and the ability to translate them into action. It may be added to any magickal working, for it will increase the potency of the energy. Taken internally, with caution, it will make the practitioner more psychically aware, capable of clairvoyancy and other psychic skills.

In spell magick, Mandrake is used to increase sexual desire, potency, and to work a charm to cause another to fall in love with you, although I have seen none who pursue that process find a happy

231

ending. Mandrake can be used to seal the commitment made between lovers, although it is very binding to the agreement.

The root may be carved into an amulet. When this is to be done, it should be gathered with care with an appropriate ritual and magickal knife. For the most potent work, the knife would be used to pierce the practitioner's finger, and a drop of blood left in the space vacated by the root. The practise of carving amulets out of the root is ancient, and said to be widely practised under the reign of Henry VIII.

Amulets made of the root may be hung in the home, as a powerful Herbe of Protection, or may be worn to attract love, to keep one's aura pure, or as a sign of magick.

The apples are sometimes gathered, dried, and used in magickal potions. This is a more appropriate use for Mandrake as a Visionary Herbe. Either the apple or the root may be dried, powdered, and mixed into incense for any workings of magick. Doing so will intensify the ritual. To properly dry a root for magickal use, it should be slowly turned above a fire of vervain leaves.

To capture your loved one's heart, the root is engraved with magickal symbols beneath the fulll moon. A warning to any one who attempt this: you then must be exorcised with Mandrake, for it is wrong to 'possess' another's soul and heart.

MARIGOLD

This is an Herbe of Consecration. The incense may be used (the petals used alone or mixed with a dry incense) to consecrate tools of divination, and the petals may also be macerated in sunflower oil to make an oil of consecration.

Marigold blossoms may be used to decorate an altar in rituals to the Goddess. The flower is appropriate to plant upon sacred burial sites as its energy will bless departed souls. The flowers are sometimes used in the celebration of Beltane, strewn about the Circle to purify it.

Visions of one's enemies, or of someone who has taken your possessions may be had by collecting the blossoms when the Moon is passing through the sign of Virgo. Jupiter should not be in the same sign as the Sun.

Visions of one's beloved may be had by mixing Marigold with marjoram, thyme, and absinthe, and meditating after drinking this beverage.

MARJORAM

Marjoram was considered sacred to the Goddess Venus by the Romans. It is still used in rituals in her honor, and by those who desire

232

to find romantic fulfillment.

As a Funereal Herbe, Marjoram is planted upon graves. As it flourishes, it brings spiritual bliss to the spirit of the departed. Marjoram is also associated with Thor and Jupiter, invoking their protection against thunder and lightning.

Marjoram may be used in either weddings or handfastings, the custom from ancient Greece calling for it to be woven into wreaths to crown the newly joined.

Grieve reports the following love spell from Halliwell:

> On St. Luke's Day, says Mother Bunch, take marigold flowers, a sprig of marjoram, thyme, and a little wormwood; dry them before a fire, rub them to powder, then sift it through a fine piece of lawn, and simmer it over a slow fire, adding a small quantity of virgin honey and vinegar. Anoint yourself with this when you go to bed, saying the following lines three times, and you will dream of your future partner 'that is to be'. "St. Luke, St. Luke, be kind to me; In dreams let me my true love see . . ."

MARSHMALLOW

Marshmallow is sometimes used to cure impotency, and is sometimes used as an Aphrodisiac. The seed of the herbe may be gathered beneath a full moon, and this made into an oil which is used upon the genitals. An amulet may be made of either leaf or root, and its energy kept near the genitals to achieve the same purpose.

As a Funereal Herbe, it may be used in rituals for the dead, or may be grown upon the grave.

MARSHWORT

This herbe is used in the magickal healing of animals. One manner would have you place both leaves and flowers at the four directions beneath either altar or altar stone. The animal is kept in the center of the Circle and the ritual of healing is performed.

An amulet may also be made, and secured within the building or near the sleeping place of the animal to keep it in good health.

MEADOWSWEET

This herbe has long been sacred to various Goddesses, and later was sometimes connected with the Virgin Mary. It is also known as

'Lady-of-the-Meadow', and Bridewort, held sacred to the Goddess Blodeuwedd. It is a favorite of Brides, and included in a bouquet will bring happiness to her and her marriage. A favorite flower of Queen Elizabeth the First, an oil made of the blossoms is said to give special joy when a woman uses it nightly before bed.

MESCAL

Mescal has a long history as a Visionary Herbe and a Religious Herbe. It must be used with extreme care, in either of these manners. It is capable of provoking visions of various dimensions of time, of other-life experiences, and of one's spiritual potential. As an herbe of Neptune, great care must be maintained after the experience to keep reality and visions separate. This is a most serious herbe of the practitioner, and must never be taken lightly. There are said to be spirits associated with Mescal who can plague those who use the buttons for pleasure rather than for serious religious experience, and they will bring confusion and illusion to the abuser.

MILKWEED

This herbe, often thought of as a common weed is used by Herbalists to remove warts. As the patron herbe of the Monarch butterfly, it is also partial to the little people, and growing it in the garden will encourage the presence of elves and fairies.

MINTS

Mints may be used as a Greene Herbe, bringing kitchen magick and pleasure to all guests of the household. Used in amulets and spells, mints carry the qualities of success and protection.

Mints are held sacred to the deity Mintha, once a lover of the God Pluto. They were also chosen by Solomon when he constructed his ritual sprinkler. Mints were anciently an honored herbe, considered worthy of use as payment to the Pharisees, and used by the Romans to crown themselves at great celebrations.

MISTLETOE

There are many uses for this herbe, it being one of the primary herbes of the practitioner. It is used to bring fertility, for either a child-to-be, or for a personal project of creativity. The berries represent sexual potency, serve as an Aphrodisiac, and are used with frequency in amulets for heightened sexual experiences. Mistletoe has also been used to manipulate another into falling in love with you (a nefarious practise, indeed).

An Herbe of Immortality, Mistletoe is seen as a symbol of rebirth, its energy containing the secrets of life beyond this, carrying the soul far into the future. It is used as an Herbe of Protection in nearly any manner imaginable and is traditionally hung over a doorway with red thread or cord to bring harmony and protection to the home. Recent custom gets us extra kisses when we pursue this practise.

Should you find the stalk of sufficient size, it would make a very powerful magickal wand. The wood of the herbe is also used to fashion the handle of ritual knives. Mistletoe banishes all evil and negative energy, and brings good fortune and joy to the user. Mistletoe used for magick should be gathered at Midsummer, and household amulets are traditionally hung at Midwinter.

Mistletoe was held in such virtue by the Druids that they would sacrifice two white bulls and gather the herbe with a gold blade. This herbe may be used in rituals sacred to Odin.

As a Magickal Herbe, Mistletoe may be used in any positive workings.

MOTHERWORT

This is a strengthening herbe, giving a person a sense of purpose, and joy in the completion of the work needed. It brings an attitude that all will succeed, and allows for the growth of inner trust, knowing that all will work towards a good and positive conclusion.

Motherwort is also used as an Herbe of Protection and Countermagicke.

MUGWORT

This herbe is nearly essential to any modern practitioner. A Visionary Herbe, Mugwort has been long used in the making of a dream pillow. A small pillow should be made of two squares of purple velvet, and sewn shut with Mugwort stuffing inside. Sleeping with this beneath your head or even near your bedside, will bring dreams of the future, of great mystical experience, and of inner enlightening.

An oil made of Mugwort is used in the consecration of crystal balls, prisms, and divinatory tools.

This Herbe of Protection keeps you safe from all forms of evil, and tossed into a burning fireplace or cauldron will keep a house safe against lightning during even the fiercest of storms. Amulets made of Mugwort are sent with loved ones when they set out on a journey, to keep them safe from all trouble and misfortune. It will also give them stamina to continue their journey and return safely.

A little Mugwort burnt in a room brings protection to one's children and Mugwort is an herbe revered by many all-women covens.

Mugwort is used to consecrate tools of silver, and is in affinity with both Moonstones and pearls. It is used as a Religious Herbe for Midsummer rituals, and is held sacred to Diana and used in rites of Her honor.

Taken twice daily, as a magickal tonic, it heightens one's psychic awareness and leads to a sense of inner vision.

MULBERRY

In ancient times, this herbe was consecrated to Minerva, and may be used to understand what She stands for, and may also be used in the study of other Goddesses.

Mulberry is considered a tree of wisdom, and a leaf pressed and dried is excellent for having in personal books of wisdom. Mulberry may be used to protect children, but, used for any magickal purpose, should be gathered before the Sun sets in the western horizon.

MULLEIN

Although ruled by Saturn, this herbe is often associated with fire. It may be used to invoke the fire elementals, and the dried leaves often kept, and used to light sacred fires. The large flower stalk may be dried, soaked in vegetable oil or tallow, and used as torches. As such, they are most appropriate for Hallow's Eve.

Mullein is an Herbe of Protection, and an herbe garden is blessed to have at least one of the tall, proud, plants growing. The leaf is dried, and carried as a talisman of safety. It is said that monasteries often grew Mullein to protect them against manifestations of the Devil.

Mullein is sometimes used in rituals for women.

MYRRH

Since ancient times, this has been a Magickal Herbe. Mixed into incense, it brings communion with spiritual awareness, and a better understanding of the currents of energy which flow through a ritual. It heightens the magickal awareness of any spiritual experience. Myrrh is very appropriate to burn when attempting to understand personal sorrow, as it has an aspect of peace and solitude about it.

An oil made from Myrrh is used to dress a candle. When burnt, it will bring peace to the situation intended by the practitioner. As a Religious Herbe, Myrrh as been used to celebrate Juno, Saturn, Demeter, Cybele, Hecate, and Rhea. The Egyptians revered Myrrh as a Funereal Herbe, using it in the embalming process, and also burnt in the funeral ceremony.

Myrrh should be used to consecrate pearls, and may be used in Tarot to study the threes and the queens.

Myrrh was also a holy herbe to the Hebrews and the Ethiopians.

NARCISSUS

This herbe is used to invoke Isis in Her Maiden aspect. The Greeks used it as a Funereal Herbe, and planted it near the burial site. In Tarot, it is used to understand the Hermit card.

The sexual lore of Narcissus sets it apart from nearly all other herbs. It is said to contain the magick of parthenogenesis, and as such may be used to create inspiration and creativity. The narcotic constituents of the herbe function as an anaphrodisiac, quieting desire, and allowing one to turn to less physical sources of inspiration.

Narcissus should be stored with a Peridot.

NIGHTSHADE, DEADLY

This herbe, also known as belladonna, is one of the more dangerous herbes of the practitioner. It was Deadly Nightshade which Juliet took as a potion, and brought sorrow and death to herself and Romeo.

There is lore which says Deadly Nightshade may only be gathered on Walpurgis Night, for that is the only night the devil lets go his watchfulness over the herbe. It was also used to invoke Bellona, and other Goddesses of War.

Deadly Nightshade may be used to invoke Circe, and is the appropriate herbe used to consecrate ritual tools made of lead. It has affinity with onyx, and may be used in the consecration and charging of that stone. They do well stored together.

OAK

The Oak was a most sacred tree to both Romans and Druids. It is considered sacred to Jupiter and Zeus, and the acorn may be worn as a symbol of fealty to those Gods, or also to Blodeuwedd or Odin. The bark may be dried, ground, and used as an incense to honor these deities.

To keep yourself surrounded by good luck, take two pieces of a small branch, equal in length, and tie them crossed with red yarn to represent keeping oneself in perfect balance.

Never gather from an Oak which is host for the mistletoe. These trees are best served by doing ritual beneath the branches, but the tree itself should be left undisturbed. The mistletoe, however, may be gathered, and is highly prized.

OLIVE

This has been a most sacred herbe for many cultures. It is held sacred to Athena, Poseidon, and Zeus, and may also be used in the honor of all Solar Deities. The oil of the Olive was preferred for the sacred temple lamps of the Greeks.

Olive Oil is used to consecrate incense burners and thuribles.

Interestingly, it is said that Moses granted military exemption for those men who worked in the Olive groves cultivating the herbe. Honor is usually associated with Olive, and it was used to crown the Olympic victors.

Olive, either the leaf or the oil, may be used in rituals to honor either human or deity. It may be used to dress the candles, to anoint the person, or to bless the holy water. Olive is one of the traditional fixative bases for ritual oils.

ORCHID

This herbe is sometimes known as Satyrion Root, and it is the tuberous root which is used by the practitioner. It is capable of affecting sexuality, and in a full, wholesome state is considered an Aphrodisiac, and when withered and dried it is said to quell the sexual appetite.

Orchis was born of a nymph who had been seduced by a Satyr (Satyrs are well known for their ability to seduce), and the result was this son. As the son grew, he carried a bit of the off-handedness of the

238

Satyrs, insulted a Priestess, and was killed for his rudeness. His father was very sorrowful and prayed to the Gods, who took pity on him and turned the dead Orchis into the herbe. It was long believed that Satyrs considered Orchid roots to be a delicacy and fine food, giving them sexual prowess.

Satyrion Root is best used previous to entering a ritual act of love-making. It can be sliced, and the broth shared from the same cup by the couple. It also makes an excellent ritual drink for a couple entering handfasting. The root may also be dried, powdered, and used as an Aphrodisiac.

PARSLEY

Common in the kitchen as a Greene Herbe, Parsley also has a wonderful history as a Magickal Herbe. It was long held sacred to Persephone, and later considered sacred to St. Peter. The Greeks considered Parsley an herbe of honor, and used it to fashion wreaths to crown the victors of the Isthmian games.

Currently, Parsley is also considered a favorite herbe of Venus and Aphrodite. It is believed that used for Magick, it should be gathered on any Friday, when the Moon is waxing.

When used as a bathing herbe, Parsley brings communion with the second aspect of the Goddess, that of the loving Maternal aspect of the Universe. This procedure is highly recommended when a Priestess intends to invoke this form of the Goddess, or for a woman who is with child, desirous of a healthy pregnancy.

Parsley was, in times past, given to chariot horses, and it is believed that it may be fed to a horse today, giving it sure-footedness and speed.

In ancient mythology, Archemorus was the forerunner of Death, and it is believed that Parsley sprung into existence from his blood. It was also used as a Funereal Herbe by the Greeks.

PASSION FLOWER

This herbe is used to calm, to soothe, and bring understanding to troubled emotions. It will calm anger, and replace it with an understanding of the human condition. For those prone to emotional unbalance, it will bring them to a more even state of being.

PATCHOULI

Familiar today as an oil, one may anoint the self with it in order to attract sexual love. The same effect may be had by use of the dried herbe in bathing. Patchouli may be used in rituals which will involve sacred rites of sex magick, or in which the God or Goddess will be invoked during the Great Rite.

PENNYROYAL

Albertus Magnus tells us that Pennyroyal, when burnt and the ashes still warm, is capable of reviving a dead insect. It is still known as an herbe which contains the secrets of rebirth and immortality.

The Greeks used this herbe when initiating the novice into the secret rituals of the Elusians, and it was held sacred to Demeter. Pennyroyal is associated with the High Priestess card in Tarot, and has an affinity with pearls. If a pearl is to be used as a sacred jewel, it should first be anointed with Pennyroyal when being consecrated.

PEONY

This common garden flower has a history of use as a Magickal Herbe. To use as an Herbe of Protection, the seeds should be gathered, dried, and threaded onto a white thread to wear as a necklace. This same necklace may be used as a ritual necklace.

The roots were gathered, dried, and carved into amulets, in similar fashion to the mandrake. When this Pagan custom became Christianized, the roots were carved into beads for rosaries. Beads made thusly make an excellent necklace for wear in rituals, or for general use to keep one safe from all negative energy.

An old bit of folklore warns against gathering the Peony in the sight of a woodpecker, believing that you will lose your eyes if you do so. It is recommended, as it is with most herbes gathered for the practitioner, that it be done during the night, preferably beneath a waxing Moon.

Although Peony is ruled by the Sun, it is of Lunar origin, thus maintaining in its energy the balance of both sources of light. It was thought to have been created by the Moon Goddess, and to reflect Her light during the night. It is used to keep away all the unpleasant associations of darkness.

240

There are even some sources which say that the Peony should be gathered in like fashion to the mandrake.

PEPPERMINT

Peppermint is a Visionary Herbe, and should be used as an incense at sunset, and then on into the evening to bring dreams of prophecy. It is used in divination, and may be taken as a tea to increase one's skill with the art.

Peppermint is held sacred to Zeus, and may be used in rituals in His honor, and may also be used in rituals to honor any male deity.

Peppermint is associated with both topaz and chalcedony, and may be used to magickally charge the stones, and is ideally stored with them. In studying the Tarot, Peppermint is helpful to understand the Fool card.

PERIWINKLE

One of the common names, 'Sorcerer's Violet', is a clue to the magickal uses of this herbe. It is considered a patron flower of the 'Wicca, the Wise-Folk of villages and cities, known for their healing skills and magick. Periwinkle has been used in many love spells and beneficial charms. It is said to banish all negative energy, and has been used in exorcisms to drive away evil.

The flowers are primarily used, and may be gathered, dried, and ground into a powder. Thus, they may be made into potions, or placed in an amulet to bring love into one's life.

German custom says that this is an Herbe of Immortality, and in other places it is a Funereal Herbe, woven into wreaths and placed upon the coffins of dead children, possibly to hasten them into their next life.

Grieve quotes Apuleius, in the manner of gathering Periwinkle, as follows:

> *I pray thee, vinca pervinca, thee that art to be had for thy many useful qualities, that thou come to me glad blossoming with thy mainfulness, that thou outfit me so that I be shielded and ever prosperous and undamaged by poisons and by water.*

241

PIMPERNEL

This herbe was chosen by Solomon to use in the consecration of his sacred knife. It is still used as an Herbe of Consecration today. Formerly, the juice of the pimpernel was mixed with the blood of a young goose at the time of a full moon, and used to anoint the blade. Sacrifice is not practised today, and dragon's blood may be substituted for the blood.

Wearing an amulet with Pimpernel will keep one safe when journeying, and will protect one's physical self from accidents, poor health and misfortune.

PINE

The resin of Pine may be gathered, dried, and used as an incense. It has the quality of cleansing a space of negative energy. Pine is also very effective as a Countermagicke Herbe, repelling evil energy and returning it to its source.

Pine is held sacred to Poseidon, and using the pitch of the tree to caulk a boat gives it magickal protection upon the waters.

POMEGRANATE

This herbe has an ancient history of magickal use. It was used by the Hebrews in their ceremonies, and was considered sacred by Solomon. Today it enjoys use in women's rituals, held sacred to Persephone. Pomegranate may also be used to invoke Saturn.

PRIMROSE

This herbe is held sacred to the Goddess Freya. It may be worn when invoking this Goddess, or used to decorate an altar. Frequent use of Primrose as a bathing herbe increases beauty and the ability to attract love.

Magickally, Primrose is one of the Herbes of Immortality, holding within the secret of eternal bliss. Upon being Christianized, Primrose was thought to grant one access to heaven.

PURSLANE

This is an herbe for those who fear the darkness of the night. It will protect you from all bad dreams, and from any strange spirits that roam the darkness. It is most frequently used for this purpose by being made into a dream pillow. The fabric may be blue, soft pink, or off-white.

Purslane may be taken as a daily tonic, for it attracts positive energy, and will bring a more wholesome outlook to the mentality and emotion. For those who pursue astrology, Purslane is said to be most effective when undergoing difficult and dangerous transits.

QUINCE

Many images of Venus show Her holding Quince in her right hand. She is said to have received this from Paris, as a token of love and esteem. Quince is still held sacred to Venus, and honors Her even today. It is also used as a token of lasting love, sometimes shared by a couple upon completing the ceremony of either marriage or handfasting. Thus, they will share love and joy in their union, and it will be blessed by the Gods.

Quince is also used to protect one from another's evil intent, and is known as an Herbe of Protection.

RED CLOVER

Although we all know the luck to be had if you find a four-leaf variety of Red Clover, did you know that a three-leaf Clover is one lucky for those who study magick?

A four-leaf clover may be placed beneath the pillow before going to sleep, and it is said that you will then dream of your beloved, even if you have not yet met.

Red Clover was a sacred herbe among the Celts, and was widely used by Anglo-Saxon practitioners of herbal magick. It is best gathered within two days of a full Moon, and kept out of the sight of the Sun.

Red Clover holds energy that is benevolent for animals, and has been used in the ritual healings of domestic animals and pets. It is said that Red Clover is an Herbe of Immortality, and this applies to both animals and humans alike. Steeping the blossoms and drinking the draught is an excellent means of getting in touch with one's eternal soul.

As an Herbe of Protection, the dried blossoms may be used in amulets as well as the three-leaved greens. It is said to keep one in good health, and protect you against consumption, cancer, and other wasting diseases.

ROSES

Roses are sacred to Aphrodite, Goddess of Love, and represent beauty, which is capable of winning over evil and adversities. A Rose is also a symbol of secrecy, and was once suspended from the center of the ceiling at important meetings of confidence, that none would break the trust.

If you have a magickal stock of Rose petals, the appropriate stone to keep with them would be an emerald. The oil of Rose is the best herbal mixture you might find to consecrate the emerald with.

When meditating, anointing the heart chakra with Rose oil is a means of learning the manifestation of love, and the perfect balance to be kept within the world when giving love to all humanity.

To magickally attract a lover, remove all of your clothing and jewelry and walk through a garden scattering Rose petals as you walk. It is said that your lover will soon appear. Don't be surprised if you find a midnight voyeur . . .

Roses bring with them the ability to learn the balance of giving, how to do so selflessly, and to take joy in the process, rather than expecting a return. They represent all aspects of the Goddess, the ability to love and nurture, and to see beauty in all things.

In Tarot, the Rose represents the Seven of Cups.

ROSE GERANIUM

This herbe has such a magnificent scent, that merely growing in your garden is enough to spread its fragrance. The leaves are gathered, dried, and ground into love philtres. The oil, which may be either extracted or commercially prepared, is worn by those who seek sexual fulfillment and represents sexual maturity, and a great joy taken therein.

ROSEMARY

This is the herbe that even Shakespeare says is for 'remembrance'. This herbe is capable of increasing the power of memory, and is also brought into use when a particular occasion merits special remembering.

In some places, all guests to a wedding are greeted with a branch of Rosemary. Some say it should be decorated with gold and ribbon, others, more practical, leave out the gold. Grieve also tells of taking the branch of Rosemary and dipping it into a mixture of herbal oil, perfume and water, and the Rosemary then being woven into the bride's wreath.

Rosemary has also been used as a Funereal Herbe. It has sometimes been mixed into the incense for the ceremony, and has often been cast upon the coffin, when it is slowly lowered into the burial place. Thus will we all remember with love and fondness the one who is passing into another life, and thus will we also remember that we inhabit mortal bodies as we walk this earth. For a long time Rosemary was a symbol of cemetaries and funerals, and seeing it grown or worn would bring to mind the loved ones who had passed beyond.

As a Magickal Herbe, Rosemary is used as a religious incense, and will enhance the sacredness of any occasion. It is an Herbe of Protection against evil, and has been used as incense in places of illness, mixed with juniper, to cleanse and purify the air. It is sometimes placed beneath the bed, and this is said to protect you from frightening and evil dreams. It was chosen by Solomon for his aspurger so that these qualities would work their magick when he sprinkled holy water about his temple.

Rosemary has been worn when going to face enemies, and might be an excellent herbe to use for fortification when going on job interviews. It is also wonderful to use as a Greene herbe at family gatherings.

ROWAN

This lovely tree, known in the United States as the European Mountain Ash, is both an Herbe of Protection and a Visionary Herbe. It may be used ritually to invoke the Goddess and ask Her for help, direction, and bounty. The leaves are commonly used, but the berries may be gathered, dried, and when ground, added to the incense.

Rowan has been used to call up magickal spirits, familiars, spirit guides, elementals and the like, but it also has the ability to banish any type of energy undesired by the practitioner. For the poet, Rowan is a sure herbe to enhance creativity and set the creative process flowing. Rowan has also been used to divine future loves and mates.

A familiar tree in the lores of Scotland, it is said that once there were nearly no homes without the tree growing nearby, for it brought protection against evil energies and bad times. A Scot saying is "O

Rowan tree, O Rowan tree, thou'll aye be dear to me."

Taking two small twigs of Rowan, equal in length, and bound into a cross with red twine is a sure means of keeping negative magicians and those who work evil away from one's life. A ritual beverage was once brewed of the berries by the Welsh, although the recipe was lost in the passing of time. This would be an excellent goal for the practitioner.

RUE

This Greene Herbe of the kitchen belongs also in the magickal closet of the practitioner. It is an Herbe of Protection, and is most useful in bringing benevolence and good to one's family. It is sometimes hung in a small bunch in the kitchen, and other times made into an amulet with a morsel of bread, some ash from the hearth, and something personal of each member of the family, and secreted someplace within the house.

As a Countermagicke Herbe, Rue may be used to exorcise any item which has been in contact with negative feelings or unknown energies. Rue has also been used to attract love, and the easiest approach is to use it as a bathing herbe.

Sometimes called 'herbe of grace', Rue was once commonly grown around the temples of Rome. It is considered sacred to the God Mars, and as a Religious Herbe may be offered in His honor. For those who study the astral realms, it is said to take your vision out into places of purity and vision.

During the Middle Ages, Rue was strewn about, thus protecting the home from plague and disease. This may be done in conjunction with angelica. For those who channel visions, Rue is an excellent herbe to protect a medium, to keep the seer safe from influence from the visions and messages.

Rue is used to consecrate tools of iron, and is associated with the ruby, used in cleansing the stone. Magickal Rue is best kept with a small ruby in the container.

SAGE

This has been a most sacred herbe among many tribes of North America, who regard it as a highly Religious Herbe. It is used in purification, healing and cleansing. A most powerful broom to sweep away undesired influence from a Circle would be made of Sage. Sage carries the virtues of strength, mental health, wisdom, and banishes all evil.

246

When growing Sage, to keep its energies pure it should be planted near rue. As a magickal tonic, it is nearly unsurpassed. One method is to drink it after sunrise for nine consecutive mornings. Another is the following charm, found in several modern sources: "Sage make green the winter rain, Charm the demon from my brain."

When a practitioner grows Sage, the health of the live plant is seen as a reflection of the grower's personal affairs and business. Sage is the appropriate incense for meetings of business and important decisions. It invokes the deity Consus, who is the ruling God of councils. Solomon included Sage in the making of his aspurger, and it also is used today to increase longevity.

SAINT JOHN'S WORT

Used primarily as an Herbe of Protection, it should be tossed into the hearth or fireplace and allowed to burn, bringing protection to the home against lightning and severe storm.

Saint John's Wort is best gathered at Midsummer, and may be used as an amulet at this time. It is associated with the element of fire, and may be magickally worked to commune with the fire spirits.

The Greek name for this herbe means 'over an apparition', a reflection of its protective virtues.

SANDALWOOD

This herbe may be used to invoke the Goddess Venus. In Tarot, it works with the Empress card, and its gems are emerald and turquoise. It was a Funereal Herbe in the Orient, used in embalming the body and carrying the soul into the next life.

Sandalwood may be used in all forms of meditation, divination, and trancework. It calms the mind, and allows the spiritual aspects of the self to do their work with confidence and ease. It carries the virtue of success with it, and may thus be added to any magickal incense.

Sandalwood is the appropriate herbe to consecrate the altar cloth It vibrates with Hod on the Tree of Life.

SAVORY

A Greene Herbe, it may be used in kitchen magick to bring joy and good times to a feast. The Romans believed that Savory was an herbe of the Satyrs, and called it Satureia. Added to the cooking, it will lighten the mood of the meal and increase the sense of mirth.

SENNA

This is the herbe for a diplomat, or a person who manages people. It is said that carrying a few leaves with you will emphasize the positive qualities of those you meet. It is a good herbe, and may also be used to promote compassion among a group of people, and a willingness to cooperate.

SESAME

The seed of this herbe is used as an Herbe of Protection, functioning primarily to preserve the health and vitality of the reproductive and sexual systems of the body. The oil is used, and is regularly used to anoint the external parts. It may also be taken internally for the internal organs. An oil of the Sesame seed may be used as a lubricant for sexual activities.

SKULLCAP

This herbe carries the virtue of fidelity, but caution must be had for those who would use it to bind their promise, for should the promise be broken this herbe commands a severe penalty. Skullcap may be used in the binding of a handfasting for a couple willing to pledge their commitment for the rest of this life. It is also used by those who desire to commit themselves to a relationship which will extend beyond this life.

SNAPDRAGON

This lovely flower is an Herbe of Protection. A bouquet given to a friend will keep them safe from harm. The flower may also be worn fresh, as an amulet against all unwanted occurrences. They are grown about a house to keep it safe.

SOLOMON'S SEAL

This Herbe of Protection is one of the most powerful Herbes of Consecration available to the practitioner. It is used in ceremonial magick to bind magickal works, and to make sacred oaths and promises, and to keep them everbinding. The flowers and roots have been used in Aphrodisiacs, and sometimes the herbe is found in recipes for love potions. Its primary use is in the consecration of temples, and all the sacred tools which would be used in the Circle. If you are considering making a sacred oath, it could be sealed with this herbe of Solomon.

SOUTHERNWOOD

This herbe is sometimes used as an Aphrodisiac. It has other associations with sexual desire and attractiveness, and is said to increase the potency and sexual skills of a male. It has been claimed that used as a wash it will inhibit the balding process.

Absolutely fascinating common names for this herbe include 'lad's love' and 'maiden's ruin', a very interesting and colorful pair of labels.

SPIKENARD

This is the herbe of the student, for it increases mental clarity. In early magickal training, Spikenard may be taken as a tonic to help one in remembering the details of one's study, and to more quickly learn from the experiences one undertakes. Spikenard is sometimes associated with Hod on the Tree of Life.

STORAX

This is the herbe for opals and turquoise. It carries the virtues of truthfulness and honesty. As a Religious Herbe, Storax may be used in rituals to honor Hermes, Loki, Mercury, or Thoth. The lessons of truthfulness are also shown when studying the Tarot, and Storax is best served to understand any of the Eights of the suits.

SUNFLOWER

Sunflower was a Religious Herbe of the Aztecs. They would carry the flowers and adorn themselves with them in honor of the Sun God. Sunflowers were often found around the temples of Peru.

Sunflower may be used as a bathing herbe, to bring increased happiness into one's life, and to attract joy to fill the emotional spaces where there is sorrow. An oil made of this herbe is used to consecrate ritual robes.

As an Herbe of Protection, Sunflower keeps the soul safe against malicious energy, and may be used to consecrate stones and gems which will be used in healing. It corresponds to the Sun card of the Tarot.

Sunflower is also an Herbe of Immortality, and carries the virtues of adoration and worship. It is used to honor all Sun Gods, particularly Apollo, and is said to be a patron herbe for Leos and Virgos. It is an herbe which is excellent for those choosing to preserve their virginity, and to those who wish to have dragons and lions about. As it relates to the Goddess, it is most like Demeter.

TANSY

Tansy is an Herbe of Immortality. As such, it was associated in many areas in the Christian festival of Easter, added to the batter for small cakes to represent the eternalness of life, exemplified by Christ.

Tansy is used in women's rituals, and as such shares its virtue of celebrating womanhood. It would be appropriate to give the live flowers as a blessing to one's mother, or another woman held in esteem.

Tansy was also an embalming herbe, the tannic acid in its constituents keeping the corporal safe against decay (up to a point).

Tansy is often seen as an herbe which honors the Virgin Mary and other Goddesses.

TARRAGON

A Greene Herbe of the kitchen, Tarragon is sacred to the feminine aspect of the Universe. In particular it is used to invoke Lillith, and may be used in kitchen magick to calm, nurture, and make the guests more compassionate to one another. It should be gathered after Midsummer, but yet before Michaelmas.

THISTLES

Thistles represent the virtues of endurance, and the ability to survive. They are used in ritual healings for animals, both domestic and wild. Within a healing Circle a red Thistle is placed at each of the four directions to invoke healing powers for the animal.

THORNAPPLE

Also commonly known as Jimson Weed, this is a Visionary Herbe, and should be used with care. It has long been associated with the working of spells and the seeking of visions, and is used in similar fashion today. Large quantities of the herbe are dangerous.

THYME

One of the most popular Greene Herbes of the kitchen, Thyme is most fun when used to invoke the faery folk. When added to the cooking, it will help guests reclaim their childlike sense of fun, letting go the 'serious' cares of the adult. Thyme also carries the virtues of courage and ambition.

As a Funereal Herbe, Thyme is used to re-establish communion with those friends and relatives who have passed into death, to ask advice of them or to send them blessings. As an incense, Thyme is an Herbe of Protection, used to bring protection against all dangerous creatures, insects, and animals.

Once, Thyme was part of a design embroidered for valiant knights, shown with a bumblebee flying over it. The Greek word for Thyme describes its use for incense, and it works to consecrate pearls.

TOADFLAX

This is an herbe of Witches, according to folklore, grown everywhere in their gardens to encourage the presence of toads. It is still in use as a Magickal Herbe and may be included in any amulet. It is also used by those who work with familiars and grow magickal gardens.

UNICORN ROOT

The true Unicorn Root is used by those who keep one or more astral unicorns about, and is the patron herbe of the magickal tradition of Lothlorien. It is a Visionary Herbe, used by those who enjoy an element of joyful fantasy in their visionary workings.

UVA URSI

For those who wish to increase their psychic ability, this herbe may be used in small daily amounts as a tonic. It was a Religious Herbe to Native Americans, who included it in the pipe-smoking mixtures, and in some tribes used it to train Shamans in skills of divination and prophecy.

VALERIAN

This is known as an 'herbe of witches'. It was included in Solomon's sprinkler, and is known as an Herbe of Protection. It may be used for cleansing any space, and is often used in self-purification. This must be done with care, and only small amounts taken daily.

Valerian is an herbe of Virgo.

VERBENA or VERVAIN

Although there seems to be much misconception, these two names refer to the same herbe. This is one of the few herbes which can be used in almost any magickal situation. As a Visionary Herbe, it may be mixed with others in either incense or beverage, or it may be used as either oil or fresh juice to anoint one's divinatory tools. It has been used by those who follow a dream quest, to divine one's future love, and the Pawnee thought it an excellent choice of herbes to enhance the dreaming process.

Vervain enjoys many delightful common names, such as 'fer faen' among the Celts for its ability to relieve us of emotional pressures and unnecessary burdens; 'llysiaur hudol', or the enchanting herbe, among the Welsh, and one of my favorites, 'lustral water'. It has been a Religious Herbe for many peoples, among them the Druids, the Celts, the Welsh, the Greeks, the Romans, and nearly any culture that grew this herbe in their gardens.

Vervain is an Herbe of Immortality, containing the essence of this mystery and regular work with the herbe can bring an understanding of this secret. It is also an Herbe of Protection, added to numerous recipes for spells and amulets to keep the practitioner safe against various negatives influences. It is used to reverse bad spells, and to keep one safe against all negativity. It is used to consecrate tools of magick, and keep them safe from evil. In times past, a priest or priestess performing an exorcism might wear a wreath of Vervain about the head. It was used by the Druids in their ritual sweeping to cleanse the altar, and is of particular virtue in consecrating the altar stone. It is also used to consecrate tools of Mercury. If mecury is stored with Vervain, the mercury should be in a sealed glass vial.

Vervain or Verbena is also an herbe of romance. It is found in a great many recipes for attracting mates, love, and sexual fulfillment. It is ideal for the ritual drink in rites of love and sexual magick, and was often worn by brides. It is sacred to the Goddess Diana, and may be used to ask Her for favors. Vervain was used to honor the Sun by Persian magicians who would gather bouquets of it to hold in the newly-risen Sunlight. Thus, the Vervain and the Persian magi were totally bathed in sunlight, wearing nothing else, as a magickal preparation for the day. This custom is still preserved in some places today.

An herbe of Midsummer, this is the best time to gather it. It is also dried, and tossed into the Midsummer fire at the gathering for the following year, and is an appropriate incense for any of the eight major festivals.

An ancient recipe for a Draught of Immortality contains Verbena and this herbe is used in conjunction with opals and agates. Some say a magickal wand should be cleansed with Verbena before the consecration, and it was one of the Herbes used by Solomon to aspurge his temple.

Vervain is the herbe of poets, singers, and bards, and should be worn when performing, bringing inspiration and increased skill.

VIOLETS

As a Funereal Herbe, Violets are used when a young child passes away. They will bring comfort to the hearts of those left behind. This virtue is not limited to these times of sorrow, but may be gained by either tending a bed of violets, or by collecting the fresh blossoms and using them, such as sprinkling them on a salad.

Violets carry also the virtues of modesty, simplicity, serenity, peace, and are particularly a source of inspiration and good fortune for women. Violets originate from the nymph Io, a daughter of the river god Inachus. She and the god Zeus were developing a romance, when another of Zeus' lovers became so jealous that she cast a spell and changed Io into a heifer. Poor Io was left with grass to munch, and a god who really loved women rather than cows. In His great compassion, this benevolent god changed her, not back into a young woman, but into the Violet.

WATERCRESS

This is a true herbe of the water creatures, magickally symbolized by elementals called 'undines'. Magickally, Watercress is carried in a bit of red flannel to bring safety for those traveling in boats, or flying across the waters. Watercress is also known as a Visionary Herbe; if included in the morning breakfast at daybreak, visions and dreams may result the following night. In Tarot, this herbe helps to understand the Chariot card.

Watercress may be made into a wash to anoint and stimulate the third eye for a better balance of energies and understanding of the human condition.

WILLOW

Among the Chinese, the Willow is an Herbe of Immortality, for even the smallest piece of branch is capable of bringing forth another tree. It is said the Hebrew peoples, as they wandered through Babylon, came to the Willow and hung their harps upon them, and wept to return to their homeland. The Druids used the pussywillow, and thought it appropriate for charms and protection. There are many who think a pussywillow makes an excellent magickal wand, and others who take their tool from the mightier tree.

Anciently, it was the Willow which was site of the birth of Hera, a most honored Goddess. It is said that Orpheus turned to the Willow when passing through the underworld to receive the virtue of eloquence. The Willow is today a patron herbe of those involved in communication.

Willow is sacred to Hecate, Hermes, and all deities of the otherworlds, and may be used as a Funereal Herbe. For safe passage into another life, one must plant a Willow during their lifetime so that it will still be alive at their death.

Willow is the herbe to work with rock crystal, to charge the stone and give it protective and healing virtues.

WISTERIA

This is an herbe of all students, scholars, and those pursuing intellectual development. It will stimulate the brain, aid in keeping thought organized, and will aid in helping achieve educational goals. The oil may be used, or the flowers made into a tea.

WOODRUFF

This is the herbe of May wine, that wonderfully flavored wine used to celebrate the joys of Spring. It was once used in Christian magick, hung about cathedrals and churches as a protective charm against evil.

WORMWOOD

This herbe is sacred to both Artemis and Diana. A most potent herbe, it is used in less common works of magick. For those who seek to vent their anger in a peaceful, creative means, this herbe is appropriate to use. It is also used when a group works magick to stop war, or to inhibit the enemy.

This herbe is a patron of Herbalists. It is said that Artemis gave this herbe to Chiron as his primary healing herbe.

Wormwood can be used to banish anger and negative energy. In Tarot it may be used with the Lovers card. It is a visionary Herbe, and is used in prophecy and divination.

YARROW

The use of this herbe is most ancient, said to have been used for healing by Achilles. In the Orient it is highly respected and used in divination with the I Ching. For this purpose, the most prized Yarrow is that which grows upon the burial site of Confucious.

These flowers are used in handfastings and weddings, worn by guests and added to the bouquets.

Yarrow is sacred to the horned god of Pagan mythology, the male principle of the Universe. One lovely folk custom is to watch the Yarrow patch, and to make a wish upon the first blossom of the summer.

HERBS AND ASTROLOGY

HERBS AND ASTROLOGY

lthough the connection between herbs and astrology may seem new to the novice, these two sciences have a long history of working together. Even in modern times, when astrology is often relegated to the realms of the occult, Carl Jung says that astrology "is assured of recognition from psychology, without further restrictions, because astrology represents the summation of all the psychological knowledge of antiquity." This is one of the numerous statements Jung makes favoring astrology, and is found in *The Secret of the Golden Flower.*

There are many quotes, ranging from Hippocrates through Culpeper, which state, unequivocably, that a physician must have an understanding of astrology. Hippocrates says that "A physician without a knowledge of astrology has no right to call himself a physician," and Culpeper says that the practise of medicine "without astrology, being like a lamp without oil," is something not to be done.

There are many approaches to this combination, from prognostics, the art of reading a natal chart to determine the stress and tension causes of illness, to the following approach, in which the various energies may be brought as healing elements to the patient. Keep in mind that modern medicine itself states that a good portion of illness is caused by hypochondria or is psychosomatic, which really is magick turned against oneself in a negative sense.

Following are a list of the planets and their energies. Should you desire to bring energy to a person, it may be done by preparing a tonic of herbs associated with that planet which would by taken daily, either in the morning or before bed, or even both. This is not a complex method and is worth exploring.

THE SUN

Herbs of the Sun give our inner self a sense of future. They will help us to better realize our goals. In prognostics they are said to heal the sides of the body, the right eye of men, the left eye of women (which may be sexist and needs exploring on a personal level), and the back.

Solar herbs are excellent for those who have trouble with their self-image, and who suffer illness because they are afraid of dealing with the public. Herbs of the Sun will build self-confidence and an ability to complete one's goals. Remedially they also govern the spleen, thyroid, spine and the vital fluids of the body.

For those of us who have trouble understanding our place in the world, these herbs will help us to realize how we are one of many, and know that there is divine work. It helps the individual to see his or her life as being part of a large plan in which each person is essential to the harmony of the universe. These herbs help to strengthen the ego. They are often associated with Christ and other Sun Gods, helping us to be strong in our purpose, and good in our intent. These are recommended for depression, inferiority complexes, and fear of the world around. They help us to be generous with our love and our energy, and seeing all, even those of whom we disapprove, as part of life, each essential and capable of choice.

For those in need of ambition, independence, and the ability to take charge, solar herbs should be taken with the sunrise. These are the herbs which help us to get in touch with the self, and to find that process joyful. Even though we may be fault-finding when examining the self, we know that growth is a life-long process, and we should see the self compassionately as evolving gradually toward perfection. We may be joyful creatures, if we view ourselves as becoming better and better.

THE MOON

These herbs are for emotions and instincts. They help us to realize our ability to love. Their energy is like divine ecstasy. For the prognostician, these herbs remedially govern the uterus and ovaries the breasts, the stomach and parts of the brain, and the esophagus. They are often used to treat coughs and colds.

These herbs work with the subconscious mind, and are of value for those who work to develop their intuition. They may help us to understand our childhood, even those parts which we hated, yet are essential to our health and maturity as adults. Thus, we are better able to understand those feelings which cause fear and inhibit our ability to love and be loved.

They bring a higher degree of sensitivity, and increase the childlike wonder of imagination. They are excellent for diseases caused by fear of change or lack of imagination. They are good for those whose limited vision causes stress and inflexibility.

These herbs help us to flow with the rhythm of life about us, just as the ocean and earth flow with the tides of the Moon. They are good for soothing domestic troubles, and for the woman who serves a family and is not appreciated.

MERCURY

These herbs have been associated with the brain, nervous system, respiratory system, throat, nerve sensations, defects of speech, memory, and of the tongue. They are essential for those who have difficulty in thinking or communicating. Some say the Mercurial planets govern the bowels (particularly for Virgos), lungs and hands (particularly for Geminis).

The herbs of Mercury will have an effect upon the intellectual processes, such as those of thinking, logic, reasoning, and conclusion -reaching. Regular use of these herbs makes the process more facile, keeping the mind sharp and alert. This is particularly effective when working on books or a particular project, but not for prolonged use, for then they lose their effectiveness.

For those who pursue spiritual paths, these herbs help one to understand the balance of conscious and subconscious, and should be taken in equal mixtures with solar and lunar herbs. This brings to the person a sense of integration, and an ability to flow with the meaning of life.

For the magickal practitioner, these herbs do well to be balanced with lunar herbs or Uranian herbs, thus enabling the self to bring forth the ideas and answers found through intuition. Usually, one of the stumbling blocks in this process is learning to translate intuitive feelings into conscious words. In ritual use, the power of the word is learned, and also the value of holding true to the words we have given.

VENUS

These herbs are highly recommended for those sullen and unhappy, particularly when those states of distress are caused by a lack of social grace. They will make us feel more attractive, and freer in giving of a sense of joy. They are for persons desiring to be more outgoing and social. They give us a sense of self-comfort which leaves us more open (yet safely) to the vibrations of others.

Herbs of Venus are recommended more in healing for young people than for old, but are not recommended for anyone when the ailment is caused by love. In that case herbs of Jupiter are the best, for Venus will only increase the longing, whereas Jupiter will allow us to see other options.

These herbs have remedial associations with the blood, kidneys and urinary system, the tactile nerves, complexion, throat, and skin. Many ailments of the reproductive system are connected with Venus.

These herbs work to refine our sensory perception and aesthetics. They often have with them energy which increases our ability to attract those things we desire. They are best used in this manner to attract imagery such as sought by artists, musicians, and others involved in the creative arts. They affect our sense of taste and value judgement of beauty.

They also increase psychic perception, opening our awareness to many other senses. They have been used successfully for those who work on the astral planes.

MARS

These herbs are used to heal muscle strain, external sex organs, and for force and vitality. They add a desire for momentum to one's life, and are used to cure lethargy, although the mixture should include other herbs to bring a sense of direction and focus, as well.

These herbs are very basic, as they relate to the sexual organs, and as they affect the inner person, for they contain energy similar to that of survival. They release the instinctive quality of the Moon in order to preserve the self.

If one desires a great tonic, try herbs of the Sun with herbs of Mars. Martial herbs always impart a strong energy, and when combined with those of the Sun, it is more focused and directed. It is easier for the self to manifest the energy to accomplish goals and achieve desires.

Magickally, Martial herbs relate to manifestation, by learning how to be the 'divine' and see magick occur on the physical planes. Hurley tells us that for powerful manifestation, mix herbs of Mars, the Moon, and Mercury.

The herbs of Mars give us more activity, and a sense of being with other active people. They are recommended for those suffering from apathy, a sense of uselessness, boredom, wastefulness, and are most useful for athletes and those whose jobs require physical exertion.

JUPITER

These are the natural benefactors of all the herbs, having an innate sense of bringing into our lives just what we need. (Also needed is the awareness to perceive these opportunities and benefits.) Remedially, they rule the liver, blood (along with Venus), vitality, attitudes, the manufacture of adrenalin, and fats. Jovian herbs (herbs of Jupiter) are good for those desiring growth.

Taking these herbs as a tonic brings an understanding of how the individual relates to the 'system' and to make use of it for personal advantage without violating ethics. They are excellent for those who pursue the study of ritual, for they provide a conscious link between the microcosm of the Circle and the macrocosm of the Universe, with understanding of how they are both part of the perfect balance.

Herbs of Jupiter are said to give tact, and are excellent for office managers, diplomats, and any professional who must give knowledge and advice to people.

These herbs are recommended for those unable to give of the self, or who go through emotional upheaval on occasions of gift-giving. They allow people to both give and receive with good feelings and an understanding of karma.

For those trained in serious magickal workings, I would highly recommend reading Hurley's *Herbal Alchemy,* in which he gives several planetary formulae for Jovian herb mixtures.

SATURN

These herbs deal with structure. Remedially, this means the skeletal system, ligaments, teeth, and possibly hearing and the gall bladder. Esoterically, their energy proves a source of grounding, or bringing one's feet back to earth. They will settle our attitudes, making us more willing to be stable, and are recommended for those given to excessive daydreams and who get lost in their flights of fancy.

These herbs balance karma, helping us to understand cause and effect, and showing us how to bring discipline into our lives to accomplish goals that will give us increased freedom. They are recommended for those unable to complete projects, and for those who are unable to translate ideas into manifestation and action.

Elixirs made of Saturnian herbs help us to manifest our magick on the earth, and when mixed with Mercurial herbs give us a sense of tradition, as handed down through mysteries, magick, and religion.

Working with Saturn must be done with caution. These herbs can be used to induce change when a person is too caught in a rut, but it will involve letting go of much of the past, until dependency upon the past is alleviated. Only then will the person be free, and able to take both from the future and past to achieve a new and better life.

URANUS

These herbs govern the nervous system, many areas of the brain, and nerve impulses. They are used for those suffering from agitation, a too inflexible attitude, and a need for mental freedom.

Working with these herbs brings inspiration and an ability to follow one's feelings in trying new endeavors. They bring a lighter approach to life, and are useful in alleviating depression.

Magickally, they allow us to trust our impulses, and to follow divine insight. They are good in learning to work with symbols, and to trust initiatory paths. They work with the child within, resurrecting those delightful aspects of one's self.

They may be used when one's thinking is stuck, going round and round in the same old circle, unable to break old mental patterns. They are good for relationships that have become based upon habit and need an injection of new vitality, and work well followed by herbs which will stimulate sexual enjoyment.

NEPTUNE

These herbs should work well with the kidneys and systems which pass fluids within the body. In some ways they work in similar fashion to those of Venus. They also rule the spinal canal and the parathyroid.

For those who have a limited sense of vision, Neptunian herbs open the mind to a greater sense of vision, in which we may find avenues to escape destructive boredom. They bring an ability to dream, both when asleep, and awake. They increase creative imaginative processes, and are the herbs of artists seeking new ideas. They lead to the visions, and other herbs will enable one to put them into manifestation.

Herbs of Neptune have been used to enhance astral travel, but may only do so when reality is held in one's mind at the same time, for they can lead to dependency. They are best used as a key, learning as one flows through the astral realms, but only for brief periods at a time, for that form of psychic travel is only of value when it can be experienced independently of physical assistance, including herbs.

PLUTO

These herbs affect our sexual drive and desire to procreate. They work upon our deepest senses of motivation, based upon childhood training and influences, and can have a real and profound effect upon our lives, although the changes which will manifest do so slowly.

They affect our understanding of the need to preserve life, not self preservation, as with Mars, for herbs of Pluto relate to generations. Thus, they help to understand racial and cultural preservation, and the reaching out to embrace humanity.

They are recommended for those who have lost sexual desire and drive, and for those who feel frustration when working with groups of people. Remedially, they are used to stimulate sexual drive, and to increase procreation.

PROGNOSTICS

Prognostics is the art of diagnosis through the interpretation of a natal birth chart. The method I will describe is very easy to work with. It is an exploratory science, first used for oneself and then, in time, with study, may be used with other people.

A natal birth horoscope is easy to acquire these days. There are astrological societies, astrologers, and computerized charts readily available in nearly every city, and there are also a number of mail-order services. Use one of these methods to acquire a copy of your own natal chart. Constructing the natal chart oneself would be the best, but this would require additional study.

Go to an inexpensive copy shop and have anywhere from fifty to a hundred copies made of your chart. Place these in a loose-leaf notebook, and you have most of the work done. The other 'tool' you will need is an ephemeris. These may be purchased for large spans of years, or for a single year. Probably the most economical would be one of the astrological calendars now available. There are several brands which have the ephemeris printed for each month. (An ephemeris is a list of planetary positions printed on a daily basis. All you need to do is read the minutes and degrees of a planet, and know the symbols for the signs of the zodiac, and you will be able to locate that position on your own chart.)

In looking at your own natal chart, you can see that it is divided into twelve wedges, or houses, numbered one through twelve. Each of these refers to an area of your life, and by observing the planetary motion as it passes through a house, you can better understand these distinctions. A brief synopsis of them is as follows:

FIRST HOUSE   This house immediately follows the rising sign. It has to do with one's identity, self-image, and how one projects this self-image. It also interprets our behavior as it communicates the self to those around. Planets passing through this house have a tendancy for causing re-evaluation, sometimes doubt in the capability of the self, and other ego-related situations. When the Sun passes through this house, for example, there is a stronger need for a definite sense of self, and for recognition of that worth. Planets such as Venus and the Moon tend to make the self more sensitive, needing reassurance. When these types of transits are occurring, solar herbs will give self-assurance during the times of doubt. Refer to the planetary passages to see what will fill the needs of these transits. Planets such as Mars, Saturn, Pluto, and Neptune are generally troublesome. Saturn, particularly, leads to forced change in the self-image, and herbs may be selected to ease the situation. In treating a person who is experiencing these types of change, herbs which provide compassion for the self, courage in the face of danger, and strength may be applicable.

SECOND HOUSE   This house shows how we choose to fulfill our material desires, including the money it takes to buy fun possessions, and much of the furnishings of our homes. It also reflects taste. This house is reflective of our monthly budget, and activity (planetary transits) in this house is always interesting. When planets such as Venus, which seeks pleasure, moves through this house, the native (the person for whom the chart has been made) may have strong desires to purchase 'gifts' for themselves. Mars may have a similar effect. This type of impulse buying often causes internal stress, and being aware of the potential hazards and treating the situation with herbs is good preventative healing. Herbs which give a sense of stability, discipline, and opportunity are appropriate. When a planet such as Saturn moves through the second house, it often implies a period of minor financial hardship. Perspective is needed, for we are forced to trust our abilities to weather the situation, and in doing so, when the financial situation improves, will have learned how to budget, and will be able to use the money to its best advantage. When Saturn is transiting the second house, herbs of Jupiter are good, for they show us how to find opportunity in all situations, and perhaps that bookcase you have been wanting to purchase for two hundred dollars may turn up slightly used at a garage sale for fifteen.

THIRD HOUSE   This is the house of communication, how we speak, listen, and even talk to ourselves in our reasoning and logic processes. In many ways this is much like the discourse on Mercury. When planets move through this house, unless they be Saturn and Pluto, it usually increases the desire to communicate. In those cases, there is both a desire to withdraw (Pluto), or sometimes a harshness (Saturn). Herbs which induce tact are excellent. It is also a good time to work with herbal tonics to provoke memories of the childhood and

266

understanding of them. Herbs may be taken which provide caution, in the case of transits such as Mars, when one might too easily speak before thinking.

FOURTH HOUSE   This house deals with our families, both that of our childhood, and that which surrounds us as adults. For the single person, or the childless, this is the house of the 'chosen family' including those friends we stick with even when we do so with difficulty. They are our support group, and when planets move through this house, it affects those relationships. Some of these transits may involve stress, and should be watched carefully. Planets such as Venus and the Moon may cause us to overextend ourselves, and these situations are often the stressful ones which can lead to nervous stomachs and tension.

FIFTH HOUSE   This is the house of 'love, pleasure, sex, and all the things which make life worth living', as a wise woman friend of mine once said. It is also the house of personal freedom, showing us how much space we allow ourselves for exploration of our fantasies. Planets moving through this house affect our sexual drive, and must be understood, for in doing so much fear can be alleviated. It seems that a change in our sexual drive often brings fear, for we are a sexual society, despite our puritan ethics. This is the house in which that dichotomy is worked out. Planets such as the Sun, Mars, Venus, and Jupiter may increase sexual activity. If a person is in a relationship and such desires are not reflected in the partner, a sudden increase in the desire for sex may go unfulfilled. When this is not understood, all sorts of strange games may go on in the mind which will lead to various manifestations of illness. When understood, communication between the partners may be enhanced by either counseling or herbs, and the situation defused. Planets such as Saturn and Neptune often lead to changes in sexual exploration of fantasies and what is sometimes thought of as 'kinkier' types of sex. In any transits of this house, herbs which reassure the patient are workable, and in extreme cases, herbs which calm the sexual desire may be advisable. A couple of planets, such as the Moon, and occasionally Pluto (which moves very, very slowly, and would take a long time to move through this house), may lead to decreased desire.

SIXTH HOUSE   This house has several characteristics, one of them being the job. This word is distinct and different from that of career. An example is a person whose job is selling shoes, but whose career is writing poetry. This is also the house which shows changes in health, perhaps more quickly than any other. As the last of the houses beginning with the first, and moving through the bottom, more

267

personal part of the horoscope, it is a reflection of how 'in balance' we are. If there are any internal problems, this is the house in which we may see them manifest as physical problems. This is also the house of the hypochondriac, or of psychosomatic illness, and it is easier, with the aid of prognostics, to better understand the true cause of the disease/stress. Planetary transits often lead to a restlessness, a desire to change jobs, or see a change within the employment situation. Frequently they cause the patient to consciously realize that they are not fulfilled and happy; that the job is not a career. Herbs which bring subconscious and intuitive reasoning to the conscious mind are appropriate. Herbs which give a sense of stability and a means of weathering change are also good.

SEVENTH HOUSE   This is the house of relationships, and transits moving through this space are often very fragile, for they lead to changes. This type of situation often can create doubt and fear, both of which are quick to cause illness. Herbs which promote understanding and communication are excellent. Frequently the passage of Saturn through this house is one of the most difficult, for it may seem that the relationship will be ended. Herbs of compassion are good for both persons, and if treating only one, herbs which allow us to see our personal integration with society are excellent.

EIGHTH HOUSE   This is the house which indicates one's ability to undergo deep, internal change, and to take risks in the world around. Regarding money, it talks about the type of money one would invest, or risk, in order to make more. It refers to money inherited through death. Personally, it refers to those internal changes which are akin to initiation. Only in time, as they manifest outwards, do they become understood. This is the house of psychic ability, and magick, and the occult. Planetary activity can lead to restlessness, a feeling that things should be changing. Planets such as the Sun tend to make us think about large sums of money, unless we are skilled at internal changes, in which case it seeks manifestation and an assurance of the process. This is an appropriate time, for any planetary passage,for herbs which lend their energy to smooth transitions, to profound revelation. Visionary Herbes are most appropriate. Herbs which dispel fear are usually recommended.

NINTH HOUSE   This is the house of learning, particularly those things which we choose to learn. Within the system, this refers to post high school education, but can also refer to apprenticeships and learning from an employer. It even includes learning in the streets. For many, it includes religion and travel. Activity is desired when any planet passes through this house, although difficult to achieve when the planet is Saturn or Neptune. Herbs which promote communication are always effective. Herbs of Mars, which lead to activity are also effective.

TENTH HOUSE   This is the house of career. It will show us, when undergoing transits, how we feel about what we are doing. This house indicates our ability to complete our deepest goals, and to enjoy the recognition which results. When planets transit this house, it is wise to select herbs which will allow us to focus this energy, and discipline ourselves to make great strides in moving forward. Herbs of Saturn are good, unless the planetary transits dictate otherwise (see following section). If we have previously been feeling unmotivated, herbs of Mars may provide the drive. Make no decisions when the transiting planets relate primarily to feelings (such as the Moon).

ELEVENTH HOUSE   This is the house of socializing. It deals with the aspects of the self when it is with others, both friends and strangers. Frequently when planets transit this house, a person's thoughts turn more to phone calls, visits, and parties, resulting in feelings of guilt from neglecting those we care about. Herbs which promote internal understanding are good for most transits. If the sign of the cusp is Cancer, and the transiting planet is Venus, herbs which aid the self in being strong and independent are appropriate.

TWELFTH HOUSE   This is the house of our fears. In interpretive astrology, we use this house to find which things are our greatest limitations. These are the forms of self-limitation usually perceived by the native as coming from external sources, but are completely self-induced. Often the 'system' is blamed, but there should be no blame placed anywhere. Herbs which stimulate the imagination and a sense of divining the true abilities of the self are often needed. Frequently there are problems with motivation, which can be helped with herbs. Major transits of this house often will provoke an increased desire for herbs of Neptune, and an ability to fall prey to chemical dependency, and must be watched very closely.

TRANSITS

This term refers to a planet's motion across the same position as was held by another planet (or even the same) when you were born. When this is the same planet, this is often called a 'return', such as on your birthday when the Sun is in the same position of the sky as the day you were born, often called a solar return.

269

When one planet moves across another, it most often manifests stress, and an internal feeling of uneasiness. There are two types of transits. In the first, a planet moves directly across a natal planet (a planetary position from your natal chart). When you were born, a map of the sky based upon that time and position on the earth produces a natal chart. You might think of it as your own claim to the universe. Each point in the zodiacal circle around the earth which held a planet was 'yours', and you are very sensitive to these positions. You will notice during your life, that anytime a planet moves through one of those positions, you might not realize what is occuring, unless with the aid of astrology.

The second type of transit involves retrograde motion. You will notice that sometimes the ephemeris lists a planet moving backwards, that is, the degrees and minutes of its motion are decreasing, and there is a small "R" along the numbers indicating its motion. This is caused by the irregular orbits amongst the various planets. If they were all in concentric circles about the Sun, there would be no retrograde motion, but this is not the case. Frequently a planet will move across, or transit a planet, only to soon turn retrograde, back up across it (for its second passing), and then, when it turns direct, may move across for the third time. Sometimes retrograde motion will cause a planet to sit within a degree of a natal planet for a long time; in the case of Neptune and Pluto, their transits may last a couple of years. Of the planets we observe in astrology, only the Sun and Moon never move retrograde.

Transits of the Sun often indicate an increased ability to bring hidden parts of the self to consciousness, which can be enhanced by herbs. They often give the native a desire for recognition, which can lead to out-of-control emotions when that is unfulfilled. When the Sun transits itself (a solar return), there is a strong desire for self-recognition, and honor given by friends. Truly, our birthdays are special. For the person who wants to deny this energy, herbs of Aquarius will bring them out of their self-denial. When the Sun transits the Moon, herbs which help the self understand the balance between conscious and subconscious are of particular value. All transits of the natal Moon are usually difficult, for they are emotional, and herbs are needed which calm, soothe, and bring a bright outlook to the native.

The transits of Saturn can be the most difficult, giving Saturn a much-maligned reputation. In all cases, herbs which bring patience, discipline, and the ability to clearly discern physical reality, are essential. Saturn's transits of the Moon and Venus can be very painful and need herbs which are soothing. When Saturn contacts the Sun, it is hard on the ego, and inner strength should be included in the tonic. When Saturn transits either Mars or itself, herbs which protect the person against all physical harm are essential.

270

In like manner, by studying more about astrology and watching the planets transit your own chart, can you learn the essentials of prognostics. It is most important that your record the transits, and the feelings and events associated with them. Transits of the Sun, Mercury, Venus, and Mars happen very often, once a year, except Mars which passes all the way around the chart in about two years. The slower the planet, the more profound the transit, and those of Jupiter and Saturn are much stronger. Jupiter is beneficial, and the herbs needed are those to make permanent the opportunities and expanded vision. Saturn is often difficult, taking 28-30 years to move its sickle path around the chart. It is helpful to go to a library or purchase an ephemeris to consult those years since your birth, and check which transits Saturn has made since your birth. When you see the startling and accurate connection with events in your life connected with enforced change, death of friends and loved ones, and times of severity, it becomes easier to use your herbal wisdom to sooth the afflictions of others.

Planets such as Uranus, which takes 84 years to move around one's chart, are more difficult to use prognostics with, for the amount of time they may affect a natal planet is greatly increased. It will take Pluto nearly 250 years to move around one's chart, making a Pluto return most unlikely (even with herbs of longevity). Of the three slower planets, Neptune is the most difficult, particularly because the patient will feel that everything is fine, caught in the illusive web of Neptune. Herbs which ground and which deal with reality are essential. Visionary and Magickal Herbes should be avoided.

Herbal Prognostics require several years of study before they may be put into practise. These sections are merely to provoke your studies. If you, as an Herbalist, desire to work with prognostics, it is mandatory to have a solid training in astrology. That skill should be developed to the ability to do professional interpretations, for it is tricky business, and one in which you should not allow any margin of error. However, it is rewarding, and perhaps the most ancient and purest form of preventative medicine available. Within its realm is the ability to foresee stress and tension, and in working with these primary causes of disease, to treat the person long before any illness is manifest. It also allows you aid the person in becoming a healthy, well integrated and successful individual. These are very high goals for the herbal healer, indeed.

HERBS AND TAROT

HERBS AND TAROT

here are a number of ways in which the Traditional Herbalist can use herbs to enhance the study of Tarot. Tarot is a much younger art than the science of herbs, but within the last couple of hundred years there are a number of herbs which have become associated with particular cards. In the list of correspondences which will follow, half of the herbs have been associated with certain cards for over fifty years.

Perhaps the simplest means of attuning a card with an herb is to take a small piece of the herb and to set them both in a conspicuous place where they will catch your attention. In some cases, an herb works with the Tarot because it has a similar energy to the card. In other cases they are not of the same energy, but one unlocks the other. It would do the student well to also take into study the astrological correspondences of both.

For the serious student of Tarot, a great deal of time is spent meditating upon each card. It is suggested that in the process, a tea be made with the herb (or herbs) assigned to the card, and that ingested in conjunction with the meditation.

In the same manner, the herb might be used as an incense, burnt upon a glowing block of charcoal. Then may the card be passed through the gently wafting smoke. This combination of the scent reaching the brain as the image of the card is before the student can be very powerful, and together will stimulate accurate interpretations of the symbols and excellent recall of the meaning later when doing interpretations for others. As the smoke moves along the image of the card, study all of the symbols within its images. Look for as many symbols as you can within the card, and remember how they strike your inner voices. It is helpful to learn at the same time the traditional interpretations, but far more important to learn how to interpret symbols, for that is the skill which can be used in dreams, Tarot, religious studies, and many other subjects. Each symbol represents a concept, and one can learn to understand the patterns of the symbols. Using the herbs in your study will aid in learning to work with the symbols, for the herb does not translate the card, but works with the symbols, each representing a concept, a feeling, a need which can be shown to the subconscious through a simple picture.

Here then, is the list of the major arcana, and the herbs which may be used in conjunction with them. In those cases where gems and stones have also been used, and non-herbal substances such as animal oils, they have been included in order to give a more complete set of references. The numbers are those of the cards.

1.	The Magician	Mercury	gold, fenugreek, horehound
2.	High Priestess	Moon	emerald, pennyroyal, peony
3.	Empress	Venus	coral, sandalwood
4.	Emperor	Aries	dragon's blood
5.	Hierophant	Taurus	borage, periwinkle
6.	The Lovers	Gemini	cinnamon, wormwood
7.	The Chariot	Cancer	anise, camphor, watercress
8.	Strength	Leo	catnip
9.	The Hermit	Virgo	jade, narcissus
10.	Wheel of Fortune	Jupiter	horehound
11.	Justice	Libra	amber, hyacinth
12.	Hanged Man	Neptune	fern, lotus
13.	Death	Scorpio	basil, lapis lazuli
14.	Temperance	Sagittarius	dill, parsley, garnet
15.	Devil	Capricorn	asafoetida, diamond
16.	The Tower	Mars	eyebright, onyx
17.	The Star	Aquarius	cloves, pearl
18.	The Moon	Pisces	elder, moonstone, mugwort
19.	The Sun	Sun	bay laurel, sunflower
20.	Judgement	Pluto	chervil
21.	The World	Saturn	lovage, mandrake
0.	The Fool	Uranus	adamant, opal, peppermint

In studying the minor arcana (the suits), there are several ways to approach the herbs. The same techniques may be used, but the study is approached either by card (all of the fives, for example), or by suit, of which there are four. Each of the four suits corresponds to one major tool of ritual, and is similar in those concepts to the four directions and the four tools of ritual discussed in those passages of this book.

The swords are said to be learned through work with garlic and mistletoe; wands through almond and cedar; cups through hemp and marjoram; and pentacles through ivy and mulberry. Use either one of the two or both of the herbs. For the individual cards, it applies to all four of the suits, as, in the case of the sixes, frankincense may be used with the six of swords, six of wands, six of cups, and six of pentacles.

- Kings . . . . hyssop, musk
- Queens . . . . myrrh
- Knights. . . . . musk
- Pages . . . . blessed thistle
- Tens. . . . . dittany of crete
- Nines . . . . broom, catnip
- Eights. . . . . elecampagne, storax
- Sevens . . . . benzoin
- Seven of Cups. rose
- Sixes. . . . . frankincense
- Fives. . . . . clover
- Fours . . . . cedar
- Threes . . . . myrrh
- Twos . . . . musk
- Ones/Aces. . . . . ambergris, lady's mantle

Using an herb to study Tarot is an excellent way of learning for those who enjoy both. The flavor, scent, or texture of the herb will stimulate a specific portion of the brain, and that stimulus will join the images of the card to bring wisdom from the subconscious.

Not only is this a great source of wisdom, but is an enjoyable approach as well.

AMULETS:
THE APPROACH OF THE
TRADITIONAL HERBALIST

AMULETS: THE APPROACH OF THE
TRADITIONAL HERBALIST

n amulet is a very magickal tool. It is ancient, perhaps nearly as old as the craft itself. It may date back to the finding of a very potent and powerful plant, when the Herbalist, living in a time when all parts of nature were seen as alive and vital, thought to gain the magick of the herb simply by carrying it around.

Humans, and they are not the only creatures on earth who do so, are continually fascinated with brightly colored stones which look different than the rest of the surroundings. They pick them up, put them safely in a pocket, and, even as time moves on, keep them as a source of enchantment and wonder. There are few of us who have not collected feathers, bits of string, or other curiosities on our journeys. These are the ingredients for the Traditional amulet.

Amulets have acquired an unfavorable reputation, most likely from the Middle Ages, when the practise of herbs included poisoning the enemies of royalty, stunting the growth of children to produce novelties for the courts, and other nefarious practises. That perspective is inaccurate, and needs a new outlook. It may well be that the making of amulets is found in nearly all religions (even the Christians in their rituals work with forms of amulets) and cultures because they are powerful and because they work.

In the making of a Traditional amulet, a definition for it is simply "a container of magick." Amulets are constructed in a ritual situation. They are not made idly, for all of the concentration put into the construction is a most important part of the effectiveness.

An amulet, once finished, is a tool. It has a purpose and it is designed, both physically and spiritually, to carry out that purpose. They are not handed out indiscriminately, but only to those capable of using the energy wisely. Even though an amulet may experience ritual energy only once, in its consecration (although there are amulets made to wear only during rituals), it is still a tool of magick. One should not be made and given to someone who will discard it, for they are also discarding your energy. They do not belong in the hands of those who laugh at them, for then they are laughing at you. It is your concentration and your energy which is placed inside with the herbes,

281

stones, and other ingredients, and they are to be taken seriously. As do all magickal tools, an amulet requires a ritual of consecration to purify, cleanse, then to empower and seal the magick inside.

In many ways, an amulet is a microcosm of you. It might also be constructed to be a microcosm of the person who will receive it, or it may even be made to be the microcosm of the situation. An amulet is like the Cauldron of Cerridwen, like the secret infinity of the Universe. Once an object is placed inside, it is there forever.

We might think of an amulet, in another sense, as a black hole in space, for it is a time warp, and properly constructed is capable of drawing the healing and loving energies of the Universe through it, channeling it to the recipient.

THE CONTAINER

Traditionally the container for an amulet is made of natural materials. A metalsmith might make a metal capsule, which might be worn linked to a chain, carried in purse or pocket, or even buried in a magickal garden. Some might choose to make it of a piece of cloth, sewn by hand into a small bag. The color would be carefully chosen to correspond to the need. The fabric should be of natural fibres, and sewn with cotton thread. This form is easily embroidered with thread to carry a symbol of its power.

Another form, and that of the Traditional Herbalist, is a piece of leather, sewn or tied shut, cut in a magickal shape and sealed with blessings. Those items which will go inside, the ingredients, are those of which only the practitioner has knowledge. An exception to this is when making an amulet for a particular person; they may choose to have the practioner include a particular personal item, such as a piece of jewelery no longer worn. These ingredients are called the Secrets. Secrets are the herbs, chosen with care, or the stones, selected for their special properties, sometimes by the inner voice of the 'child within' for their ability to catch the imagination. Other times they might be a gemstone, selected for the special magickal lore of its energy. The Secrets might be things of any sort, a lucky penney, a feather, a piece of jewelery being 'Recycled into the Universe', a wishbone, or whatever strikes your fancy.

One might also choose to use words, for there is much magick within the word. These might take the form of characters, symbols, sigils, designs, or personal names of power.

THE PENTACLE

Personally choose a circular piece of leather. It should be supple and workable, for you must be able to draw it up into a baglet when it is done. The Traditional size would be the same size as your magickal tool, the pentacle. These are often six to eight inches in diameter, which might seem large, but when sealed will be small enough. This will represent various concepts, all of which you should be conscious as you do your own work. It is the Magickal Circle, or the circle of death and rebirth. It represents the turning of the seasons, each dying into the birth of the next, going on for all ages into timelessness.

There are some serious thoughts to remember when working with this piece of leather. Leather is a gift of the creatures of the Earth. It represents the physical existence, the body. The body is the temple for the soul, and must be treated with reverence. Thus, again we find the concept of the microcosm and the macrocosm. This leather is the exterior of the temple within. Making an amulet of leather is not to be lightly undertaken, for it is a symbol of the wisdom of being at one with all creatures. It represents life, for it was once a living part of a creature, and it also represents death, for that creature has passed on into another state of being. Thus, with life and death, it represents the two of the most powerful mysteries of all being.

You must keep in your mind an image of ancient times, when holy men and women were called upon to make a sacrifice to appease the Gods and Goddesses. This is about as close to sacrifice as the Traditional Herbalist will ever come, unless it be the tossing of herbes into the fire in a solemn rite.

Pierce the perimeter with holes. This can be done with the white-handled knife, which is invariably difficult, or it can be done with a leather working awl. A less reverent, but far more practical means is to use a paper punch. Near the edge, but leaving at least a half-inch margin around the pentacle, you will surround the perimeter with holes, spaced about three-quarters of an inch apart. Lace these holes with a cord, or a piece of rawhide lacing. When this cord is drawn tight, it will pucker the edge of the pentacle, and you can tie it shut, having formed a small bag.

CONSECRATION OF THE AMULET

Once complete, the amulet should be cleansed and blessed as you would any tool of magick, by air, fire, water, and earth. Cleanse it of all negative energy, of impatience, of misunderstanding, and so on. Do this realizing that even the argument of your neighbors sends out bad energy, and you want only good within the amulet. Then, it will be consecrated and blessed. Once the pentacle has been cleansed, place it on your altar if you have one, or on some stable piece of furniture where it will not be disturbed. Lay it out flat, and upon it set a small wooden box with a flat lid. Upon the lid, you will keep a small candle in a glass holder, such as a votive candle; one which can be allowed to burn safely for many hours.

RITUAL SWEEPING

This cleansing should be done under the new moon, and you then have two weeks to complete the amulet. However, for a more complex working, you might start it on a full moon and work for two weeks cleansing it, and then at the new moon, begin assembling the 'Secrets'.

From new moon to full, bring the ingredients, one at a time, and place them in the box, lighting the candle. Thus, as you go about your other work, each time you see the candle, it will remind you of the amulet under construction, and you may focus your will and energy into the secret workings. Work on the amulet should be done each day of the waxing moon. At the same time, you will assemble the items you need to seal and consecrate the amulet in the full moon ritual.

In the selection of herbes, read through the magickal herbal of this book. There are a great many herbes, and a great many purposes. Choose carefully. Each evening (or morning, if you are a day person), you will place another ingredient into the magick box resting on the leather pentacle. It is almost like making a magick stew, adding ingredients one at a time to let them cook into a tasty broth.

During this time you might also wish to inscribe your amulet with the words. There are different inks associated with magick you might purchase, or even make yourself. You might choose ink by the color, to correlate with the color magick correspondences. You may wish to make an herbal ink, which is quite simple. Select a commercial ink, and place into it a piece of moonstone and a piece of herbal root. This ink must remain steeping for at least one full lunar cycle (28 days) before it may be used, so plan well ahead of the amulet. There are the very serious practitioners who would use their own blood for any inscriptions, but not all of us are that brave.

One of the more common inscriptions is a copy of the natal astrological chart of the person who will be using the amulet. If the amulet is for a specific event (such as a good luck amulet for a friend's graduation) you might make an astrological chart of that date. Some

284

amulets are for a new sense of direction, to utilize higher inner qualities and bring them to light. In those cases, one might inscribe a card of the Tarot or a hexagram from the I Ching. You might just write a wish for the person, which also constitutes very potent words of power.

THE RITUAL

In order to perform a ritual to seal and consecrate the amulet, you may follow the following procedure. It is a ritual based upon the practices of several Native American Tribes, upon the Tibetan mystics, and the ancient European Priests and Priestesses of the Old Religions.

THE CIRCLE

You must have a sacred space in which to seal the ritual, for you want only good energy to be within it, once sealed. The best way to create this space is to scribe a circle about yourself. Traditionally, one would use a ritual knife or a wand to do this, but you may use even your fingers. This is your space, once you have defined it by facing the East, and drawing the circle all the way, through the South, West, and North, and coming back to the East. This Circle is your sacred space. It is equidistant from you, and you have separated it from the outside world, from the garbage you forgot to empty, from the job that tires and bores you, from the bills that need paying. But all of that is outside the Circle. Within it, you will now concentrate, and focus all of your attention on the process at hand.

This Circle is another tool. As such, it also needs cleansing. Part of your ritual sweeping during the waxing moon would have been to bring a chalice and a small container of seasalt. The chalice, or bowl, you would have filled with water. To cleanse the Circle, sprinkle some salt in the water. Even in the days of the Old Testament, salt was believed to contain natural purity, and was used in ritual cleansing. Go to the East, for that is your starting point, and sprinkle this saltwater solution around the Circle. Since magicians of all cultures believe that all things animal or mineral have consciousness and spirit, you might even wish to tell the Circle that you are cleansing it. Choose any words you wish, for it is only the meaning and intent which matters.

Ritual cleansing involves all four elements. You have just mingled Earth and Water and used them. In order to cleanse the Circle with Air and Fire, you may use incense. This, too, would have been prepared previous to the full moon.

Once the Circle has been cleansed with all four elements, it is time to balance it. This is done again with all four elements. Some of the

Native Americans would smoke a pipe to the four winds. The choice is yours, for you might also light four candles, a yellow in the East, red in the South, blue in the West, and green in the North. Mentally, all you need to do is to imagine that you have brought each of these four elements, each in turn, to the edge of your Circle. You may wish to do so in reality, lighting some incense in the East, a small iron pot of fire in the South, having a bowl of water in the West, and a pot of Earth in the North.

Now, you will take the pentacle and place upon it all of the ingredients from the box. Then, very carefully, take it around your circle, pausing at each of the four directions to give it positive and psychic balance. As you face each direction, imagine that you can reach out into infinity, until a large circle has been completed, coming up behind you. Science has said that a straight line extended into space will eventually circle around and touch itself. Along this line, you can draw upon your own belief in the Divine, and ask for the blessings for the recipient.

Being careful not to spill either the 'Secrets' or the energy, continue your way around the circle. When you have done this in all four directions, bring it back to the center. Now you should place some of your own energy into the amulet. A simple way is by singing to it. You need not have a professional voice, but rather the magick of singing to it as a child would. Sing about the goodness you wish for, the protection and the healing energies. Then, when you feel the time is right, pull the cord, and draw it shut.

SEALING THE AMULET

Knot the cord tightly. Then, to seal it, you may use some wax, dripped from a candle. You might prick your finger and seal it with blood. You might, for a friend, seal it with a kiss. A very, very important fact: once sealed an amulet is never again opened.

Should the time come when the amulet is no longer needed, it might be consigned to a fire, or it might be buried in the Earth where it will never be found. But, it is never opened or carelessly discarded. All of the magick, all of the energy must be allowed to be absorbed back into the Universe.

CLOSING THE RITUAL

When the amulet is sealed, then again go to the four directions, East, South, West, then North. Give thanks to the Universe for its beauty, love, and healing powers at each of the four directions. Then, beginning in the East, unscribe your circle, bringing yourself back into connection with the world around you. You have now created an amulet of magick and power.

HERBS AND GEMSTONES
MISCELLANEOUS CORRESPONDENCES

HERBS AND GEMSTONES
MISCELLANEOUS CORRESPONDENCES

 have decided to include in this book a list of gemstones and some of the lore and history that goes with them. As with the herbes, this is by no means a comprehensive list, but part of a working herbal. Even as I write this introduction to the stones, I have found more material, which will some day be included in a revised edition of this book.

Some may wonder why an Herbalist would collect information on stones. As you read through these pages, you will see a number of stones which have direct connections with herbes. Then, as the Herbalist works with the traditional approach to this craft, the making of amulets and other forms of healing come up in reading, and begin to prick the interest of an inquisitive mind. Most of us who are fascinated by those things growing upon the earth are also intrigued by those stones and crystals She has produced, for many of them 'grow' in like manner. A crystal is nearly a 'live' growth, continuing to add to its size until disturbed and taken by the collector. Just as the study of herbes adds to the wise person's knowledge of the Earth, so too, does the study of minerals and stones add to that same understanding.

In addition to the gems and stones, I have used this section to include some information on various metals, and also a couple of oils used frequently in the making of potions by the Herbalist, such as ambergris and musk. When the Herbalist embarks upon the making of amulets, there are many times when we want more than an herbe to release its energy for the recipient, but also an object to place within the amulet which is capable of storing the magickal energy raised in ritual and/or meditation. Thus, the crystal is a likely object.

When a stone is placed within an amulet, it is capable of channeling the magickal energies of the practitioner, so that an amulet made to keep a friend safe upon a journey may continue to do so.

For those who wish to keep their magickal herbes highly charged, it is desirable to collect the various stones associated with herbes and keep them together in storage. If there is an herbe associated with a stone, this is the primary way in which they can be easily used.

That same herb can be made into either an oil or a wash, and used to consecrate a special piece of jewelry, according to the correspondence between stone and herbe. Thus, the piece of jewelry is ever different, its purpose set in motion by the consecration, and the jewelry then made into a proper tool of the practitioner.

In this manner do many Herbalists have a particular ring, worn when they do healings, or a neckpiece which they wear only when entering a sacred ritual to work with their herbes magickally.

It is delightful information, and sure to stimulate the curiosity. Enjoy it, and reflect upon some of the lore which dates back to many, many centuries before the time of Christ. For those interested in exploring a more esoteric form of healing, the ancient custom of grinding gemstones and using their powder may be studied. Much of the knowledge has been lost, but can be, and should be, resurrected. Joyful reading to you all.

ADAMANT

Paracelsus describes this stone as a black crystal. It is transparent blackness, rather than opaque. Difficult to believe is its legendary ability to dissolve in goat's blood, but this may be the lore of the alchemist. Reputedly the hardest of stones, it may really be a black diamond.

Wearing the Adamant brings a better awareness of the joy that is inherent in all things.

AGATE

Agates are said to be ruled by Mars. These are very attractive silica-based stones, multi-colored, in a variety of hues. This was one of the stones of the Hebrew High Priests, and has many qualities associated with it. In accordance with the ancient practise of ingesting powdered stones, doing so will aid in the healing of many gum diseases, and helps the body to better absorb and utilize calcium.

Agates are said to magickally aid vision, and protect the wearer against venemous bites. They carry the energies of vigor for one in need of energy, and in the hand of an adept are said to be able to calm the fiercest of storms. The moss agate is said to be a talisman for a successful harvest. Some associate the agate with the planet Mercury.

AMBER

Amber is primarily associated with the Sun, but other planetary associations include Venus and Saturn. Since Amber is not literally stone, but is fossilized resin and of organic origin, it is soft and care must be taken to avoid scratching it when being worn.

Amber is said to soothe one's disposition, calming the nerves, and helping one to feel well balanced. Ingested, it is said to cure throat disorders, and as an amulet it prevents a variety of disease, such as eye troubles, rheumatism, pains, bleeding, etc. Gazing through a piece of amber is said to bring strength of vision and to correct eye trouble.

Brought into magickal workings, Amber will bring the practitioner success in the intent of the ritual. Powdered amber is used in incense for rituals to bring good fortune.

AMBERGRIS

Ambergris is a waxy substance found floating along the coastal waters in which the sperm whale plays. It will prolong sexual desire, arousal, and is well known as an aphrodisiac.

Spiritually, it is used as a potion in order to ensure that your next incarnation will be a most attractive one. It also symbolizes the ability to maintain conscious awareness of the Divine within. It may be either worn or mixed into incense to invoke the deities of Jupiter and Zeus.

When brought into meditation, it allows one to perceive the Divine source of all power, and to bring that wisdom into benefiting one's own Pathwork. As such it represents the color of hidden light and a dot (.). It aids the student in learning the lessons of the Aces in Tarot, and is used in the consecration of Diamonds. If possible, store a small uncut diamond in your container of Ambergris.

The most powerful Ambergris is that which the user collects beneath the light of a full moon as it reflects upon the water and brings the substance visible to the naked eye.

AMETHYST

Amethyst has two ruling planets, both Jupiter and Mercury. One of the most fascinating bits of lore is that Amethyst will prevent drunkenness, thus were many goblets set with faceted pieces of the stone. Some sources say that the stones should be engraved with symbols of Bacchus.

Amethyst is said to bring the wearer peace of mind, and in time, to increase one's beauty. Frequently the stone was given to a spouse or lover, for it is said to keep the love alive.

It is used as a talisman and worn to bed, where it brings the most pleasant of dreams and a good night's rest. When awake it improves the mind, keeping a healthy sense of humor and a good, keen memory.

Some say that Amethyst should be worn by those who wish to maintain chastity or celibacy. It is thought to control passions, and was accordingly a stone used for the making of rosaries. Other religious uses include the placement as the third stone in the third row of Aaron's breastplate, and the invocation of the Gods Mars, Hermes, and Mercury.

The color comes from the presence of manganese oxide, and can fade when too frequently exposed to the sun.

AQUAMARINE

These stones are thought to be associated with Pisces and the planet Neptune. They are related to the emerald, and said to bring courage, bravery, and the ability to make quick decisions in times of need. They are particularly recommended for those who are prone to procrastination and need motivation. Aquamarine is a form of beryl.

BERYL

Beryl is a varied form of gemstone. It is found in various colors, which are known by different names:

Heliodor - golden; Goshenite - clear; Verobyerite - rose; Morganite - pink (this and Verobyerite are basically interchangeable); Aquamarine - pale blue; Beryl - blue-green.

There is much lore associated with the stone. It was one chosen for the breastplate of Aaron, and appears as one of the stones of the Apocalypse. It has been much used in healing, for gas, melancholy, liver disorders, and throat complaints. Not only that, but it is said to cure stupidity.

Positive energies connected with Beryl are that it brings marital joy and the ability for the partners to work together towards common goals. It also brings motivation for one who wears it. As an amulet, it is said to be most powerful when engraved with a crow on one side and a crab on the other.

BLOODSTONE

These are beautiful stones, usually deep-green with flecks of vivid red. They are mixtures of quartz and jasper. The iron compounds found within are most similar to that of our blood, hence the name.

Sympathetic magick uses Bloodstone to stop cuts and bleeding, to heal wounds, and protect warriors. They have long been talismans for soldiers.

Worn as an amulet by the peaceful, it is said to bring recognition, fame, and a long life in which to enjoy those rewards. Placed under your pillow at night, you will have visionary dreams of the future.

It is thought that an expectant mother should wear the stone on her left arm until labor in order to prevent miscarriage, and then place it upon her right arm to have an easy delivery.

Bloodstone is said to bring wisdom, and in the past they were polished to use as mirrors in which to watch solar eclipses.

CARNELIAN

Wearing this stone will bring one into harmony with the energies of the Sun. It has been used as an amulet to bring one into communion with the Goddess Venus.

CHALCEDONY

This stone of Mercury balances the mental processes, and has even been said to cure insanity and madness. It has also been used to invoke the healing presence of the God Mercury, to heal and bring understanding. It also carries compassion, and is said to be associated with the zodiacal sign of Cancer. The stone carries a strong reputation of being able to heal through its presence, or by drinking water steeped with Chalcedony.

It is also one of the stones symbolic of the mystical city of the Apocalypse in the Book of Revelations.

CHRYSOLITE

This is usually a stone of magicians and mystics. References to its long history are found in both the old and new testaments of the bible, for it is one of the stones of Aaron's Priesthood, and is also one of the stones of the Apocalypse.

CHRYSOPRASE

Although this stone is said to be of the planet Saturn, it is used to invoke the Goddess Vesta, to give the user control and understanding of fire. It carries with it a lore for healing, and for protecting the wearer from ill health. It is one of the twelve stones of the Apocalypse, and Paracelsus describes it as appearing like fire at night, surely a similar attribute to its association with Vesta.

COPPER

Although Copper is associated as representing Earth as one of the four traditional elements, it is ruled by the planet Venus, which makes it warm, easily conductive of energy, and pliable.

Copper is one of the more unusual materials other than wood for the making of a pentacle, one of the four suits of Tarot and also a tool found within many practises of ritual. It invokes the element of Earth to balance the ritual with the other three and may be used to focus energy. Some magicians use a disc of copper upon which to rest the stand for their crystal ball, to stablize the energy within.

CORAL

Coral appears to be associated with either Mars or with Venus. Wearing it as a gem is said to protect a swimmer from danger in the water. It has also been used by those who desire to communicate with sylphs, the spirit creatures of the water. In this case, it may be worked with the planet Neptune.

There are several healing properties associated with Coral, as it is said to cleanse both liver and blood of impurities and disease. Wearing it is said to beautify the skin, and keep it clear and healthy. Wearing it as an amulet is a means of promoting fertility, for it keeps one from losing potency, from contracting sexual diseases, and will keep men potent and women fertile.

This is truly a stone of protection, keeping away all negative energies, undesirable problems, and protects the psychic self, the soul, and the spirit of the wearer. It has been used over many years, beaded into amulets and rosaries.

Red is the appropriate color to use when desiring to attract love and romance.

DIAMOND

This is a fascinating gem, and has an involved history about it. Primarily seen as ruled by the Sun, others place this stone under the dominion of Saturn, due to its amazing hardness. The Diamond has been perceived as a stone of power for many ages. Moses is said to have used a diamond to cut the pieces of his priestly robe, and this same stone is supposed to have passed on to Solomon, who worked with it as a key to understanding the wisdom of the Universe. It was one of the stones of the Hebrew priest, Aaron, who wore it to divine the state of his people: it was brilliant and clear when they obeyed sacred laws, and when they were in violation, it would cloud and darken.

The healing properties of this gem include protection against poison and taken ground, internally, an antidote for those unlucky enough (obviously those without a diamond) to have ingested poison. They are said to keep one alive into a wise, old age, and to heal damaged tissue, bones, and afflictions of the skin. They are also said to have cured nearly any disease known to humans!

Many perceive the diamond as the jewel mentioned in the sacred texts of Tantric Buddhism, "Om mani padne hum," which translates as "Oh, jewel in the lotus."

A warning should be posted on each piece of Diamond jewelry, for it is said that the spirit of the stone will haunt and plague any who steal the stone from the rightful owner. Diamonds have also been used in battle, worn usually upon the left arm, to bring the warrior back victorious. The stone is said to give the wearer above-average strength and great courage in the face of difficulty.

Not only do Diamonds confer blessings to lovers and their union, but it is said that it will help a troubled relationship. For the single person, it is said that wearing the stone will keep them from wandering into temptation, yet this has not interfered with the stone's popularity, and I know many who wear it who would seem unaffected by this lore.

Diamond is a cubic form of crystal, and comes in an amazing array of colors: black, blue, green, yellow, rose, and brown. It is often seen as a symbol of eternal fire.

Diamonds are recommended for those suffering from paralysis or epilepsy.

EMERALD

Much has been written about the Emerald. These are stones of royalty and have a long and ancient history, appearing as a stone of Aaron's priesthood and also as a stone of the mystical Apocalypse. The Moslem peoples would have them inscribed with verses from the Koran, and use them as powerful amulets. The Chaldeans felt that the Emerald was a key to the Goddess, who was able to channel Her energy and Divine Will through this gem. It was thus often associated with Venus.

The healing properties of the Emerald have it capable of protecting the expectant mother, bringing her safely through childbirth and labor. Hippocrates would take an Emerald and steep it in water, producing a wash which he claimed was excellent for his eyes and vision. Emerald is one of the many stones said to be an antidote against poisoning. It also has been used to cure skin problems, colic, ulcers, and tension. As a remedy, it has been ground and taken internally, steeped in water, and worn next to the troubled condition. Gazing through a cut stone, or meditating upon one is another way of protecting the eyes and improving sight.

Symbolically, the Emerald is given to represent healthy romance, love which brings fulfillment and happiness, and joy and peace throughout the household. It would seem to be a stone more used at weddings, handfastings, and unions. It is ruled by the planet Venus.

Paracelsus agrees with the Emerald's healing power for the eyes, and says that it also strengthens the memory. He notes that it is also used to help a person maintain their vows of chasity.

Some Emeralds are able to change hue, losing the deep color when exposed to lies, treachery, and evil intent. Emeralds are highly valued, sometimes said to help the liver and cure dysentery.

Religiously, the Emerald may be used to invoke the Goddesses Venus and Ceres. They banish all evil, quiet the worst of storms, and even are supposed to keep you free from insects.

GARNETS

The Garnet is akin to the planet Mars, bringing the ability to hold true to fidelity, friendship, and the commitment made to loved ones, to take those words and bring them into action.

This form of silicate is often used to represent love, and is associated with the month of January.

GOLD

Gold has long been associated with the Sun, both by color and by energy. It balances silver, which is used to represent the Moon. Gold is best used as the metal in amulets, when seeking those things which reflect to us ego accomplishment, such as in matters of fame, success, and earthly fortunes.

The wearing of Gold brings a long life for one's physical body. It is often the metal of adornment for the wand of magick. In many ancient civilizations, Gold was a symbol of the king, who was given his power from the Sun God.

HYACINTH

This is somewhat a mystical stone, and according to W.B. Crow may be used to invoke Diana, the Moon Goddess. It is ruled by Jupiter, and is of particular value to Sagittarians, keeping them from running off the edge when pursuing their dreams.

IRON

This metal is attuned to Mars. It is often used in the construction of amulets which are to be buried in the Earth. Magickally, it may be considered attuned to the element of Earth, sometimes used in conjunction with copper.

IVORY

Some consider this stone to be ruled by Jupiter and others by the Moon. Ivory is often used in the making of talismans, easily scribed or engraved. Ivory should be stored in a cloth, and may be consecrated with oils made from Herbes of Immortality.

JACINTH

This is a stone of the ancients. It has been used in healing, particularly for its ability to work with cancer, tuberculosis, and other wasting diseases. It brings comfort and understanding to the user. It also brings sleep, peace of mind, and cures insomnia. Early

Catholicism is said to have thought the stone carried the virtue of humility.

As an amulet, Jacinth is said to bring protection against violent storms, lightning, plagues, and poisons. It is sometimes worn by expectant mothers, to carry them safely and easily through childbirth.

JADE

Jade may be considered a patron stone of gardeners. All who desire to become Master Herbalists should have one special piece of Jade, to make certain that both their gardens and wisdom flourish.

Jade was one of the most important stones to the Chinese, who said that it carried five cardinal virtues within it: charity, modesty, courage, justice, and wisdom. They used it in their rituals, carving elaborate ceremonial knives with it, and sometimes making large prayer gongs with it, which when rung, would instill virtue in all who heard the tone.

Jade has a large reputation for healing, is said to cure kidney disease, to aid in the passing of stones, and to keep one's eyesight in top shape. Jade has also been used in the treatment of many other illnesses.

Magickally, Jade is said to have the power to raise the dead, although this seems to remain unproven. It is used in countermagick, to reverse negative energy and return it to the one who sent it.

Jade is attuned with Venus in Libra.

JASPER

Jasper is an interesting stone to see. It is one of the stones of the Apocalypse, and is also said to invoke the God Jupiter. Jasper is a form of red silica, which gives it its appearance, and is under the dominion of the planet Pluto.

Frequently worn as an amulet, Jasper is the stone for things 'that go bump in the night', for it will protect you against nightmares and evil shadows. It is said to be most powerful when engraved with a hawk holding a serpent in its beak. It is very potent in protecting the wearer against black magick and evil. It is recommended for those who practise ceremonial magick, as it will keep one safe against entities which have been ritually evoked.

In healing, Jasper has been used as a haemostat, to stop bleeding, and to give ease in childbirth. It has also been used against consumptive disease and cancer.

JET

Jet, being mostly carbon, is a stone of the planet Saturn. It is of vegetable origin, and is really an evolved form of coal. It is said to work against pain, and has been used to calm both toothache and migraine headache. It has been used in the treatment of epilepsy, and, ground, made into an ointment with beeswax to treat tumors.

During Victorian times the color of Jet led to its association with mourning. It has also been often used in the making of rosaries.

Magickally, Jet is used to banish all evil and negation, for protection, and in order to hear clearly one's intuition and inner light.

LAPIS LAZULI

This handsome blue stone is associated with both the planets of Mercury and Jupiter. It is said to be one of the stones of which the Earth Mother is particularly partial to, and may be worn in rituals in Her honor.

Lapis Lazuli has a history of use in bringing psychic safety, having been used by the Egyptians for psychic protection, and still being used today for the same purpose. It does not have a history of healing physically, but a most interesting use has been found in which Lapis Lazuli is worn by a person suffering from the shock of incest. Wearing the stone will calm the person and help them to clear their psychic energy of the trauma.

This form of calcite is said to be a stone of Alchemy, capable of causing transmutation, and often worn by practitioners of that art. It is also said that magickally used it will bring material wealth, which would be the aspect of Jupiter, the psychic workings being more akin to Mercury.

Lapis was so highly regarded by the Egyptian priests that Tutankhamun's mask was made of both the stone and gold inlay.

LEAD

Lead is associated with Saturn. It is used in grounding energy, and may be worn by a person who needs to bring their feet and mind back to earth-plane reality. It may thus be worn as an amulet, or interestingly, a small piece of lead may be placed in each shoe.

301

LODESTONE

These are the natural magnets of the Earth. They are traditionally used to charge a magickal blade. In doing so, they give the blade the ability to attract energy, power, and magick, which will then be channeled by the practitioner.

Lodestones have been used in healing. Sometimes they are used to draw off energy which is harmful and causes illnesses.

As talismans, lodestones are often included in amulets. These are said to bring a person safely home again, and usually include a bit of home soil or ash from the hearth.

MALACHITE

This beautiful green stone is a carbonate form of copper. It is in tune with the planet Venus, vibrating in like manner. It is said to carry healing abilities, and may be worn in jewelry by someone ill who desires the return of health and well-being.

Malachite is an ancient stone, important in Moslem magick and religion. It is said to work specifically against the diseases of cholera and colic.

MOONSTONE

This stone is directly associated with the Moon, and has been for many ages. It is also known as 'Selenite', named for Selena, one of the aspects of the Moon Goddess. It is said to change color with the phases of the moon, although when a stone becomes particularly attuned to the wearer, it will change its tint with the well-being of the person's aura.

These stones are often associated with the month of June and represent good things such as happiness, health, good fortune, and companionship. They are good stones for those who need to dispel a troubling, internal fear, particularly for those afraid of the night and darkness of the unknown. Moonstone brings peace of mind and inner security. They are often worn by Priestesses and those who channel healing energy.

Wearing a magickally prepared Moonstone will strengthen your psychic abilities, and bring strength to emotions and will. Care should be taken in wearing them, for they are of soft texture, and will easily be marred.

MUSK

This oil, associated with the planet Pluto, is much associated with its reputation as an aphrodisiac. It is used in the making of lubricants, or worn as a perfume. Both uses will allow one prolonged arousal, increased desire, and greater sexual fulfillment.

Musk is also used to consecrate jewelry set with turquoise, and is used in rituals to invoke Thoth, Athena, and Shiva. Rubbing a small amount of oil on the third eye and meditating upon the Tarot cards of all four kings, knights, and twos, will bring better comprehension of those cards.

OBSIDIAN

Obsidian is a beautiful black stone when polished. It is of the same nature as Saturn, and a small piece of Obsidian should be placed within containers of the herbs of Saturn to enhance their spiritual properties.

Obsidian is sometimes used for the black handle of a magickal knife, and is sometimes set into a magickal wand. This is to bring the practitioner more control over the energies, to channel and focus them, and also to keep from becoming too directly involved with the power.

ONYX

This is one of the stones of Aaron's priesthood. It is often thought to protect against negative energies, evil and black magick, yet there are many cultures who regard the black stone as just the opposite. Some feel that wearing it will bring misfortune, bad luck, and will attract mental demons to plague the mind and the dreams.

It is thought by some that Onyx given to a friend will cause a parting of the ways, but this also has its opposite, for some give it as a token of magickal friendship, to seal and protect the relationship.

Onyx is a stone of Saturn.

OPAL

These magnificently beautiful stones are considered to be akin to Venus in Libra by some, and to the Moon by others. These stones are often brought from Australia, and are a form of silica.

Opals are said to protect the wearer from an interesting variety of things, including drunkenness, blindness, from death by fire, and bad health. A stone which has been magickally charged is said to build your sense of self esteem and to bring enjoyable dreams. Opals are said to change color and brightness, turning pale and wan near danger and shining brightly when near good energy.

Some compare the Opal to the rainbow, and say it represents hope.

PEARL

Pearls are organic, grown by oysters. As jewels of the sea, they are associated with the Moon. Pearls have been used as symbols of Christ and also of Unicorns. They have often been powdered and taken internally to treat a host of illnesses, among them insomnia, asthma, diabetes, and consumption. Pearls have also been used to treat disorders of internal organs, and to strengthen the heart after it has malfunctioned.

Pearls represent purity, peace, tranquility, and wisdom. They are often worn by a person who is recognized as a leader, trusted and loved for compassion and knowledge.

An interesting historical fact is the use of Pearls to pledge honor and loyalty to another. Cleopatra is said to have dissolved a Pearl in acid, and then drank it in honor of Antony.

PERIDOT

This stone is associated with the month of August and with Leo. It carries the vibrations of the Sun, and as such is used to bring a sense of security which banishes fears of the dark and unknown.

Carrying a Peridot in one's pocket will attract attention, bringing love and recognition. It may also be used to bring about change, and encourage a flow of money into one's life.

QUARTZ

Clear Quartz is a stone of the Moon, whereas Smoky Quartz is a stone of Mercury , as is chalcedony, which is a white Quartz. Smoky Quartz is used to prevent argument, and to keep peace and harmony in conversations and business meetings.

Clear Quartz is the stone of crystal balls, working as a channel of energy. Quartz has 'piezo-electric' properties, which allows it to convert physical energy into electrical energy, or the other way around. The crystal radios operated by a Quartz crystal are examples of this function. If a Quartz crystal is used for psychic or magickal workings, it should be kept out of direct sunlight.

QUICKSILVER

This substance, also known as Mercury, is also attuned to the planet Mercury. It is often used in Alchemical workings, and is magickally used to charge tools of communication or divination. When boiled, Quicksilver gives off a beautiful violet vapor. Both the metal and the vapor are potential health hazards, and great care should be taken in working with Mercury.

ROCK CRYSTAL

Rock Crystal is associated with either the Moon or with Uranus, depending upon the nature of the work being done. It is used in divination and in enhancing communication.

Rock Crystal has been used to invoke Juno, Ra, Helios, and Apollo. Some consider the Moon aspect of this stone to make it particularly a favorite of those born under the sign of Cancer. The crystals are used in psychic healing, to channel energy, and also as stones of protection against dark and worrisome energies.

When working with the Uranus energies of Rock Crystal, it represents the fifth element, Spirit, which may also be seen as inspiration.

RUBY

The Ruby is kindred to the Sapphire. Its brilliant red color comes from the presence of chromium oxide, and has fascinated mankind for centuries. Over the ages, the Ruby has come to represent freedom, charity, dignity, divine power, health, strength, and wearing a Ruby is said to keep sadness away from your life.

Rubies have been used in healing, said to heal the heart, wounds, anemia, and other circulatory system afflictions. They are used to prevent and cure paralysis, and one ancient system of healing used the ash of this gem to treat wasting diseases, poison, and ulcers. Pliny felt that Rubies were either male or female, and recommended using the male stones against the plague and to banish all evil.

305

This is the gem of the wand, staff, and sceptor, symbols of balanced divine and earthly powers. They are said to show the presence of evil, clouding and darkening when the owner is threatened. Traditionally, Rubies have been worn as amulets to bring success in business, war, and other endeavors. A Ruby should always be treated with respect.

SAPPHIRE

Sapphires are considered under the rulership of either Mercury or Jupiter, and W. B. Crow also says they may be used to invoke Neptune. One of the stones of the Apocalypse was a Sapphire, and there are some of the Jewish religion who believe that Sapphire was the stone of the two tablets of the ten commandments.

There are many virtues associated with the Sapphire, and the long list includes wisdom, mental tranquility, faithfulness, sincerity, truthfulness in speech, and the Sapphire is considered the appropriate stone for the ring of a Catholic cardinal. The Buddhists believe that wearing the stone will aid in keeping you devoutly on your path, and will promote spiritual enlightenment.

Sapphires have been much used in healing, used to dispel fever, eye disorders, rheumatism, and ulcers. They are also a stone of tranquility, used to dispel all fears and bring inner peace, and to cure mental and nervous disorders. The Sapphire which is the lighter blue is considered male and has been used in healing, sometimes powdered and mixed with milk as an ointment to treat ulcers of the skin, sometimes mixed with vinegar to stop nose bleeds and to cure eye infections.

The deeper blue Sapphire is considered the female, both male and female receiving the blue tint from titanium found within the crystal. The female Sapphire is considered a potent amulet against all forms of fear.

SARD or SARDIUS

This stone was chosen by Aaron for the breastplate he wore when performing as high priest of the Hebrew peoples. It has also been said that this stone invokes the Goddess Minerva. Generally associated with the planet Mars, some also consider it under Aries.

Wearing a Sard is said to keep one safe from the bites of venomous snakes.

SARDONYX

This stone is associated by jewelers with the month of August. Astrologically, it may be associated with the planet Mercury, and the zodiacal sign of Virgo. This stone was chosen both by Aaron, and also is in Revelations in the Apocalypse. It has been considered magickal for a long time. It is often taken, and one side engraved, to render the stone into a talisman. The most common symbol carved into the stone is that of a quail. Wearing such a talisman is said to allow the person to pass through the world, unseen, as if invisible.

Sardonyx is said to also promote warmth and friendship.

SEASHELLS

Seashells are variously associated with the Moon most commonly, and also with Venus. They are seen as direct magickal connections with the Goddess aspect of creation, and the maternal energies of the sea, the tide, and the pull of the Moon.

When included in an amulet, they can make the magickal project fertile, and bring those things needed to give fulfillment and peace of mind. They are also used as one of two ingredients in an amulet to represent the God and Goddess, or male and female principles of all creation. (A stone is often included to represent the male.)

SILVER

This metal is directly associated with the Moon. It is often chosen to balance Gold, which is solar in aspect. Whereas Gold is associated with the conscious ego and outward manifestation, Silver reflects the inner self, the subconscious, and those things which are unseen within the personality.

Wearing Silver promotes harmony and peace and keeps one in balance with the feminine aspects of the Universe, and able to get on well with women relatives. Silver is the metal of the Goddesses, and balances the Gold of the Gods.

For ritual use, Silver is most appropriate for the chalice or ritual cup. It is also appropriate for the container for sea salt, and a small piece of Silver may be secluded within lunar herbs, which are reserved for magick.

TIN

Tin is under the rulership of the planet Jupiter, and is an excellent metal to use when making amulets to attract better fortune, good luck, and an inflow of money or goods. Do not use Tin out of greed, merely to satisfy needs, or it will throw you into further imbalance.

TOPAZ

This is the stone that Paracelsus says will shine at night. The Topaz is said to hold some aspects of the sunlight, and carry it through all times, even though the yellow color of the stone comes from the presence of iron oxide.

Many virtues follow the Topaz: wisdom, beauty, strength, loyalty, knowledge, enlightenment, and others. The stone is placed under the rulership of the Sun, and has been used to invoke Apollo and other Sun Gods.

Topaz appears as one of the stones chosen by Aaron, and is also listed as one of the stones of the Apocalypse. It is said to increase joy and happiness, and to cause depression and down-hearted spirits to pass away.

As a talisman, Topaz has been variously used to control lust and greed, to cure insanity, to calm anger and prevent its arousal, and to stop insomnia and bring refreshing sleep. It is capable of giving off an electrical charge, and this property is seen as its means of passing on the goodness of radiant solar energy.

Medically, Topaz has been used to aid the heart, stop bleeding, and correct poor vision. W. B. Crow says Topaz may be used to invoke Gemini.

TURQUOISE

This is definitely a stone of protection. It is said to protect the wearer against snakebite, poisons, blindness, black magick, and gives one the ability to stand in the midst of dangerous and wild beasts, and remain unharmed.

Turquoise is the stone chosen by Moslems, upon which they inscribe verses in tiny script, as talismans of their religion and of protection. In the west, Turquoise is believed to protect both the horse and the rider against all danger.

This is a hydrated phosphate of aluminum and copper, and has been magickally used to banish evil, to protect against all negative energies, and to attract both love and money.

It is said to keep the wearer in good health, and will change color with the aura of the wearer, moving from light to dark. Among its healing virtues are the abililites to treat both melancholy and malaria.

THE RITUAL USE OF HERBES

THE RITUAL USE OF HERBES

Ritual is a highly personal means of reaching out to experience the Universe. For some it is the only means of religious expression possible. For others, it may be adjunct to religion as a means of channeling the healing energies of the Divine for personal use, such as healing, house blessing, and celebration of special days. Ritual is a means of preparing a temple space in which one has total control over all the energies, in order to open one's most inner, divine self to the Mysteries of the Universe.

Ritual is an art and a skill; thus all are capable of learning safe and sane procedures and using the tool of ritual to expand levels of consciousness. Each time the practitioner casts a Circle and reaches out, the limits are taken further. Each time a ritual coincides with the harmonious junctions of the solar system (such as lunar changes and those points on the Wheel of the Year), the self is brought more fully into natural rhythms, and becomes more than an egocentric individual.

For those who develop the arts and skills inherent in the adept practise of ritual, there are great changes to be gained in terms of personality, ego, and self-knowledge. The ego becomes perceived as a tool, rather than that willful master which controls a life. Responsibility is taken for all that is encountered in life, for we come to understand that *we* are the true masters of our lives. We *do* get what we want, even during those long and dark periods when we heap negative wishes upon the self; when we unwittingly make endless statements of self-negation, and then beat our breasts and wonder why we are getting less than our neighbors. Psychic energy is totally psychosomatic. Ritual is capable of being a path for many (although not for everyone) in which we learn to generate only positive energies toward the destinies of our lives.

Although it is possible to touch and to have access to great amounts of energy within ritual, you will not have this power unless it is sought. You will not encounter demons unless they already lurk in your mind. Ritual merely focuses and intensifies that to which you already have access. For that reason, heed this advice: Never, never treat ritual casually and without forethought. Always do thorough ritual sweeping, and be certain that you have meticulously examined your motives. Should you enter a cast Circle with anger in your heart, you will find that anger magnified in the depths of the Universe. Should you carry dark and lurking fears, you will have to confront them. And also avoid taking ritual too seriously, for it is when we dance the ancient dance that we are as children playing theatrically.

Follow your script carefully, for then you may set aside the ego, and play as one of the God/desses. It is then you may wear the shoes of the Ancients, and dance as one who has lived many lives and will dance again and again in joy upon the Earth. In many senses, ritual is making believe, much as you did when a child. In Christian words, we must take back the child-within, in order to reach those joys which exist beyond this life. Thus it is: ritual may be as simple as a meditation upon a leaf slipping from a tree, and it may be lavish with drifting plumes of incense and hand-sewn robes. There may be masks, props, songs, feasting; there may be the use of traditional ritual tools such as those described within this chapter; you may find that tools used in other Traditional approaches suit your needs and work for you. You may also find that those which are yet to be borne of your imagination are the ones in your future.

IMAGICK

Words create thoughtforms; thoughts create images and symbols. Symbols are the true channels of the inner vision of our minds; the ultimate being and power of the mind talks with the Universe through symbolic images. Within this concept are some of the greatest lessons of esoteric orders and magickal traditions.

In the same manner, we are able to use herblore as a means of communicating with the subconscious. The potency of Magick is defined by the worth of the imagery and symbolic input of the inner mind. For one who would become an Herbalist Adept, the ritual is ever connected to the use of Magickal Herbes. They can be the means of casting the Circle (in the Ritual of Handfasting within the Tradition of the Rowan Tree, the Circle is cast by strewing flower petals). They can be placed in water used to bless the Circle; they are the incense; they are the ritual cup; they are the means of saying "I am One with the Earth." Use them wisely and the Herbes will be your greatest teachers. And always they will say "work in love."

PREPARATION OF RITUAL TOOLS

TEMPLE   The actual space in which you cast your Circle or set your altar, or worship in your own manner, may be cleansed and purified with the following herbes. You may use them in water for cleaning, or bunch them to aspurge the space with sacred water, or in any manner you choose. You may also use them as incense.
  • Broom, Camphor, Fumitory

CANDLES   Everyone loves the glow of a candle. In most ritual practise, candles are prepared by lightly coating them with an oil so that the candle is dedicated to ritual use and will not also be lit for a party. There are some herbes traditionally used for this purpose. You may purchase an extracted oil, or macerate your own.
  • Balm of Gilead, Jasmine, Lotus Flower, Myrrh, Olive

RITUAL KNIVES   The use of a sacred blade in a ritual is of long-standing history, from the athame of a Witch to the sacred sword of a Catholic Bishop. These are one of the four tools of Tarot, and represent one fourth of the manifest reality we encounter in our lives. Various herbal woods are used for the handles, with mistletoe being most prominent. The following herbes are used in the consecration of the knife.
  • Ginger, Holly, Mistletoe, Nettles, Pimpernel, Wolfsbane

WANDS   Wands and staves (the plural of staff) are also tools of Tarot. They date to before the time of Aaron, and are still in use today. One of the powerful symbols of Christ was the shepherd's staff. Herbes often chosen to be made into a wand are:
  • Almond, Ash, Bamboo, Mistletoe, Oak, Thorn, Willow
      Once made or adapted, the wand or staff must be consecrated for the sacred purpose. Its use in a ritual is to take control over the space which was 'carved' out of the mundane for sacred use. These herbes which will help consecrate a wand to that use are:
  • Asphodel, Cedar, Frankincense

CHALICES   Perhaps the most graceful of the four tools of Tarot, the Chalice is used to contain the holy water, and (in a different Chalice) the ritual cup. The ritual cup is the beverage which is taken by the Priest and/or Priestess, and may or may not be shared by other participants. In many religions this drink is wine, but for the Traditional Herbalist, we cannot miss a chance to partake of earthly wisdom. Herbes used to consecrate Chalices are:
  • Anise, Verbena, Tarragon, Watercress

PENTACLES   The last tool of Tarot and of the classic four would be the pentacle. The blade represents air (in most practises), the wand, fire, and the chalice is associated with water. The Pentacle is a symbol of the element Earth. It is a round, flat disk, much as the Earth appears to our eye. A common traditional approach would have the Pentacle made of copper, but there are other options open to the practitioner: Herbes used in the consecration of the Pentacle are:
  • Clover, Ivy

Similar to the Pentacle, yet of a different purpose is the altar stone. Should you have one, the appropriate herbe to use in its consecration would be Verbena. If you choose to have a special cloth to cover your altar and altar stone, consecrate it with Sandalwood.

SACRED BOOKS   If you keep a personal book of your ritual and sacred materials, there are several herbes which are associated with this tool. Dragon's Blood makes an appropriate ink for writing in your Book, and Dogwood and Mulberry are used in the consecration. Take a Mulberry Leaf, and press it someplace and keep it within your book to guard its secrets. Dogwood makes a fine incense for the consecration.

THURIBLES & ASPURGERS   The preparation of a sacred space usually encompasses two processes. One is to aspurge the space, usually with water which has a bit of salt mingled with it, to combine Earth and Water. This is done to cleanse the Circle or Temple. One manner of aspurging, or sprinkling, is to take a bunch of herbes, bind them with a ribbon, and dip them into the water chalice. Herbes used thusly are:

- Fennel, Hyssop, Lavender, Mints, Rosemary, Sage, Valerian, Verbena

The other process in the preparation is to cense the space. For the use of herbal incense, place a charcoal block in a thurible, and sprinkle loose incense on top of it. The thurible must be made of a material able to withstand intense heat from the burning charcoal, and should also be equipped for carrying, so you can take it about your sacred space. In consecrating a thurible, which will carry both Air and Fire, use Olive oil.

OTHER TOOLS   Herbes which are used in the consecration of tools in general are:
- Burnet, Caraway, Dragon's Blood, Fumitory, Gum Mastic, Solomon's Seal

RITUALS OF HOUSE BLESSING

These are rites conducted in and around the home, to cleanse a new residence of old energies left behind by previous and possibly unknown tenants. The purposes of these rites are to cleanse (exorcise) old and negative energies, and to bring in those energies which will protect and bless the home and those who will both reside and pass through it. A ritual of Home Blessing should involve all members of the family, but may be performed by a trusted family Priest/ess.

BASIL   Basil should be added to the water used in scrubbing the floors, walls, and in any cleaning of the home previous to unpacking and getting settled. An often used part of a house and home blessing is a planting ceremony. Basil is an herbe to plant, for it will bring protection and good fortune to those who live within.

BAY LAUREL   Bay Laurel should be hung someplace in the home. It can be included with other hanging herbes, or a leaf can be secreted here and there.

BITTERSWEET   This is a hanging herbe, and should be tied alone or with others, with brightly colored ribbons.

CAMPHOR   This herbe is used in cleansing. Some of it may be added to the cleaning water. When the home has been thoroughly cleansed, but before any possessions have been moved in,

317

a thurible should be set in a central location, and camphor burnt upon a glowing block of charcoal. The smoke should be allowed to fill all the rooms of the residence, which is a sure way to exorcise old and unwanted energies. As we so rarely have the opportunity to go about cleaning in this manner, Camphor is excellent when added to the incense for the ritual.

CARAWAY   This herbe is best used in the initial cleaning. It may also be made into a wash which will be used in the aspurging of the Circle, Temple, or entire home during the ritual.

CORIANDER   This is a hanging herbe, tied with ribbons.

COWSLIP   Hang Cowslip, preferably with other herbes.

DILL   Dill may be planted, used in cleaning, or added to the incense. Dill-seed cakes make a good ritual bread for all to share at the bread-breaking part of the ritual.

ELDER   Small, equal-armed crosses of Elder are placed in each room. The same method is used to protect household pets. Elder blossoms make an excellent fixative for the incense, and may be added to the beverage which will be shared by all as the ritual cup.

FLAX   The dried flowers of Flax may be scattered throughout the house as part of the blessing ceremony.

HOREHOUND   This herbe is best used in the ritual cup, although its extreme taste requires moderation.

MINTS   These make wonderful planting herbes, but may be used in any manner in any part of the house blessing.

MISTLETOE   This herbe should be tied with red ribbon and hung at Yule. Not only does it fill your home with extra kisses; it also brings protection and good fortune. Leave it up all year. The following Yule, the old should be placed in the Yule fire and the new hung in its place.

ROWAN   If possible, this should be planted, as a young tree, to grow with the family. Small crosses will make talismans of protection.

318

RUE   This herbe is best when placed in a small bag to hang as an amulet. Seal the bag with red thread, and place within it something personal of each family member (even, as the witches do, a hair.)

SAINT JOHN'S WORT   This herbe should be tossed into the fire. The ideal would be a hearth fire, in the fireplace which will be most used. If this is not the case, take a cauldron and set it in the room which will be the center of family activities, and perform this protection ritual there.

THE GREAT RITE

This is a very solemn and joyful ritual, performed traditionally by a man and a woman. There are many theories surrounding this ritual, and they are personal. The woman ritually embodies the principal of the Goddess, the feminine aspect of the Universe, the element of Yin. The man ritually takes on the other half of all being: the male aspect, the God manifest, the element of Yang. The coming together of these two persons sexually is perceived as representative of the creative forces of the Universe, and is done for reasons beyond the personal. The energy tapped into by this mating is often used for healing, spiritual transformation, for transcendental achievements, and for healing the Earth. Under no circumstances should this ritual be taken lightly or for carnal experience, for as in the sexual forms of Yoga, the goal is internal.

CORIANDER   Excellent in a ritual beverage, this may be shared in the ritual cup by both.

CUBEB BERRIES   These may be macerated into an oil, used for lubrication. Do not use excessively, for they are rubefacient and irritant in nature.

DAMIANA   This herbe may be made into a ritual beverage, but may be taken even prior to the ritual. Some use it as a douche (either vaginal or anal) to increase sexual pleasure.

HENNA   This is made into either oil or ointment, and is seen as primarily for the male organs. It will leave color behind.

KAVA KAVA   This herbe is best taken in the ritual cup. It can be steeped quite strong, and may also be taken at least an hour before the ritual.

LEMON   The peel of the lemon is dried, and ground into a powder. This is excellent in the incense for these rituals.

LOVAGE   This herbe is best used in the ritual bath, as a bathing herbe. This bath is most fun when shared, but each can take it separately, if that is seen as better mental preparation.

MANDRAKE   There are a number of ways this herbe can be used. Each may wear a piece of the root as a ritual necklace. The ritual cup may be made of Moon Water or Mandrake. A piece of the root may be added to the herbes used in macerating a lubricant. Use no more than one small piece.

MARSHMALLOW   This herbe makes an excellent lubricant.

MISTLETOE   Add several of the berries to the mixture being made into a lubricant. A few of the berries, dried, may be ground and added to the incense.

ORCHID ROOT   A slice of the fresh root, taken from a healthy, firm, and full-grown root may be eated as the ritual food, shared between the two persons.

PATCHOULI   This herbe is best used in the form of oil, used to dress (anoint) the candles, and may be used to anoint the two bodies following the ritual bath. It may also be added to lubricant.

ROSE GERANIUM   This herbe may be used in like fashion to Patchouli, but the two do not blend well.

SESAME   The oil of this herbe makes an excellent fixative for lubricants.

SOUTHERNWOOD   This herbe is used in the ritual bath for men.

RITUALS OF PURIFICATION

These rituals are generally performed for two purposes. The first is to rid the self of a period of self-negation, doubts, fears, or troublesome negative energies that follow the self around like a minor plague. In this case, the ritual is seen as a minor exorcism, or cleansing. In the other case, the ritual is performed in preparation for an event one wishes to enter in a spiritually clean manner, such as an initiation, handfasting, or the like. Some view a ritual of purification in similar manner to a baptism, but this is a personal view and not a general theory. A Ritual of Purification should only be performed for the self, or for another *if* it is requested by that person. To perform the ritual for someone who has not requested it, is psychic manipulation, and will cause trouble for the ritual practitioner. The ritual is most effective performed solitary. If you feel a need for purification, and do not feel capable of performing the ritual, seek out your Priest/ess.

ANGELICA This herbe may be used in the ritual bath preceding the rite of purification. It is also excellent in the ritual cup, and may be added to the incense.

ASAFOETIDA This herbe may be used to cense the ritual Circle or the temple. For self-cleansing, prepare your thurible and stand over it, allowing the smoke to swirl all about your body. Keep your eyes closed, and your mind focused.

BASIL This herbe is one of the best, and may be used in nearly any manner. You may bathe with it, drink it, burn it, wear it, or anything you imagine. It is very cleansing, and prepares you also to embrace the new.

BLESSED THISTLE This herbe is best used added to the Ritual Cup, and consumed as the beverage.

ELECAMPAGNE This herbe is excellent in the incense, and may also be taken in the ritual cup.

FRANKINCENSE This herbe is best used as an incense for the Circle.

FUMITORY   This herbe should be used to cense the body, and in turn will cleanse the aura.

HYSSOP   This herbe is one of the best bathing herbes for purification. It may also be added to wash water for your clothing, and placed in an amulet to wear. It may be incorporated easily into any part of the ritual of purification.

MANDRAKE   This herbe is most effective if taken in Moon Water, that is by placing a small piece of the root in a container of water at the new moon, and leaving it until the Full before drinking it.

SAGE   Sage is excellent for cleaning the self of negative energies. It may be taken as a magickal tonic, or in the ritual cup.

TANSY   Take this herbe as a daily magickal tonic, beginning during the ritual and continuing for a full lunar (28 days) cycle.

VALERIAN   This is an herbe of cleansing, and may be drunk in moderation only, during the ritual. You may also use it in the water used to aspurge the Circle, and the self.

RITUALS OF THE DEAD

These rituals are also known by some as Requiems. They are performed for a two-fold purpose. On the one hand, they are seen as a source of comfort for the living, but the primary purpose is for the spiritual essence of the loved one whose body has died. There is no culture nor religion that does not have rituals for this purpose, and this is verification of the effectiveness. The rituals are variously seen as giving peace to the departed, keeping the departed from hell or other forms of evil, and guiding the departed's spirit towards a joyful existence, or heaven, or the Summerland, as one's personal beliefs may prefer.

ACONITE   This herbe has been administered as a ritual cup when a person was dying (at the moment of death). For those who practised euthanasia, this was the herbe they dispensed. Following burial, this herbe would be planted on the grave. It may be used in the incense during the ritual.

ANEMONE   The flowers may be tossed into a cauldron fire during the ceremony, indicating the passage of the body into a new existence as pure energy, with the wish for reincarnation.

ANISE, STAR   This herbe is excellent for the ritual cup, for incense, and if the climate permits, for growing on the grave.

ASPHODEL   Traditionally grown on the grave, this herbe is excellent for bathing the dying body, or washing the corpse. It may be gathered into a bunch, tied with a ribbon, and used to aspurge the body during the ritual.

BASIL   This herbe is excellent in the incense. It is unsurpassed for bringing courage and dignity to one facing death.

BLUEBELLS   These are grave flowers, planted to bring peace and blessings. They may also be used to decorate the altar.

CHERVIL   This herbe should be taken as a ritual cup, to aid in the communion with the soul of the departed, to guide the spirit to peace and serenity.

ELDER   For those desiring cremation, this herbe makes the best wood for the pyre. As this is rarely feasible in these times, those personal belongings which need to be sent with the soul should be burnt over a fire of Elder wood. A sprig of Elder may be buried with the body.

LOTUS   The pod of the blossom should be used as an incense burner to aid the soul in seeking reincarnation.

MANDRAKE   Bury some root with the body to protect the spirit, and send it safely on its way.

MARJORAM   This should be planted on the grave.

MYRRH   This herbe has been used in embalming, and now is used in the incense of the ritual.

PARSLEY   If the body is to be transported, Parsley is strewn in the path. It should also be planted on the burial site.

PENNYROYAL   Bathe the body of the dead with this herbe, and it will assist the soul in being reborn.

PERIWINKLE   This herbe should be woven into a wreath, and placed upon the coffin. It is of particular value for deceased children.

TANSY   This herbe was, in times past, used for embalming. It is now used to aspurge the temple, and the deceased.

THYME   This herbe makes an excellent ritual cup to take before communing with the deceased.

VIOLETS   These are best planted on the graves of children, and may be used to decorate the altars at the rituals.

WILLOW   It is said that you should plant a willow during your life-time, and its life at your death will ease the soul. Willow branches may be planted on the grave site, or buried with the casket.

RITUALS OF BABY BLESSING

These rituals are performed to welcome a new spirit into the world. Some religions call this rite baptism, others wiccaning, and some have no name for it. Some use this ritual to dedicate the baby to the religion of its parents, or to provide for alternative care and responsibility in case the parents are lost. The primary purpose of the ritual may be perceived as a welcoming of the new child into the social life of the family, and to give the child its name.

CEDAR   This makes an excellent incense ingredient.

DAISIES   These flowers should be used to decorate the altar and the crib.

ELDER   The flowers make a fixative for the incense, and the wood may be made into a wash to bathe the child prior to the rite. A wash of Elder may be used to symbolically or literally bathe the baby during the ritual.

ELECAMPAGNE   This herbe is excellent added to incense.

FLAX   Prior to the ritual, a baby should be allowed to nap in a field (or patch) of flax.

IRIS   A small patch of Iris should be planted the day of the ceremony. This may be done as part of the rite, or not, as you wish. This will bring happiness to the growing child.

LAVENDER   This herbe is traditionally used as incense when the child is being born. It may be used in any manner during the ritual.

MILKWEED   The juice of this herbe may be used to anoint the child during the rite, bringing inspiration, imagination, and creativity.

MULBERRY   A leaf should be placed near the crib to protect the baby.

PARSLEY   The expectant mother should bathe in parsley root water, thus bringing extra care and protection for the baby. Some parsley root water may be used to aspurge the baby at the rite.

ROSEMARY   This herbe should be added to the incense.

UNICORN ROOT   This herbe is excellent when made into an amulet for the baby.

RITUALS OF UNION

This ritual may be a handfasting, an old form of ritual in which the hands of the two are bound together and not released until they have later, in private, celebrated the Great Rite. This ritual may also be a legal wedding. Some use the two terms of handfasting and wedding interchangeably, and others do not. These herbes are for rites in which the two come together, make sacred vows to cherish that union and honor their commitments, and leave united by those vows.

ANISE SEED   This herbe is traditionally baked into the cake.

BROOM   This should be gathered live, and tied with ribbons to decorate the space. It may also be tied into a bunch like a 'broom,' over which the couple will jump during the ceremony, symbolically leaving their old, un-united life behind.

CARAWAY   This herbe is sometimes baked into the cake, and the seed is often thrown at the couple following the ceremony.

CORIANDER   This herbe belongs in the ritual cup.

IVY   This herbe is for decoration. Wreaths may be woven and worn by the couple, and it may be used to decorate the altar and place of the ritual.

LAVENDER   This herbe is also worn as a wreath. It may be taken in the ritual cup.

MARJORAM   This herbe is excellent used as incense in the ritual cup, or worn.

MEADOWSWEET   This herbe, gathered while in bloom, is best in the bouquet of the bride.

MISTLETOE   Two berries should be among the herbes used to make the ritual cup.

ORCHID ROOT   The flowers are appropriate for wearing, and some of the root may be added to the ritual cup.

QUINCE   This should be included among the food of the feast.

ROSES   Particularly the red varieties, Roses are best used in decoration, may be worn or included in the bouquets, and the petals may be used in the blessing of the Circle.

ROSEMARY   Tradition says that a bunch of Rosemary should be tied with a ribbon and presented to each guest. To help each person remember this occasion with special fondness, Rosemary may be added to the incense mixture, and to the ritual cup.

SKULLCAP   A small amount of Skullcap in a ritual cup should be shared as the vows are exchanged, binding them and making them sacred.

YARROW   If you wish your ceremony to be festive, include Yarrow in the bouquets, and have a small bunch of it given to each guest to wear.

LUNAR RITUALS

The most commonly celebrated ritual is that of the Full Moon. At the moments of the Full Moon, the Earth is poised in a magickal balance between the Moon and the Sun. The side bathing itself among the stars is lit by the Moon, and the opposite side is radiant in Sunlight. For those who see the practise of ritual as a means of increasing inner awareness, the Full Moon is an amazing time to be in a cast Circle or in a temple. Sacred surroundings allow the practitioner to set aside the ego and cares of the mundane world, and in this secure psychic shell (as most view the sacred Circle) reach out with psychic and spiritual awareness to feel the delicate balance of Moon and Sun, as they bathe this beautiful planet we live on. It is easy to find numerous magazine and newspaper articles describing Full Moon events; the busiest of times in emergency rooms, more babies being born and higher tides. The Moon's gravity is strong enough that there are places on Earth where the crust (not waters) is raised nearly twelve feet beneath a Full Moon. No wonder that for many thousands of years the Full Moon was held as particularly mystical.

Where does the Full Moon come from? This is in terms of magick and astrology, and is a rhetorical question. She, for only in feminine terms can we see something so graceful and beautiful, begins at the New Moon, when we cannot see Her, for she is in the same place as the Sun. The New Moon is second in intensity to the Full Moon, and is seen as the beginning. In ancient times, the Moon would be missing from the night-time sky, leaving it particularly dark and awesome. And, on those special occasions when the Moon and Sun were in a very exact line, an eclipse would occur. In some cultures this was terrifying, in others it was a time of the most incredible magick. The most common association with the Moon was to refer to her as a Goddess. Much of human history is filled with human interpretations of the Divine in masculine and feminine symbols, and the most prominent symbol of the Feminine Divine was as Moon Goddess.
Those who thus perceived the Moon felt the Goddess also as Earth, and as other aspects of nature . . . "I am the beauty of the green Earth, and the white Moon among the skies, and the mysteries of the waters, and the desire in the hearts of humans," speaks the Goddess in modern literature.

The other half of the Divine was seen as the male principal, and was embodied by the Sun. Lunar celebrations, then, are particularly focused on the relationship between Moon and Sun, and their effect upon the Earth.

CHAMOMILE   This herbe may be used to invoke the God. It should be made into a ritual cup and taken by the Priest.

CHASTE TREE This herbe may be used to invoke the Goddess. It should be made into a ritual cup and taken by the Priestess.

CORNFLOWER This herbe may be used to invoke the Goddess. It may be taken by one reaching out to the Moon.

CUCUMBER Tradition would place pieces of the peel upon our eyelids as we lay in the temple, meditating on the energy of the Universe.

GARLIC This herbe is appropriate for use during the waning moon and at New Moon rituals.

MANDRAKE Take a piece of mandrake root and place it in a container of water. A chalice or special vase would be appropriate. This should be set in 'moonlight' each night until the Moon is full. In practise this means to set it out from twilight to just before dawn, keeping it away from sunlight. This, when done, is known as Moon Water.

MOTHERWORT This herbe is excellent for inclusion in the ritual cup.

PEONY ROOT Pieces of the root make an excellent ritual necklace.

POMEGRANATE This herbe is known for its use in rituals of all-women.

YARROW Yarrow is a fine herbe used to invoke the God aspect of divinity.

THE WHEEL OF THE YEAR

In ancient times, the passage of time was marked by eight great festivals. These existed in various forms in nearly all countries, and we find them even today. They have been Christianized, they have undergone transformation in cultures just as politics and religion have changed over the ages, yet they persist. Four of them are quite specific, as they mark the beginnings of the four seasons, and are determined by the passage of the Sun. The other four are determined in a more arbitrary fashion, and have shifted dates a bit over the years. They go by countless names, each culture having several names for each holiday, and they are rich in mythology, filled with stories of Gods and Goddesses, and told in order to pass on the mystical interpretation of how life functions, of the passage of time, and even of how all must die in time, but yet has a promise of something more.

SPRING

The beginning of the zodiacal year is at Spring, when the Sun moves into 0 degrees Aries. This is not necessarily the beginning of the Wheel of the Year, for it is perpetual, and the beginning holiday varies in different places. Traditionally, this is a season of birth, of resurrection following the winter. Among the names for this season is Eostre.

ACORN   An acorn can be planted as part of the celebration of Spring. It should have been gathered the previous year and saved, and will represent the beginning of the planting season, and also those attributes you wish to increase internally this growing cycle.

BULBS   Any flowers grown from bulbs, daffodils, crocus, and the like are most appropriate for altar and temple decorations.

CELANDINE   This herbe should be included in the ritual cup.

CINQUEFOIL   A pinch of the dried leaves will help the incense.

DOGWOOD   This herbe is one of the best for Spring, the flowers bringing beauty to the temple, and the dried bark being ground into the incense mixture.

HONEYSUCKLE   To display the promise of Spring, no matter how severe the winter, the flowers should grace the sacred Circle.

IRIS   The ground, dried roots are desirable for the incense mixture.

JASMINE   Although excellent in the incense, Jasmine, as a tea, makes a good ritual cup.

ROSE   Yellow Roses are appropriate.

SEEDS   Any seeds from the previous harvest should be brought into the ritual, to bless them for the Spring planting, that the crops be bountiful and healthy.

TANSY   Ritual cakes for Spring and Easter should have some Tansy in them.

VIOLETS   These delicate flowers make wonderful altar flowers.

MAY EVE

Who can resist the pleasures of May? The Sun in romantic Taurus, the seeds planted in the fields, and the work of weeding and tilling balanced by rapture, for the trees are lush and the Earth is in bloom. An old rhyme goes "hooray, hooray for the month of May, outdoor loving starts today." At last it is warm enough that it almost feels like Summer, and we celebrate the changes in the weather and energy. May Day has become very political in many countries, but there are still many who celebrate the old festival of Beltane, which is but one of the names for this turning point in the Wheel of the Year.

ALMOND   If you are fortunate to have flowering Almond for your celebration, use it to decorate your temple.

CINQUEFOIL   Add a pinch of Cinquefoil to ritual cup and to incense.

FRANKINCENSE   As we celebrate the growing Sunlight, use Frankincense as a main ingredient in your incense.

IVY   Wreathes of Ivy should be worn around the head, and Ivy may be used for decoration.

MARIGOLD PETALS   Gathered the previous Autumn, use Marigold petals to purify your Circle.

MAYBASKETS   This is a tradition that should be kept: place little baskets of flowers and homemade treats at the doors of your friends. It is best done anonymously, so that it will seem more like a gift from the Universe rather than an individual.

MEADOWSWEET   Do some magickal work with Meadowsweet if you want to make a May Eve wish for a romantic mate.

ROSES   Any roses are appropriate for this ritual.

SATYRIAN ROOT   This herbe should be added to both ritual cup and to incense.

WOODRUFF   The best way to use Woodruff in your Circle is to have some delicious May Wine, which can be found at most liquor stores.

MIDSUMMER

What a curious name is Midsummer, for it is not the middle of summer at all, but the beginning. It feels like the middle of summer fun and warmth, however, for this is the longest day of the year, when we have more sunlight than any other time. From Midsummer on, we find the days too hot to do much work, and we bake beneath the sun until we are lightly browned. Midsummer's Eve has long been celebrated, as we find it even among Shakespeare's works. Who can resist going out to play when we can frolic in the woodlands until late at night?

CHAMOMILE   Used to invoke the God, Chamomile will make us aware of the Father of Nature.

CINQUEFOIL   As in the preceeding two festivals, we add a pinch of Cinquefoil to the ritual cup and incense.

ELDER   If you have enough of the child in you, go stand among the Elder groves on Midsummer's Eve, and you are sure to see the little people and the faeries.

FENNEL   This is the night to have bunches of ribbon-tied fennel hanging at the portals of your home.

HEMP   An interesting divination is to sow Hemp seed around a church; the first person you see will be your new love.

LAVENDER   A bonfire is a very common element of the Midsummer rituals. Traditionally, you would toss some lavender into the fire to ensure a safe year.

MALE FERN   This is the night to gather Male Fern.

MISTLETOE   If you desire any Mistletoe for magickal purposes, you should gather it this night.

MUGWORT   Use this herbe for your ritual bath, and for the ritual cup.

ROSES   Decorate with red Roses. You may use red Rose petals in your incense and to bless the Circle.

SAINT JOHN'S WORT   This is the time to gather this herbe, and also to cast some into the fire.

VERBENA   At Midsummer, gather the new Verbena you will need for coming year, and throw the old into the fire.

LAMMAS

Lammas marks the beginning of the harvest cycle, for the days are growing noticably shorter. With the nights longer, we have respite from Summer's heat, and though we toil in the fields all day, we can sleep soundly with the cooling nights. From this day, we harvest and work to gather our crops, both literally and spiritually, until the first frost of Autumn.

FENUGREEK   As we note the waning of the Sun, Fenugreek may be used to invoke the God.

FRANKINCENSE   Long associated with solar deities, Frankincense may be used to cense the gardens and fields at the beginning of the harvest.

HEATHER   Heather may be used to decorate, along with various grains from the coming harvest: wheat, rye, and the like.

HOLLYHOCK   One long stalk of Hollyhock may be carried by the children, at the beginning of the ritual procession to the fields.

MISTLETOE   Two of the berries should be added to the ritual cup.

OAK   Use some leaves to decorate, and some of the bark in the incense.

PRODUCE   A few samples of the first produce should be brought into the rite, both for decoration, and as part of the feast.

SUNFLOWER   This magnificent blossom may be used for decoration, or in any other manner.

AUTUMN

We hope that our harvest is complete at Autumn, although with modern technology and hybrids this is rarely the case. Autumn marks the halfway mark from the longest day to the shortest day, and is a sign that we need to begin preparations for the darkest half of the year. With the main work done in the fields, Autumn marks the beginning of a season in which we must busy ourselves outside, and complete our projects before Winter's cold arrives.

ACORNS   Acorns make excellent decorations, and may be strung into necklaces.

BENZOIN   Used in the incense, it makes us more aware of the balance of light and dark.

FERNS   This is an appropriate time to gather Ferns.

HONEYSUCKLE   The dried, ground wood and bark make excellent incense.

MARIGOLD   Decorate with the blossoms, which are very full at this time of year.

MILKWEED   There are faeries and little folk about at Autumn, and Milkweed is the herbe to help you see them.

MYRRH   Use Myrrh for your incense, and some of it for the ritual cup.

PASSION FLOWER   Place the flower petals in your incense.

PRODUCE   The custom of fairs, in which your best produce is taken to show with pride the harvest, is carried through in the ritual, where the best of each crop is brought into the ceremony.

ROSE   White Roses are appropriate.

SAGE   Use Sage in the ritual cup.

SOLOMON'S SEAL   Use this herbe to cast your Circle.

THISTLES   These herbes are appropriate to show the endurance it will take to outlast winter.

HALLOWS

This night of pumpkins and ghosts has ancient origins, for all around us we can see the Earth pass into a dying cycle. The grass turns brown, the leaves fall from the trees, and more than likely the first snows of winter will arrive long before the Sun reaches Capricorn. Ancient tales teach us that on this night we move into the space of the underground. In order that the Sun will begin growing again at Yule, and that the Earth will return fertile and growing at Spring, we must pass through the valley of death. No wonder that we light pumpkins with candles to keep safe our homes.

ACORNS   Symbolic of life contained within, Acorns are much used at Hallows for decoration.

APPLES   Apples are used for the feast, the bark ground for the incense, and they are pretty. Bobbing for Apples is traditional for this holiday.

CORNSTALKS   A few bundles of Cornstalks stir the right imagination for this night.

DITTANY OF CRETE   Some of this herbe should be tossed in the fire, for it is traditional on this night to share with those of our loved ones who have passed into death.

FUMITORY   Use this in your incense.

MULLEIN   Spears of Mullein should be gathered in advance, and dried. The flower tops may be soaked in oil or fat, and then you have torches which provide good light and Hallows atmosphere.

NIGHTSHADE, DEADLY   This is the night to gather this herbe.

OAK   The leaves should be used in decorating.

PUMPKINS   Probably the most frequent symbol of Hallows other than Witches, we can both decorate with them and eat them!

SAGE   Use Sage in the ritual cup.

YULE

The celebration of Midwinter begins as the Sun moves into zero degrees Capricorn, and we have the beginning of this season. It is the shortest day of the year, and from this night on, the Sun grows in strength and duration until the zenith of Summer. It is traditional for this to be the birth of the Sun God, and of God Manifest. The tradition is so strong that the Christian church chose this time of year to celebrate the birth of Christ, for it is common among religions to celebrate the birth of the God at this time of year. Christmas as we celebrate it today is a rich mixture of old, Pagan traditions and newer Christian.

BLESSED THISTLE   This herbe, taken by the Priest from the ritual cup, is used to invoke the Sun God, who will grow to become the Father of the harvest.

CHAMOMILE   This herbe is also used to symbolize the Sun God, and may be used to cast the Circle, in the incense and cup, and may be used prior to the ceremony as a bathing herbe by the Priest chosen to represent the new Sun.

EVERGREEN   The only plants which look as if they enjoy this weather, Evergreens are used profusely at this time of year. Boughs are hung about, and a Yule tree is traditional in nearly all homes. The needles make excellent incense.

FRANKINCENSE   This solar herbe is excellent incense.

HOLLY   Use Holly to decorate your entire home.

MISTLETOE   Add Mistletoe to your incense, and hang it in doorways to fill your home with extra kisses. Each person at the ritual should toss a Mistletoe berry into the fire, to represent those personal things one desires to increase as the Sun grows towards Summer.

PINE   Pine is often used as a Yule tree and is excellent for incense.

SAGE   Taken in the ritual cup, Sage helps us to stay bright and sunny in disposition, even though the days of Sunlight are short.

CANDLEMAS

Candlemas is also known by some as the "Feast of the Waxing Light," for it marks that time of year when everyone is talking about increasing hours of daylight. Even though we still have half of winter to endure, Spring's promise cannot be far behind, for we can see it with the lengthening days.

ANGELICA   Best used as an herbe in the ritual cup.

BASIL   Candlemas is a traditional time of the year for initiations. If you are preparing for initiation, Basil is perhaps the best herbe to take as a magickal tonic.

BAY   If your Candlemas ritual is peaceful and solemn, you may chew one (no more) fresh Bay Leaf, and meditate on the growing light.

BENZOIN   Use Benzoin in your incense.

CELANDINE   In addition to use in the ritual cup, some Celandine may be tossed into the ritual fire.

HEATHER   Heather is one of the best herbes for decoration. There are several choices: some of us are fortunate to find it at a florist this time of year, and others will need to collect it when available, and dry it. Heather is very attractive when dried.

MYRRH   Myrrh may be used in the ritual cup or in incense.

APPENDICIES

APPENDIX I
HERBAL/PLANETARY CORRESPONDENCES

Herb	Botanical Name	Planetary Ruler
Acacias	leguminosae	Mars
Aconite	aconitum anthora	Saturn
Acorns	quercus robur	Earth
Adam & Eve Root	*	Neptune
Adder's Tongue	ophioglossum vulgatum	Moon/Cancer
Agaric	agaricus	Mercury/Leo
Agaric	agaricus	Pluto
Agrimony	agrimonia eupatoria	Jupiter/Cancer
Alder (Black)	alnus nigra	Venus/Cancer
Alder (Common)	alnus glutinosa	Venus/Pisces
Alexander	smyrnium dusatrum	Jupiter/Sagitarius
Alfalfa	*	Jupiter
Alkanet	anchusa tinctoria	Venus
All-Heal	prunella vulgaris	Mars
Allspice	pimento officinalis	Uranus
Almond	anygdalus	Sun
Aloes	aloe vera	Mars, Venus
Alstonia	alstonia scholaris	Mercury
Ambergris	*	Pluto
Amaranthus	amarantus hypochondreacus	Saturn
Anemones	anemone nemorosa	Mars
Angelica	angelica archangelica	Sun/Leo
Anise Seed	pimpenella anisum	Moon
Anise, Star	illicuim verum	Moon/Aquarius
Apple Blossom	pyrus amlus	Venus/Taurus
Apricot	prunus armeniaca	Venus/Neptune
Arbutus, Trailing	epigaea repens	Uranus
Arnica	arnica montana	Saturn
Arrowhead	sagitarria sagittifolia	Jupiter
Arrowroot	maranta arundinaceae	Jupiter
Artichoke, Jerusalem	helianthus tuberosus	Sun
Artichoke, Globe	cynara scolymus	Pluto
Asafoetida	ferula foetida	Pluto
Ash, Mountain	pyrus aucuparia	Moon
Ash Tree	fraxinus excelsior	Sun
Asphodel	asphodelus ramosus	Pluto
Asparagus	asparagus officinalis	Jupiter
Avens	geum herbanum	Jupiter

Azaleas .... • .... Mercury

Balm .... melissa officinalis .... Jupiter/Cancer
Balm of Gilead .... commiphora opobalsamum ...... Venus, Jupiter
Balmony .... chelone glabra .... Neptune
Balsam, White .... gnaphalium polycephalum .... Mercury
Barberry .... berberis vulgaris .... Mars
Barley .... hordeum vulgaris .... Saturn
Basil .... ocymum basicum .... Mars/Scorpio
Basil .... ocymum minimum .... Mars/Scorpio
Bayberry .... myrica cerifera .... Mercury
Bay Tree .... laurus nobilis .... Sun/Leo
Beans .... • .... Venus
Beans .... vicia faba .... Venus
Bearberry .... arctostaphylos uva-ursi .... Mars, Pluto
Bedstraw .... galium verum .... Venus
Beech .... fagus sylvatica .... Mars
Beets .... chenopodiaceae .... Saturn
Belladonna .... atropa belladonna .... Saturn
Benzoin .... styrax benzoin .... Mars
Bergamot .... monarda didyma .... Venus
Betony (Water) .... betonica aquatica .... Jupiter/Cancer
Betony (Wood) .... betonica officinalis .... Jupiter/Aries
Bilberry .... vaccinium myrtillus .... Jupiter
Bindweed .... convolvulus .... Saturn
Birch .... betula alba .... Venus
Bishop's Weed .... ammi majus .... Venus
Bistort .... polygonum bistorta .... Saturn
Bittersweet .... solanum dulcamara .... Mercury
Blackberry .... rubus fruticosus .... Venus/Aries
Bladderwrack .... fucus vesiculosis .... Jupiter
Blessed Thistle .... carduus benedictus .... Mars/Aries
Bloodroot .... sanguinaria candensis .... Venus/Scorpio
Bluebell .... scilla nutans .... Saturn
Boneset .... eupatorium perfoliatum .... Venus, Jupiter
Borage .... borago officinalis .... Jupiter/Leo
Box .... buxux sempervirens .... Pluto/Saturn
Brack Fern .... pteris aquilina .... Mercury
Briony .... byonia .... Mars
Broom .... orobanche major .... Mars
Buckthorn .... rhamnaceae .... Saturn
Buckwheat .... polygonum fagopyrum .... Mercury
Bugle .... ajuga reptans .... Venus
Burdock .... arctium lappa .... Venus
Burnet .... pimpinella saxifraga .... Sun
Butterbur .... petasites vulgaris .... Sun

Cabbage .... • .... Moon
Calamint .... melissa calaminta .... Mercury
Camomile .... anthemis nobilis .... Sun
Campion .... cucubalus behen .... Saturn

342

Caraway	carum carui	Mercury
Cardamom	elettaria cardamomum	Jupiter
Carob	jacaranda procera	Saturn
Carrots	daucus carota	Mercury
Cascara	rhamnaceae	Mercury
Cashew	anacardium occidentale	Mars
Cassia	cinnamomum cassia	Mercury
Catnip	nepeta cataria	Venus
Cayenne	capsicum minimum	Mars
Cedar	thuja occidentalis	Mercury
Cedar Leaf	thuja occidentalis	Mercury
Celandine (Greater)	chelidonium majus	Sun
Celandine (Lesser)	ranunculus ficania	Mars, Sun/Leo
Celery	apium graveolens	Venus
Celery (Domestic)	*	Mercury
Centaury	centaurea cyanus	Sun
Chamomile	anthemis nobilis	Sun
Cherry Tree	*	Venus
Chervil	choerophyllum sativum	Jupiter
Chervil	scandix odorata	Jupiter
Chestnut	castanea vesca	Jupiter
Chick-pea	cicer aristinum	Venus
Chickweed	alsine media	Moon
Chicory	chichorium intybus	Uranus
Chili Powder	capsicum	Mars/Aries
Chives	allium schoenoprasum	Mars
Cinnamon	cinnamomum zeylanicum	Uranus, Sun
Cinquefoil	potentilla	Jupiter, Mercury
Citrus	*	Neptune
Clary	salvia solarea	Moon
Cleavers	galium aparine	Moon
Clematis	clematis recta	Saturn
Clove	eugenia caryophyllata	Uranus
Clover	trifolium	Venus
Cocoa	theobroma cacao	Venus
Coffee	coffea arabica	Uranus, Mercury
Cohosh	*	Pluto
Coltsfoot	tussilago farfara	Venus
Columbines	aquilegia	Venus
Comfrey	symphytum officinale	Saturn/Capricorn
Coolwort	tiarella cordifolia	Moon
Coriander	coriandrum sativum	Moon, Mars
Cornflower	centaurea cyanus	Saturn, Venus
Corn, Indian	zea mays	Jupiter
Costmary	balsamita vulgaris	Jupiter
Cowslips	primula veris	Venus/Aries
Cramp Bark	viburnum opulus	Saturn
Cubebs	piper cubeba	Mars
Cucumbers	cucumis sativa	Moon
Cumin	cuminim cyminum	Mars/Taurus
Currants	ribes	Jupiter

```
Curry . . . . . . . . . . . . . . .   *. . . . . . . . . . . . . . . . . . . . . . . . . . . . Mars/Aquarius
Cypress . . . . . . . . . . . . . cupressus . . . . . . . . . . . . . . . . . . . . . . Saturn

Daffodil . . . . . . . . . . . . . .   *. . . . . . . . . . . . . . . . . . . . . . . . . . . . Venus
Daffodil (Yellow) . . . . . . narcissus pseudonarcissus . . . . . . . . Mars
Daisies . . . . . . . . . . . . . . chrysanthemum leucanthemum . . . Venus/Cancer
Damiana . . . . . . . . . . . . . turnera aphrodisiaca . . . . . . . . . . . . Pluto
Dandelion . . . . . . . . . . . leontodo taraxacum . . . . . . . . . . . . . Jupiter/Sagitarius
Dill . . . . . . . . . . . . . . . . . anethum graveolens . . . . . . . . . . . . . Mercury
Dittany . . . . . . . . . . . . . dictamnus albus . . . . . . . . . . . . . . . . Venus
Dock . . . . . . . . . . . . . . . rumax obtusifolius . . . . . . . . . . . . . Jupiter
Dodder . . . . . . . . . . . . . cuscuto europoea . . . . . . . . . . . . . . Saturn
Dog's Grass . . . . . . . . . triticum repens . . . . . . . . . . . . . . . . . Jupiter
Dog's Grass . . . . . . . . . cynodon dactylon . . . . . . . . . . . . . . Jupiter
Dog's Grass . . . . . . . . . agropyrum repens . . . . . . . . . . . . . . Saturn
Dog Rose . . . . . . . . . . . rosa canino . . . . . . . . . . . . . . . . . . . . Moon
Dog's Tooth Violet . . . . erythronium dens canina . . . . . . . . Moon
Dogwood . . . . . . . . . . . piscidia . . . . . . . . . . . . . . . . . . . . . . . Mars, Pluto
Double Rocket . . . . . . . hesperis matronalis . . . . . . . . . . . . . Mars
Dragon's Blood . . . . . . . daemomorops draco . . . . . . . . . . . . Pluto
Dragon's Blood Reeds . daemomorops draco . . . . . . . . . . . . Pluto/Gemini, Mars
Dropwort . . . . . . . . . . . oenanthe fistulosa . . . . . . . . . . . . . . Venus
Duckweed . . . . . . . . . . . lens palustris . . . . . . . . . . . . . . . . . . Moon/Cancer
Dwarf Elder . . . . . . . . . sambucus ebulus . . . . . . . . . . . . . . . Venus/Scorpio

Eglantine . . . . . . . . . . . . rosa rubiginosa . . . . . . . . . . . . . . . . Jupiter
Elder . . . . . . . . . . . . . . . sambucus nigra . . . . . . . . . . . . . . . . Venus
Elecampagne . . . . . . . . inula helenium . . . . . . . . . . . . . . . . Mercury, Uranus
Elfwort . . . . . . . . . . . . . inula helenium . . . . . . . . . . . . . . . . Uranus, Mercury
Elm . . . . . . . . . . . . . . . . ulmus . . . . . . . . . . . . . . . . . . . . . . . Saturn
Endive . . . . . . . . . . . . . . cichorium endiva . . . . . . . . . . . . . . Jupiter
Eucalyptus . . . . . . . . . . eucalyptus globulus . . . . . . . . . . . . . Pluto
Eveweed . . . . . . . . . . . . hesperis matronalis . . . . . . . . . . . . Mars
Eyebright . . . . . . . . . . . euphrasia officinalis . . . . . . . . . . . . . Sun/Leo

Fennel . . . . . . . . . . . . . . arethum foeciculum . . . . . . . . . . . . Mercury
Fenugreek . . . . . . . . . . . trigonella foenum groecum . . . . . . . Mercury
Fern (Brack) . . . . . . . . . pteris aquilina . . . . . . . . . . . . . . . . . Mercury
Fern (Maidenhair) . . . . . adiantum capillus veneris . . . . . . . . Mercury
Fern (Male) . . . . . . . . . . dryopteris felix-mas . . . . . . . . . . . . . Mars
Fern (Royal) . . . . . . . . . osmonda regalis . . . . . . . . . . . . . . . Saturn
Feverfew . . . . . . . . . . . . matricaria parthenium . . . . . . . . . . . Venus
Fig Tree . . . . . . . . . . . . . ficus . . . . . . . . . . . . . . . . . . . . . . . . Jupiter
Fig-Wort . . . . . . . . . . . . scrophularia nodosa . . . . . . . . . . . . Venus/Taurus
Fireweed . . . . . . . . . . . . erechtities hieracifolia . . . . . . . . . . . Mars
Five-Leaf Grass . . . . . . . potentilla reptans . . . . . . . . . . . . . . Jupiter, Mercury
Flag . . . . . . . . . . . . . . . . iris pseudacorus . . . . . . . . . . . . . . . Moon
Flax . . . . . . . . . . . . . . . . linum usitatissimum . . . . . . . . . . . . Mercury
Flax Weed . . . . . . . . . . . linaria vulgaris . . . . . . . . . . . . . . . . Mars
Flea Bane . . . . . . . . . . . . senecio vulgaris . . . . . . . . . . . . . . . Venus
Flea Wort . . . . . . . . . . . erigeron viscosum . . . . . . . . . . . . . . Saturn
```

Fleur-de-lis	iris pseudacorus	Moon
Foxglove	digitalis purpurea	Pluto, Venus
Frankincense	boswellia thurifera	Sun
Fumitory	fumaria officinalis	Saturn

Galangal	hypericum perforatum	Sun/Leo
Galbanum	ferula galbaniflua	Uranus
Gall Oak	quercus infectoria	Saturn
Gardenia	*	Venus
Garlic	allium ampeloprasum	Mars
Gelsemium	gelsemium nitidum	Pluto
Gentian	swertia perennis	Mars
Gentian	gentiana lutea	Mercury
Geranium (Rose)	*	Venus/Libra
Germander	teucrium marum	Mars
Ginger	zingiber officinale	Moon
Ginseng	panax quinquefolium	Uranus
Gladiole (Water)	butomus umbellatus	Saturn
Goat's Beard	tragopogon porrifolius	Jupiter
Goat's Rue	galega officinalis	Mercury/Leo
Goat's Thorn	astragalus tragacantha	Mars
Goldenrod	solidaga	Venus
Golden Seal	hydrastis canadensis	Venus
Gooseberry	ribes grossularia	Venus
Gosmore	hypochoeris radicata	Venus
Grape, Mountain	berberis aquifolia	Mercury
Ground Pine	ajuga chamoepitys	Pluto, Mars
Groundsel	senecio vulgaris	Venus
Gum Mastic	pistacia lentiscus	Mars
Gum Thistle	euphorbia helioscopia	Mars

Hare's Ear	bupleura rotundifolium	Jupiter
Hare's Foot	pes leporinus	Mercury
Hart's Tongue	scolopendrium	Jupiter
Hawthorn	mespilus oeyacantha	Mars
Hawkweed	hyeracia murorum	Saturn
Hazel Nut	corelys avellana	Mercury
Heart's Ease	viola tricolor	Saturn
Heart Trefoil	*	Sun
Heather	*	Venus
Hellebore (Black)	helleborus niger	Saturn
Hemlock	conium macalatum	Saturn
Hemp	cannabis sativa	Neptune/Pisces, Saturn
Henbane	hyoscyamus niger	Saturn
Henna	lawsonia alba	Jupiter
Henry (Good)	mercurialis annua	Mercury
Herb True-Love	paris quadrifolia	Venus
Hibiscus	hibiscum	Venus
High Joan	hypericum perforatum	Sun/Leo
Holly	ilex	Saturn
Holly (Sea)	eryngium maritimum	Moon

Hollyhocks . . . . althea rosea. . . . . Venus
Honeysuckle. . . . . trifolium . . . . Mercury
Honeysuckle. . . . . lonicor caprifolium . . . . Mars/Cancer
Honeywort. . . . . cerinthe major . . . . Mercury
Hops . . . . humulus lupulus . . . . Pluto, Mars
Horehound. . . . . marubium vulgare. . . . . Mercury
Horseradish . . . . cochlearia armoracia . . . . Mars
Horsetail . . . . equisetum. . . . . Saturn
Horse-tongue . . . . hippoglossum . . . . Mars/Libra
Hounds-tongue . . . . cynoglossum officinale. . . . . Mercury
Houseleek. . . . . sempervium tectorum . . . . Jupiter
Hyacinth . . . . hyacinthus . . . . Saturn
Hyssop . . . . hyssopus officinalis . . . . Jupiter/Cancer, Mars

Iris . . . . iris pseudacorus. . . . . Moon
Irish Moss . . . . chondrus crispus . . . . Saturn
Ivy . . . . helix . . . . Saturn
Ivy, Ground . . . . glechoma hederacea . . . . Saturn

Jacob's Ladder . . . . polemonium coeruleum. . . . . Mercury
Jasmine . . . . oleaceae . . . . Moon
Jasmine . . . . jasminaceae . . . . Moon
Jewelweed . . . . impatiens . . . . Venus, Neptune
Juniper. . . . . juniperis communis. . . . . Mars/Aries, Sun

Kava-Kava. . . . . piper methysticum . . . . Pluto, Venus
Kidneywort . . . . cotyledon umbilicus . . . . Neptune
Kola Nuts. . . . . kola vera . . . . Uranus

Ladies' Mantle. . . . . alchemilla vulgaris . . . . Venus
Ladies' Seal . . . . bryonia . . . . Mars
Lady's Slipper . . . . cypripedium pubescens . . . . Mercury
Laurel. . . . . kalmia latifolia . . . . Saturn
Laurel (Bay). . . . . laurus nobilis . . . . Sun
Laurel (Cherry) . . . . prunus laurocerasus . . . . Venus
Lavender. . . . . lavendula vera . . . . Mercury/Virgo
Leeks . . . . * . . . . Mars
Lemon. . . . . citrus limonum . . . . Neptune, Venus
Lemon Balm . . . . melissa . . . . Venus
Lemongrass. . . . . * . . . . Venus
Lentils . . . . ervum lens . . . . Venus
Lettuce. . . . . * . . . . Moon
Lettuce, Wild . . . . lactuca virosa . . . . Neptune
Life Everlasting. . . . . . . antennaria margaritaceum . . . . Sun
Lily, Madonna. . . . . lilium candidum. . . . . Moon
Lily (Water) . . . . nymphaea. Moon
Lily of the Valley . . . . . . convalearia majalis. . . . . Mercury
Lime. . . . . citrus . . . . Jupiter
Linseed Oil . . . . linum usitatissimum . . . . Uranus
Liquorice. . . . . glycyrrhiza glabra . . . . Mercury
Liverwort . . . . hepatica . . . . Jupiter/Cancer

Lobelia	lobelia inflata	Neptune
Loosetrife	*	Mars/Aries
Lotus	*	Neptune
Lovage	levisticum officinale	Sun/Taurus
Lungwort	sticta pulmonaria	Jupiter
Lupine	leguminosae	Mars/Aries
Mace	myristica fragrans	Mercury
Madder	rubia tinctorum	Mars
Magnolia	magnolia	Jupiter
Maidenhair Fern	adiantum capillus veneris	Mercury/Virgo
Male Fern	dryopteris felix-mas	Mars
Mallows	althea	Venus
Mandrake	attropa mandragora	Uranus, Mercury
Mandrake	podophyllum peltatum	Mercury, Pluto
Maple	aceraceae	Jupiter
Marigold	calendula officinalis	Sun
Marjoram	origanum	Mars/Aries
Marshmallow	althea officinalis	Venus
Marshwort	*	Neptune
Masterwort	imperatoria ostruthium	Mars
Mastic Herb	pistacia lentiscus	Mars
Mayweed	anthemis cotula	Sun
Meadowsweet	spirea ulmaria	Mercury/Gemini
Mescal	anhalonium lewinii	Neptune
Milkweed	asclepiadaceae	Jupiter
Mints	mentha	Venus
Mistletoe	viscum album	Sun, Jupiter
Moneywort	lysimachia nummularia	Jupiter
Monk's Hood	*	Saturn
Moonwort		Moon
Moss	lycopodium	Saturn/Capricorn
Moss, Sphagnum	sphagnum cymbifolium	Jupiter/Pisces
Motherwort	leonurus cardiaca	Venus/Leo
Mugwort	artemisia vulgaris	Neptune, Venus
Mulberry	morus nigra	Mercury
Mullein	verbascum thapsus	Saturn
Mushrooms	*	Mercury/Aries
Musk	hibiscus abelmoschus	Pluto, Saturn
Mustard	cruciferae	Mars
Myrrh	commiphora myrrha	Jupiter
Myrtle	*	Mercury
Narcissus	amaryllidaceae	Neptune
Nettles	urtica dioica	Mars
Nightshade	solanum	Saturn
Nightshade	atropa belladonna	Saturn
Nutmeg	myristica fragrans	Uranus
Oak	quercus robur	Jupiter
Oats	avena sativa	Pluto/Leo

Olibanum .... boswellia thurifera................ Sun
Olive .... olea europaea................... Sun
Onion .... allium cepa .... Mars
Opium.............. papaver somniferum .... Neptune
Orange.............. citrus .... Neptune
Orchid.............. orchis .... Venus
Orchid Root .... orchis .... Pluto, Mars
Oregano .... * .... Mars
Orris Root .... iris pseudocorus................ Moon

Pansies.............. viola tricolor................... Saturn
Paprika .... capsicum....................... Mars
Paris Herb .... paris quadrifolia .... Saturn
Parsley.............. carum petroselinum .... Mercury
Parsnips............. pastinaca sativa................ Mercury
Passion Flower .... passiflora incarnata .... Neptune
Patchouli............ pogostemon patchouli .... Pluto
Peach............... purnus persica .... Venus, Neptune
Pear .... * .... Neptune, Venus
Pellitory............. anacyclus pyrethrum............ Mercury
Pennyroyal .... mentha pulegium............... Venus
Peony .... * .... Sun/Leo
Peppermint.......... mentha peperita............... Venus
Peppers .... piperaceae .... Mars
Periwinkle........... apocynaceae................... Venus
Pilewort............. ficaria verna .... Mars
Pimpernel (Scarlet).... anagallis arvensis .... Sun, Uranus
Pine Tree............ pinaceae .... Mars
Plantain............. plantago major................. Venus, Mars
Pleurisy Root .... asclepias tuberose .... Jupiter
Plum .... * .... Venus, Neptune
Poke................ phytolacca decandra .... Saturn
Pomegranate......... punica granatum .... Uranus, Mercury
Poplar .... populus tremuloides .... Saturn
Poppy .... papaver somniferum .... Saturn, Moon, Neptune
Potato .... solanum tuberosum .... Saturn
Primrose .... primula vulgaris................ Venus
Pumpkin .... cucurbita...................... Moon
Purslane............. portulaca...................... Moon

Quack Grass .... * .... Jupiter
Queen Elizabeth Root .. * .... Moon
Queen's Delight .... stillingia sylvatica............. Saturn
Quince.............. pyrus cydonia .... Saturn

Radish .... raphanus sativus................ Mars
Ragweed .... senecio vulgaris .... Venus
Rampion .... campanula rapunculus .... Venus
Raspberry .... rubus idaeus................... Venus
Red Clover .... trifolium pratense .... Venus
Rhubarb .... polygonaceae.................. Mars

348

Rice	oryza sativa	Sun
Rocket	hesperis matronalis	Mars
Rose (Red)	rosaceae	Venus
Rose (White)	rosaceae	Moon
Rose (Wild)	rosa canina	Moon
Rose Geranium	*	Venus/Libra
Rose Hips	rosaceae	Jupiter
Rosemary	rosmarinum officinalis	Sun
Rowan	pyrus aucuparia	Moon
Royal Fern	osmonda regalis	Saturn
Rue	ruta graveolens	Sun/Leo, Mars
Rye	*	Pluto/Leo
Saffron	crocus sativus	Sun/Leo
Sage	salvia officinalis	Jupiter, Venus/Leo
Saint Joan's Wort	hypericum perforatum	Sun/Leo
Saint John's Wort	hypericum perforatum	Sun/Leo
Salep	orchis	Pluto, Mars
Sandalwood	santalum album	Jupiter
Sarsaparilla	smilax	Mercury
Sassafras	sassafras officinale	Mercury
Savory	satueria	Mercury
Saxifrage	pimpinella	Sun
Sedge	acorus calamus	Mercury
Seasalt	*	Moon
Self-Heal	prunella vulgaris	Venus
Senna	cassia acutifolia	Mercury
Sesame Seed	*	Moon/Taurus
Shepherd's Purse	capsella bursa-pastoris	Saturn
Silverweed	potentilla answerina	Venus
Skullcap	*	Saturn
Skunk Cabbage	symplocarpus foetidus	Pluto
Snakeweed	polygonum bistorta	Saturn
Snapdragon	antirrhinum magus	Mars
Soapwort	saponaria officinalis	Venus, Neptune
Solomon's Seal	polygonatum multiflorum	Saturn
Sorrel (Wood)	oxalis acetosella	Venus
Southernwood	artemisia abrotanum	Mercury
Speedwell	veronica	Venus
Spikenard	aralia racemosa	Uranus/Aquarius
Spikenard	inula conyza	Mars
Spinach	spinacia oleracea	Jupiter
Spurge	euphorbia	Mercury
Squill	urginea scilla	Mars
Star Anise	illicium vera	Moon/Aquarius
Stonecrop	sedum	Moon
Storax	liquidambar orientalis	Sun
Strawberries	fragaria vesca	Venus
Sumac	rhus	Jupiter
Sundew	drosera rotundifolia	Sun
Sunflower	helianthus annus	Sun

```
Swamp Milkweed  ..... asclepias incarnata ................ Jupiter
Sweet Briar ...........*........................... Jupiter
Sweet Cicely.......... myrrhis odorata.................. Jupiter
Sycamore ............*.............................. Venus

Tansy............... tanacetum vulgare ............... Venus
Tarragon ............. artemisia dracunculus ........... Mars
Tea................. camellia thea.................. Mercury
Teazles.............. dipsaceae ...................... Venus
Thistle (Blessed) ....... carbenia benedicta .............. Mars
Thorn Apple.......... datura strmonium .............. Jupiter
Thyme............... thymus vulgaris ............... Venus
Toadflax ............. linaria vulgaris .............. Venus
Tobacco ............. nicotiana tabacum ............... Mars
Tormentil ........... potentilla tormentilla............. Sun

Unicorn Root (False) ... chamaelirium luteum ............. Pluto
Unicorn Root (True) ... aletris farinosa .................. Uranus
Uva-Ursi ............. arctostaphylos uva-ursi ........... Pluto, Mars

Valerian.............. valeriana hortensa ............... Mercury
Verbena...........,.. verbena officinalis ............... Venus, Venus/Libra
Verbena, Lemon....... lippia citriordora ............ Venus
Vervain.............. verbena officinalis ............ Venus,  Venus/Libra
Vine................ vitis vinifera .................... Sun
Violets.............. viola............................ Venus
Virginia Creeper....... vitis hederacea .................. Saturn

Walnut.............. juglans nigra .................... Sun
Watercress .......... nasturtium officinale ............. Moon
Water Lily .......... nymphaea odorata................ Moon
Wheat ..............*............................ Pluto/Leo, Venus
Wild Rose ........... rosa canina .................... Moon
Willows.............. salyx ...................... Saturn, Neptune
Wintergreen .......... gaultheria procumbens ........... Moon
Wisteria.............*............................ Neptune/Aquarius
Witch Hazel ......... hamamelis virginiana.............. Saturn
Woad............... ivatis tinctoria.................... Saturn
Wolfbane ........... aconitum anthora ............... Saturn
Woodruff ........... asperula odorata................ Venus, Mars
Woody Nightshade .... solanum dulcamara ............. Uranus, Mercury
Wormwood .......... artemisia absynthium ............ Pluto, Mars

Yarrow ............. achillea millefolium.............. Venus
Yew................ taxus baccata ................... Saturn
Yucca............... manihot utilissima ............... Pluto
```

* As mentioned in the introduction, this book is an evolving entity and a continuing process; items indicated by an asterisk are awaiting further research for completion.

APPENDIX II
PLANETARY/HERBAL CORRESPONDENCES

HERBS OF THE SUN

Almond
Angelica
Artichoke, Jerusalem
Ash
Bay Tree
Burnet
Butterbar
Chamomile
Celandine
Centaury
Cinnamon*
Eyebright
Frankincense
Galangal
Heart Trefoil
High Joan
Juniper*
Laurel
Life Everlasting
Lovage
Marigold
Mayweed
Mistletoe*
Olibanum
Olive
Peony
Pimpernel
Rice
Rosemary
Rue*
Saffron
Saint Joan's Wort
Saint John's Wort
Saxifrage

Storax
Sundew
Sunflower
Tormentil
Vine
Walnut

HERBS OF THE MOON

Adder's Tongue
Anise Seed
Anise, Star
Ash, Mountain
Cabbage
Camphor
Chickweed
Clary
Cleavers
Coolwort
Coriander*
Cucumbers
Dog Rose
Dog's Tooth Violet
Duckweed
Flag
Fleur-de-lis
Ginger
Holly (Sea)
Iris
Jasmine
Lettuce
Lily, Madonna
Lily, (Water)
Moonwort
Orris Root

Poppy*
Pumpkin
Purslane
Queen Elizabeth Root
Rose (White)
Rose (Wild)
Rowan
Seasalt
Sesame Seed
Star Anise
Stonecrop
Watercress
Water Lily
Wild Rose
Wintergreen

HERBS OF MERCURY

Agaric
Azaleas
Balsam, White
Bayberry
Bittersweet
Buckwheat
Calamint
Caraway
Carrots
Cascara
Cassia
Cedar
Cedar Leaf
Celery*
Cinquefoil*
Coffee*
Dill
Elecampagne*
Elfwort*
Fennel
Fenugreek
Fern*
Five-Leaf Grass*
Flax*
Gentian

Goat's Rue
Grape, Mountain
Hare's Foot
Hazel Nut
Henry (Good)
Honeysuckle*
Honeywort
Horehound
Hounds-tongue
Jacob's Ladder
Lady's Slipper
Lavender
Lily of the Valley
Liquorice
Mace
Maidenhair Fern
Mandrake*
Meadowsweet
Mulberry
Mushrooms
Myrtle
Parsley
Parsnips
Pellitory
Pomegranate*
Sassafras
Savory
Sledge
Senna
Southernwood
Spurge
Tea
Valerian
Woody Nightshade*

HERBS OF VENUS

Alder*
Alkanet
Apple Blossom
Apricot
Balm of Gilead*
Beans
Bedstraw

Bergamot
Birch
Bishop's Weed
Blackberry
Bloodroot
Boneset*
Bugle
Burdock
Catnip
Celery*
Cherry Tree
Chick-pea
Clover
Cocoa
Coltsfoot
Columbines
Cornflower*
Cowslips
Daffodil*
Daisies
Dittany
Dropwort
Dwarf Elder
Elder
Feverfew
Fig-Wort
Flea Bane
Foxglove*
Gardenia
Geranium (Rose)
Goldenrod
Golden Seal
Gooseberry
Gosmore
Groundsel
Heather
Herb True-Love
Hibiscus
Hollyhocks
Jewelweed
Kava-Kava
Ladies' Mantle
Laurel (Cherry)
Lemon*
Lemon Balm

Lemongrass
Lentils
Mallows
Marshmallow
Mints
Motherwort
Orchid
Peach*
Pear*
Pennyroyal
Peppermint
Periwinkle
Plantain*
Plum*
Primrose
Ragweed
Rampion
Raspberry
Red Clover
Rose (Red)
Rose Geranium
Sage*
Self-Heal
Silverweed
Soapwort
Sorrel (Wood)
Speedwell
Strawberries
Sycamore
Tansy
Teazles
Thyme
Verbena
Verbena, Lemon
Vervain
Violets
Wheat*
Woodruff*
Yarrow

HERBS OF MARS

Acacias
All-Heal

Aloes
Anemones*
Barberry
Basil
Bearberry
Beech
Benzoin
Blessed Thistle
Briony
Broom
Cashew
Cayenne
Chili Powder
Chives
Coriander*
Cubebs
Cumin
Curry
Daffodil*
Dogwood*
Double Rocket
Dragon's Blood Reeds
Eveweed
Fern (Male)
Fireweed
Flax Weed
Garlic
Gentian
Germander
Goat's Thorn
Ground Pine
Gum Mastic
Gum Thistle
Hawthorn
Honeysuckle
Hops*
Horseradish
Horse-tongue
Hyssop*
Juniper*
Ladies' Seal
Leeks
Loosestrife
Lupine
Madder

Male Fern
Marjoram
Masterwort
Mastic Herb
Mustard
Nettles
Onion
Orchid Root
Paprika
Peppers
Pilewort
Pine Tree
Plantain*
Radish
Rhubarb
Rocket
Rue*
Salep*
Sarsaparilla
Snapdragon
Spikenard
Squill
Tarragon
Thistle (Blessed)
Tobacco
Uva-Ursi*
Woodruff*
Wormwood*

HERBS OF JUPITER

Agrimony
Alexander
Alfalfa
Arrowhead
Arrowroot
Asparagus
Avens
Balm*
Betony*
Bilberry
Bladderwrack
Borage
Cardamom

Chervil
Chestnut
Cicely, Sweet
Cinquefoil*
Corn, Indian
Costmary
Currants
Dandelion
Dock
Dog's Grass*
Eglantine
Endive
Fig Tree
Five-Leaf Grass*
Goat's Beard
Hare's Ear
Hart's Tongue
Henna
Houseleek
Hyssop*
Lime*
Liverwort
Lungwort
Magnolia
Maple
Milkweed
Mistletoe*
Moneywort
Moss, Sphagnum
Myrrh
Oak
Pleurisy Root
Quack Grass
Rose Hips
Sage*
Sandalwood
Spinach
Sumac
Swamp Milkweed
Sweet Briar
Sweet Cicely
Thorn Apple

HERBS OF SATURN

Aconite
Amaranthus
Arnica
Barley
Beets
Belladonna
Bindweed
Bistort
Bluebell
Box*
Campion
Carob
Clematis
Comfrey
Cornflower*
Cramp Bark
Cypress
Dodder
Dog's Grass
Elm
Fern*
Flea Wort
Fumitory
Gall Oak
Gladiole (Water)
Hawkweed
Heart's Ease
Hellebore (Black)
Hemlock
Hemp*
Holly
Horsetail
Irish Moss
Ivy
Ivy, Ground
Laurel*
Monk's Hood
Moss
Mullein
Musk*
Nightshade

Pansies
Paris Herb
Poke
Poplar
Poppy*
Potato
Queen's Delight
Quince
Shepherd's Purse
Skullcap
Snakeweed
Solomon's Seal
Virginia Creeper
Witch Hazel
Woad
Wolf's Bane
Yew

HERBS OF URANUS

Allspice
Arbutus, Trailing
Chicory
Cinnamon*
Clove
Coffee*
Elecampagne
Elfwort*
Galbanum
Ginseng
Kola Nuts
Linseed Oil
Mandrake*
Nutmeg
Pimpernel*
Pomegranate*
Spikenard*
Unicorn Root*
Woody Nightshade*

HERBS OF NEPTUNE

Adam & Eve Root
Apricot*
Balmony
Citrus
Hemp*
Jewelweed*
Kidneywort
Lemon*
Lettuce, Wild
Lobelia
Lotus
Marshwort
Mescal
Mugwort*
Narcissus
Opium
Orange
Passion Flower
Peach*
Pear*
Plum*
Poppy*
Soapwort
Willows*
Wisteria

HERBS OF PLUTO

Agaric
Ambergris
Artichoke, Globe
Asafoetida
Bearberry*
Box*
Cohosh
Damiana
Dogwood*
Dragon's Blood
Eucalyptus
Foxglove*

Gelsemium
Ground Pine*
Hops*
Kava-Kava*
Mandrake*
Musk*
Oats
Orchid Root*
Patchouli
Rye
Salep*
Skunk Cabbage
Toadflax
Unicorn Root*
Wheat*
Wormwood*
Yucca

* Refer to Appendix I for clarification. These herbs may have more than one planet associated with them.

APPENDIX III
ZODIACAL/HERBAL CORRESPONDENCES

HERBS OF ARIES

Betony (Wood)
Blackberry
Blessed Thistle
Chili Powder
Cowslips
Juniper
Loosestrife
Marjoram
Mushrooms

HERBS OF TAURUS

Apple Blossom
Cumin
Fig-Wort
Lovage

HERBS OF GEMINI

Dragon's Blood Reeds
Meadowsweet

HERBS OF CANCER

Adder's Tongue
Alder (Black)
Agrimony
Balm
Betony (Water)
Daisies

Duckweed
Honeysuckle
Hyssop
Liverwort

HERBS OF LEO

Agaric
Angelica
Bay Tree
Borage
Goat's Rue
Oats
Peony
Rue
Rye
Saffron
Sage
Saint John's Wort
Wheat

HERBS OF VIRGO

Lavender
Maidenhair

HERBS OF LIBRA

Geranium (Rose)
Horse-tongue
Verbena
Vervain

HERBS OF SCORPIO

Basil
Bloodroot
Dwarf Elder

HERBS OF SAGITARIUS

Alexander
Dandelion

HERBS OF CAPRICORN

Comfrey
Moss

HERBS OF AQUARIUS

Anise (Star)
Curry
Spikenard
Wisteria

HERBS OF PISCES

Alder (Common)
Hemp
Moss, Sphagnum

APPENDIX IV
MYTHOLOGICAL/HERBAL CORRESPONDENCES
(Association by Deity)

God/Goddess	Herb
Adonis	Anemone (Wood); Frankincense
Aphrodite	Apple; Benzoin; Parsley; Rose
Apollo	Anise; Bay; Fenugreek; Frankincense: Hyacinth; Sunflower
Artemis	Almond; Daisy (Ox-eye); Wormwood
Athena	Musk; Olive
Atlantis	Angelica
Bacchus	Ivy; Orchid; Soma
Bael	Frankincense
Bast	Catnip
Bellona	Nightshade
Blodeuwedd	Broom; Meadowsweet; Oak
Ceres	Chaste Tree
Chiron	Centaury
Circe	Mandrake; Mullein; Nightshade
Consus	Dogwood; Sage
Cybele	Myrrh
Delphi	Bay
Demeter	Myrrh; Pennyroyal; Sunflower
Diana	Jasmine; Mandrake; Mugwort; Verbena; Vervain; Willow; Wormwood
Dionysus	Ivy
Euphrosyne	Eyebright
Flora	Cornflower
Freya	Cowslip; Daisies; Primrose
Hecate	Aconite; Almond; Garlic; Lavender; Myrrh; Willow
Helenium	Elecampagne
Hera	Iris; Willow
Hercules	Poplar
Hermes	Lotus; Storax; Verbena; Vervain
Horus	Horehound
Hulda	Flax
Hyacinthus	Hyacinth
Io	Violets
Isis	Iris; Lotus
Juno	Iris; Myrrh
Jupiter	Ambergris; Houseleek; Oak

Karnayna . . . . Chamomile
Krishna . . . . Basil
Lady of the Woods . . . . Birch
Lilith . . . . Tarragon
Loki . . . . Storax
Mars . . . . Rue; Vervain
Medea . . . . Aconite
Mercury . . . . Anise; Storax
Michael . . . . Angelica
Minerva . . . . Mulberry
Mintha . . . . Mints
Mut . . . . Benzoin
Odin . . . . Mistletoe; Oak
Osiris . . . . Dittany; Lotus
Pan . . . . Blessed Thistle
Persephone . . . . Dittany; Parsley; Pomegranate
Poseidon . . . . Olive; Pine
Ra . . . . Frankincense
Rhea . . . . Myrrh
Saturn . . . . Lavender; Mandrake; Myrrh; Pomegranate
Sekhmet . . . . Catnip
Shiva . . . . Musk
Thor . . . . Birch; Daisy (Ox-eye); Houseleek
Thoth . . . . Musk; Storax
Ulysses . . . . Mullein
Venus . . . . Anemone; Benzoin; Marjoram; Parsley; Qunice; Sandalwood
Vishnu . . . . Basil
Wotan . . . . Cedar
Zeus . . . . Almond; Ambergris; Daisy (Ox-eye); Olive; Oak; Peppermint; Violets

APPENDIX V
LAWS OF THE TRADITIONAL HERBALIST

I.   The Traditional Herbalist is aware of all four elements: there is no facet of his work which does not invoke the power of earth and water, air and fire . . . . Indeed, the wise practitioner of the Craft of Herbs knows that each facet of the Work is always a balance of the four.

II.   The more wise the practitioner, the better the balance he will keep, knowing always the Hermetic Principle, "As it is above, so it is below," or the law of cause and effect, or as Jesus of Nazareth said, "As a man soweth, so shall he reap."

III.   All creation is a balance of the four: air, fire, water, earth . . . . And a remedy of the herbalist must be in balance.

IV   The wise practitioner will only work good: the potions, decoctions, infusions, will only be made to restore health and well-being, letting the reward being in that creation of good.

V.   The poisons of the trade must only be used to suffocate and dispel that which causes harm to a fellow creature: disease, illness and that which keeps him from seeking his peace and happiness within this Universe.

VI.   There must never be employed any concoction which would impair, injure, or interfere with anyone or anything; for the creation of harm is not your realm.

VII.   The Traditional Herbalist will always find a way to work with the Universe. No matter what his religion, his Gods and Universe are the same, and wherever he looks, he sees them both.

VIII.   And so he practises conservation in all that he does: Never taking more than is to be used; Never taking anything without something being left behind, rewarding the earth with a gift or a blessing.

IX.   Because he follows the Universal Laws of Conservation, the Traditional Herbalist will never bring harm to plant, person; nor to earth and water, and will stir the fires of creation only to work good.

X.   Because he practises his Craft within both the smallest laws of the Universe and the greatest laws, even to gaze at the stars is to be aware.

XI.   The practitioner finds himself following the patterns of the moon, the patterns of astrology, the patterns of the Universe even before he is completely able to comprehend.

XII.   And he knows from doing: Everything that happens affects everything else.

XIII   The Traditional Herbalist learns from his Craft, for the act of doing will bring about even greater knowledge, even if it is difficult to put into words.

APPENDIX VI
REMEDIAL HERBAL CLASSIFICATIONS

ABORTIFACIENT

Herbs which carry this label are those likely to induce a miscarriage. This is considered highly dangerous later than twelve weeks following conception, and is dangerous during the first period of fetal growth. It must also be noted that this practise is considered illegal nearly everywhere. Herbs known as abortifacients include blue cohosh, ergot, golden seal, tansy (oil), and valerian.

ALTERATIVE

A few herbs are vaguely combined under this term. Generally, they function somewhat as a tonic, although their constituents work more directly upon the tissue, hastening renewal and healing. Some herbs are thus called because they lead to improved health. Generally, an alterative differs from a tonic, in that it is recommended to restore health, rather than maintain it. Some of these herbs include burdock, elder, and red clover.

ANESTHETIC

Herbs which cause the nerve endings to lose sensation, making them less aware of pain, are often called anesthetics. It appears that most Herbalists use this term for herbs stronger than those called 'anodyne', but this distinction is not universal. Some of these herbs include birch bark, clove (oil), and mandrake.

ANODYNE

These herbs also alleviate pain, and, as are some herbs classed as anesthetic, may be narcotic in their effect. Some of these herbs (which may also be classed as anesthetic by Herbalists) include belladonna, coca leaves, henbane, white willow bark, and wintergreen.

ANTHELMINTIC

These herbs contain constituents which deter the existence of parasitic worms, a problem common in undernourished peoples and warm climates. Some of the herbs may destroy the worms, some may cause them to be eliminated.

There are Herbalists who report successful use in the treatment of domestic pets, although close supervision must be taken, for unlike the strong commercial preparations, herbal remedies do not automatically destroy the worms. Frequent doses must be given, and capsules are the preferred manner. Some of these herbs include flax seed, tansy, and wormwood.

ANTIEMETIC

Herbs with this classification generally are carminatives and stomachics. They alleviate nausea and can stop a siege of vomiting. Some are dangerous to take, and have led to pharmaceutically developed drugs administered in controlled doses. Some are safe. Check your reference material thoroughly. Among these herbs are clove, frankincense, nightshade, spearmint. Ice, crushed and taken internally, may also be used successfully.

ANTISEPTIC

These herbs will prevent the wound or sore from becoming infected. They work directly against bacteria, some keeping it from growth, others capable of destroying it. Among these herbs are basil, eucalyptus, pennyroyal and thyme.

ANTISPASMODIC

These herbs calm the muscles, stopping spasms and convulsions. They may be employed in situations of cramps or bronchial convulsions. Some of these herbs are both cohoshes (blue and black), chamomile, eucalyptus, lobelia, skullcap, and valerian. A popular remedy is one part yarrow, two parts orange flowers (or another aromatic) and three parts valerian root.

APERIENT

Similar to the classification 'laxative', these herbs will work to produce a natural movement of the bowels. Generally these herbs are more gentle than the laxative herbs, and may be used in the less severe cases. These are such as dandelion and rhubarb.

AROMATIC

These herbs, as their names suggests, have a pleasant fragrance. Generally, they are safely added to another mixture to enhance the palatibility. They are characterized by pleasant smell and flavor, although there are some we might question, such as yarrow. There are many aromatic herbs, among them allspice, anise, catnip, cinnamon, clove, coriander, elecampagne, ginger, lemon peel, peppermint, and yarrow.

ASTRINGENT

These herbs are called binding, for they cause tissue to contract, and are often used to stop bleeding. For the skin, they are used to improve the complexion, causing a tightening of the pores. Internally, they restore tone of organs. Many of these herbs contain tannic or gallic acid. Better known herbs of this group include agrimony, alum root, bayberry, blackberry, comfrey, nettles, sage, and white oak root.

BATHING HERBS

These are herbs which may easily be added to the bath. Generally it is recommeded placing them first in a piece of gauze or cheesecloth. The consitutents of these herbs are absorbed by the bath water with ease, and then transferred to the body. They have pleasant scents and beneficial qualities. Bathing herbs include lovage and heather.

CARDIAC

These herbs have a distinctive effect upon the heart. They do not all work in like manner, so it is most important to study each of these herbs apart from the others. Cardiac herbs include foxglove, lily of the valley, rosemary, tansy, and yarrow.

366

CARMINATIVE

These herbs are all pleasant for the digestion, stomach, and work to relieve stomach gas, mild cramps, and tension. In many ways they are similar to aromatics, but are given a specified remedial purpose. Among them are allspice, aniseed, angelica, catnip, cloves, dill, elecampagne, fennel, ginger, peppermint, spearmint, valerian, and yarrow.

CATHARTIC

These herbs produce a dramatic evacuation of the bowels, and should only be used in extreme situations. They also stimulate the secretions of the intestines, and some of them may have drastic side effects. They include boneset, broom, castor (oil), mayapple.

CONSTITUENTS

The word constituent has been used in this text to refer to volatile oils, minerals and vitamins found within the herb itself. The herb extracts them from the soil, and/or manufactures them. In the case of volatile oils, great care must be taken in making preparations, lest the oil evaporate. A brief list of vitamin constituents includes Vitamin A: dandelion, alfalfa; B: bladderwrack, okra; B12: alfalfa; C: all citrus; D: watercress; E: alfalfa. Many minerals will be found listed in the index.

DEMULCENT

These are very soothing herbs. They generally contain a high amount of natural vegetable gum among their constituents, which allows them to lubricate any surface with which they come in contact. They include arrowroot, comfrey, liquorice root, marshmallow root, and slippery elm.

DEVA

One of many terms used to describe the energy field of an herb. In popular mythology, a Deva is seen as an herb spirit, capable of 'communication', although not necessarily in a literal sense.

DIAPHORETIC

These herbs cause the body to perspire. They are used in mild fevers, and in cases where the skin is hot and dry. They are generally not as strong as a 'sudorific' herb, although these terms are interchanged by some. They include angelica, boneset, camphor, catnip, marigold, pennyroyal, and yarrow.

DIURETIC

These herbs will stimulate the flow of the urine, and are most useful in cleansing the kidneys, and promoting health for that organ. It is thought by many that they also draw out waste and toxic material from the rest of the body and flush it through the body. Among them are agrimony, asparagus, burdock, dandelion, elder, fennel, piper methysticum, uva ursi.

EMETIC

These herbs cause the stomach to contract, and induce vomiting. They are useful in food poisoning, removal of a foreign substance, or in other drastic cases. Some of the herbs require large doses, others may be dangerous and should be used with extreme care. Among them are boneset, elder (root), lobelia, mustard, and vervain.

EMMENAGOGUE

These herbs stimulate the menstrual flow, and use is recommended for those who have difficulty or discomfort with the cycle. Among them are cohosh (both blue and black), ergot, motherwort, pennyroyal, rue and tansy.

EMOLLIENT

These herbs are similar to the demulcent, but are a specific remedy for external use, whereas a demulcent is often thought of as internal. They will soften roughness, and leave the area smooth. They include linseed, liquorice, marshmallow, and, of course, comfrey.

EXPECTORANT

Many of these herbs contain vegetable gum. Their designation is due to their ability to loosen the accumulations of phlegm which collects in the lungs, sinus cavities, and in the bronchial passages. Once loosened, it is easily coughed up. Please, always remind someone suffering from congestion that this process is both natural and desirable. Due to its social discomfort, many persons tend to completely suppress this process. Some of the herbs known as expectorants include boneset, benzoin, elecampagne, horehound, lobelia, marshmallow (which works particularly well with the sinus passages), and mullein.

FEBRIFUGE

These herbs are most useful in treating fever. Many of them also function as diaphoretics. This word generally refers to their ability to lower the temperature. Occasionally an Herbalist will use the term antipyretic. Some of them are boneset, sage, tansy, and wormwood.

FIXATIVE

These are herbs which have little scent, and are used primarily as a carrier for the oil or scent of another. Thus, the constituent is held in a base material. One of these is elder flower, which is excellent in mixtures in which you wish to introduce a pure herbal oil.

HAEMOSTAT

These are herbs which contain constituents which quicken the coagulent properties of blood, and are strong astringents. They are used to stop bleeding. They include corn ergot, marigold, and sage, the latter being the quickest.

HEPATIC

These herbs work directly upon the liver, the constituents allowing it to function more easily. They assist in cleaning it, and restoring health and strength. They are useful in hepatitis and jaundice. They include agrimony, celandine, dandelion, peony, and tansy.

IRRITANT

This term is used by some Herbalists to classify a group of herbs which irritate the skin, such as bryony, cayenne, poison oak, and mustard.

LAXATIVE

These herbs stimulate the bowels to action. They are not as drastic in action as a purgative, but by many Herbalists are considered stronger than an aperient. There are some who interchange the classifications of laxative and aperient. They include herbs such as boneset, dandelion, liquorice root, mandrake, mountain flax, and rhubarb.

LINIMENT

Sometimes this word is used to indicate the property of an herb used for the making of oils. Among this type of herb are the mints, which, when used externally as an oil, produce healing qualities, and also generate heat. They soothe pain and work on the muscles and joints.

MUCILAGE

This is a natural gum substance found in a number of herbs such as marshmallow and comfrey. Mucilage is soluble in water, creating a sticky goo, which is highly demulcent in nature, and also adheres to the skin, where it is able to soothe and lubricate for a long time.

NARCOTIC

Some drugs are narcotic. They create changes within the nervous system, may be addicting under prolonged use, can lead to false vision and hallucination, and generally are dangerous to ingest. Most of them have become controlled substances due to the abuse to which they have been subverted. They include some poppies (opium), hallucinatory herbs, such as mescal and peyote, and some poisonous herbal substances, such as aconite.

NEPHRITIC

This term refers to herbs which effect the kidneys, and the definition for diuretic and those herbs listed may be used in reference.

NERVINE

These herbs are calming to the nerves and soothing to the emotions. They function as a tonic for the nervous system and are the basis for many of the pharmaceutical preparations sold over-the-counter. As herbs, however, many are very inexpensive and far more natural for the body. They make excellent teas. Among this large classification are chamomile, cinquefoil, fennel, hops, lavender, marigold, rosemary, tansy, and verbena. Some herbs with stronger effects are also found classified as nervines in other herbals. Always research your herbs carefully.

NUTRIENT

These herbs are considered unusually high in their constituent amounts of vitamins and minerals. They may be taken regularly as a morning tonic, rather than the coated pills. They include comfrey, dandelion, and nettles.

PECTORAL

Many herbs which work directly upon the lungs and chest, and are particularly effective in treating congestion are known as pectorals. They are useful in treating bronchial infections, chest colds, and other respiratory infections. They include aniseed, coltsfoot (excellent), irish moss, marshmallow, mullein, and wild cherry.

PERENNIAL

These are the herbs easiest to grow, for they survive the winter and return anew each spring. Once established, they will grow a long time, requiring working through them, thinning,and giving them more space only every three to five years. They include more than half of all working herbs. Their ability to survive depends upon your climate, for some object quite strenuously to winter, and will need to be brought indoors.

PULMONARY

This word usually is interchangeable with the classification pectoral. Its use depends upon the personal use of either pectoral or pulmonary, the latter being used less among Herbalists.

PURGATIVE

These are the strongest of the laxative herbs, and will cause drastic evacuation of the bowels, sometimes with mildly uncomfortable side effects. They include bitter apple, black root, bonenset, may apple, mandrake, and senna leaves.

REFRIGERANT

These herbs relieve thirst, impart a sensation of coolness, and a few actually lower the temperature of the blood. Some of these are aconite, catnip, chickweed, and wormwood.

RUBEFACIENT

When massaged onto the skin, these herbs cause the skin to redden. In some ways they are similar to irritants. They may be used to treat painful joints caused by arthritis or rheumatism. Included are cayenne and nettles.

SEDATIVE

These herbs function somewhat as a tranquilizer. They will relax nervous tension, may induce sleep, and soothe the muscles. With some of them, it is essential to avoid excessive dosage. They include black cohosh, chamomile, jasmine, and valerian, the latter being most effective.

STIMULANT

The constituents of these herbs cause the vital signs to quicken, raising pulse, respiration, and nerve alertness. They may even raise the temperature of the body. They feel as if they produce energy, yet in actuality only ease its flow. They are non-narcotic. They include bayberry, cayenne, cinnamon, eucalyptus, horseradish, mustard, peppers, tansy, and wintergreen.

STOMACHIC

These herbs help the stomach, and are most generally employed for poor digestion, disorders arising from tension, and the like. They include angelica, chamomile, dill, pennyroyal, peppermint, sage, and wormwood.

STYPTIC

Similar to a haemostat in that it is used to stop bleeding. The blood vessels contract and the blood clots stop the flow. They include avens, nettles, and sage.

SUDORIFIC

This is a term for those herbs which induce sweating, more strongly than the diaphoretics. These include cayenne, germander, marigold, vervain, and yarrow.

TONIC

These herbs are good for you, and may be taken even when in good health. They give the body a sense of well-being, and often include those which are stimulants and nutrients. They improve the tone of the body, some produce a sensation of vigor, and some are gentle cleansers. They include agrimony, bayberry, blackberry, boneset, catnip, cayenne, chamomile, dandelion, nettles, peppermint, sage, tansy, wormwood, and yarrow.

VOLATILE OIL

This is a primary form of a major constituent of herbs. The natural healing powers of the herbs are most often found naturally in the herb as as volatile oil. The word volatile indicates their ability to evaporate easily, requiring steeping beneath a closed lid. Some may be soluble in water, but there are those which are soluble only in another oil, and require extraction other than by means of water infusions and the like.

VULNERARY

These herbs are known for their effective use in treating wounds, cuts, and burns. They include such as comfrey, marshmallow, and tansy.

APPENDIX VII
MAGICKAL HERBAL CLASSIFICATIONS

APHRODISIAC HERBES

These herbes are said to increase sexual desire, some of them working directly upon the sexual organs as stimulants and mild irritants, creating a physical drive to seek arousal and relief; some work directly by their change in a person's energy. Many of these herbes have been used in this manner for thousands of years. These herbes do not necessarily include any interaction of love or romance, and are not for those seeking a partner for a relationship, but rather to increase the delight and joy of a playmate.

HERBES OF CONSECRATION

These herbes impart a blessing, and may often have that energy which cleanses away all negative vibrations. Some of them are particularly associated with a specific tool of magick, and some may generally be used to consecrate an object. When performing a consecration, remember that the first step is to remove any previous, unwanted energy, through ritual cleansing. Only then should the object be given positive energy, blessed, and consecrated to a specific purpose, that being its sole purpose from that point onward. Some of the Herbes of Consecration may be used to seal this charge.

COUNTERMAGICKE HERBE

Due to the popular forms of magick during medieval times, most forms of which included hexing and casting spells against others, many Herbes of Protection became known as Countermagicke Herbes. Some of these will reverse the bad feelings, returning them to the original source, in a sense taking control of karma, and returning it three-fold. Others accomplish countermagicke by their strong ability to protect and keep pure the space or person with which they come in contact. Under no circumstances would a Traditional Herbalist work magick against another.

FERTILITY HERBES

These are the herbes used in fertility charms, used to guarantee abundant crops and reproductive livestock, and the herbes women turned to when they seemed unable to conceive. Although many of them have strong implications of fertility leading to birth, they may be used to bring fertility to any creative situation, such as the production of new artwork, a particular project, or the like.

FUNEREAL HERBES

These herbes have been used among various civilizations in connection with rituals for the dead, for appeasement of the gods for a departed soul, and in connection with the passage into another life, or afterlife state. Some have been found in myths, in which a deity presides over the place where souls would pass after death; some have been used in embalming the body; some have been scattered or grown over gravesites; and some have been used in the incenses, or scattered upon a funeral fire.

GREENE HERBE

These are all herbes in which the green leaf is used, particularly for culinary flavoring, yet have strong associations with magick. They can be used in what is called 'kitchen magick', in which a wise cook will leave the guests happy and content, both with full stomach and with joyful heart. Some of these herbes may be included in nearly any kitchen preparation, from salad, to casserole or meat, and will make any dinner gathering more prone to friendship or conversation. These herbes are the gentle herbes of magick.

HERBES OF IMMORTALITY

These herbes are found in ancient myths, guarding the secrets of long life. Some of them are capable of guaranteeing a pleasant reincarnation. Most of them contain energy like that of infinity, or the eternal qualities of pure love. By working with them, one can come to comprehend the quality of immortality, and learn to recognize those aspects of the self, both divine and eternal.

MAGICKAL HERBES

This is a very loose classification. Nearly every herbe listed in this section of herbal magick might be so classified. It more distinctly applies to those herbes found in folk charms and superstitious magick. There is no religious implication to this classification. These herbes have been used as amulets, talismans, in potions, and have fascinating folklore attached to them. Generally they have a history of this form of use.

HERBES OF PROTECTION

These are the good guys in the herbe kingdom. They carry with them pure, positive energy. For those able to visually perceive it, it would appear as radiant, clear, and very light in color. They can be used to protect a person in nearly any circumstances. They radiate enough positive energy of their own that negativity must remain distant. In many aspects, these herbes might be thought of as guardian angels. They may be used in any situation where the practioner feels a strong desire to help, to be able to do something for the person, but is unsure of what that might be. There is nothing as pleasant as an extra dose of positive energy. These herbes may be freely given without affecting the karma of another.

RELIGIOUS HERBES

These herbes have been selected by various cultures as having those energies appropriate for certain deities. Many of these herbes have been grown, ingested, or sacrificed in honor of these deities. Some of these herbes have been involved in the rituals of particular religious groups, to purify, cleanse, or initiate their members. There appears to be nearly no religion, other than newer sects of Christianity, which have not used herbs in their worship. There are frequent references to herbes in portions of the bible, and most major works.

VISIONARY HERBES

These herbes are sometimes those which induce vision through narcotic effects. There are also many herbes in this group used safely to enhance meditation, to gain awareness of dreams. These herbes are used to provoke mystical dreams and great insight. They are to be used with care.

APPENDIX VIII
ALTERNATE COMMON NAMES FOR HERBS

Aaron's Rod . . . . Goldenrod
Aaron's Rod . . . . Mullein
Adam's Flannel. . . . . Mullein
African Pepper . . . . Cayenne
Alcaravea. . . . . Caraway
Alehoof . . . . Ground Ivy
All Heal . . . . Self Heal
All Heal . . . . Valerian
Alsine Media . . . . Chickweed
Amantilla. . . . . Valerian
American Valerian . . . . Lady's Slipper
Arbutis Uva Ursi. . . . . Uva Ursi
Archangelica. . . . . Angelica
Ass Ear . . . . Comfrey
Ass's Foot . . . . Coltsfoot
Auld Wife's Huid . . . . Aconite
Ava. . . . . Kava Kava

Bachelor's Buttons . . . . Feverfew
Bad Man's Plaything . . . . Yarrow
Barweed . . . . Cleavers
Bay. . . . . Bay Laurel
Bearberry . . . . Uva Ursi
Beggar's Blanket . . . . Mullein
Beggar's Buttons . . . . Burdock
Beggar's Stalk . . . . Mullein
Bird Pepper. . . . . Cayenne
Bird's Eye . . . . Heart's Ease
Bird's Foot . . . . Fenugreek
Bishopswort. . . . . Betony, Wood
Black Elder . . . . Elder
Black Haw. . . . . Cramp Bark
Black Snake Root. . . . . Black Cohosh
Blackwort. . . . . Comfrey
Blanket Herb . . . . Mullein

Blind Weed	Shepherd's Purse
Bloodwort	Yarrow
Bloody Fingers	Foxglove
Blueberry Root	Blue Cohosh
Blue Curls	Self Heal
Blue Gum Tree	Eucalyptus
Blue Rocket	Aconite
Bly	Blackberry
Boneset	Comfrey
Bore Tree	Elder
Bottle Brush	Horsetails
Bouncing Bet	Heart's Ease
Bour Tree	Elder
Boxberry	Wintergreen
Bramble	Blackberry
Bramble Berry	Blackberry
Bramble Kite	Blackberry
Bramble of Mt. Ida	Raspberry
Brameberry	Blackberry
Brandy Mint	Peppermint
Bread & Cheese Tree	Hawthorn
Broad Leaved Plantain	Plantain
Bruisewort	Comfrey
Brummel	Blackberry
Brunella	Self Heal
Bugbane	Black Cohosh
Bullock's Lungwort	Mullein
Bull's Foot	Coltsfoot
Bullweed	Heart's Ease
Bumble Kite	Blackberry
Burr	Burdock
Butter Dock	Dock
Buttons	Tansy
Calendula	Marigold
Call to Me	Heart's Ease
Call Me to You	Heart's Ease
Candleberry	Bayberry
Candlewick Plant	Mullein
Capon's Tail	Valerian
Carpenter's Weed	Yarrow
Caseweed	Shepherd's Purse
Catch Weed	Cleavers
Catmint	Catnip
Catnep	Catnip

Cat's Foot	Ground Ivy
Checkerberry	Wintergreen
Cheeses	Marshmallow
Chillies	Cayenne
Chinese Anise	Anise, Star
Church Steeples	Agrimony
Cingulum Sancti Johannis	Mugwort
City Avens	Avens
Clivers	Cleavers
Clot	Mullein
Clot Bur	Burdock
Clove Root	Avens
Clown's Lungwort	Mullein
Cocklebur	Agrimony
Cockle Buttons	Burdock
Colewort	Avens
Common Celandine	Celandine, Greater
Compass Plant	Rosemary
Compass Weed	Rosemary
Consound	Comfrey
Convallaria	Lily of the Valley
Coon Root	Bloodroot
Couch Grass	Dog's Grass
Coughwort	Comfrey
Cuckoo's Bread	Plantain
Cuddle Me	Heart's Ease
Cuddy's Lungs	Mullein
Cull Me	Heart's Ease
Daphne	Bay Laurel
Darkmous	Spurge
Dead Mens' Bells	Foxglove
Deerberry	Wintergreen
Dergmuse	Spurge
Devil's Nettle	Yarrow
Devil's Plaything	Yarrow
Dog Rowan Tree	Cramp Bark
Dog's Tooth	Dog's Grass
Dracontium	Skunk Cabbage
Dracontium Foetidum	Skunk Cabbage
Duffle	Mullein
Dutch Rushes	Horsetails
Elf Dock	Elecampagne
Elf Wort	Elecampagne

Englishman's Foot . . . . Plantain
Euphrasia . . . . Eyebright
Everlasting Friendship . . . . Cleavers
Eye Balm . . . . Golden Seal
Eye Root . . . . Golden Seal

Fairy's Caps . . . . Foxglove
Fairy's Glove . . . . Foxglove
Fairy's Thimbles . . . . Foxglove
Featherfew . . . . Feverfew
Feather Foil . . . . Feverfew
Felon Herb . . . . Mugwort
Fenkel . . . . Fennel
Fettwort . . . . Mullein
Fieldhove . . . . Coltsfoot
Figwort . . . . Celandine, Lesser
Fingerhut . . . . Foxglove
Five Fingers . . . . Cinquefoil
Five Finger Blossom . . . . Cinquefoil
Five Leaf Grass . . . . Cinquefoil
Flirtwort . . . . Feverfew
Flower of Luce . . . . Heart's Ease
Fluffweed . . . . Mullein
Foalswort . . . . Coltsfoot
Fox's Clote . . . . Burdock
Friar's Cap . . . . Aconite

Gaitre Berries . . . . Cramp Bark
Garden Celandine . . . . Celandine, Greater
Garden Thyme . . . . Thyme
Gill Go Over the Ground . . . . Ground Ivy
Gill Go By the Hedge . . . . Ground Ivy
Glyrrhiza . . . . Liquorice
Godfathers & Godmothers . . . . Heart's Ease
Golden Rod . . . . Mullein
Goldruthe . . . . Golden Seal
Golds . . . . Marigold
Goldy Star . . . . Avens
Goosebill . . . . Cleavers
Goosegrass . . . . Cleavers
Greek Hayseed . . . . Fenugreek
Green Ginger . . . . Wormwood
Grenadier . . . . Pomegranate
Grian . . . . Celandine, Lesser
Grip Grass . . . . Cleavers

Ground Raspberry .... Golden Seal
Guelder Rose .... Cramp Bark
Gum Plant............................ Comfrey

Hag's Taper .... Mullein
Hallfoot............................. Coltsfoot
Halves .... Hawthorn
Happy Major .... Burdock
Hare's Beard......................... Mullein
Haw.................................. Hawthorn
Haw Maids .... Ground Ivy
Hayriffe............................. Cleavers
Hayruf............................... Cleavers
Hawthorn............................. Hawthorn
Hazels .... Hawthorn
Heart of the Earth .... Self Heal
Hedgeriffe........................... Cleavers
Hedge Maids.......................... Ground Ivy
Herb Bennet.......................... Avens
Herb Constancy....................... Heart's Ease
Herb of Grace .... Rue
Herb of Grace .... Verbena
Herbygrass .... Rue
Herbe Militaris .... Yarrow
Herb Patience........................ Dock
Herb Sacree .... Verbena
Herb Trinitatis .... Heart's Ease
Herb Veneris .... Verbena
High Cranberry .... Cramp Bark
Hindberry............................ Raspberry
Holly Leaved Barberry .... Mountain Grape
Holy Thistle .... Blessed Thistle
Hook Heal............................ Self Heal
Horsehoof .... Coltsfoot
Horse Heal .... Coltsfoot
Hypericum .... St. John's Wort

Incensier............................ Rosemary
Indian Dye .... Golden Seal
Indian Elm .... Elm, Slippery
Indian Paint .... Bloodroot
Intoxicating Pepper .... Kava Kava
Invisible Vet........................ Comfrey

Jack Jump Up & Kiss Me . . . . Heart's Ease
Jacob's Ladder . . . . Lily of the Valley
Jacob's Staff . . . . Mullein
Jaundice Root. . . . . Golden Seal
Jupiter's Staff . . . . Mullein

Karawya . . . . Caraway
King's Crown. . . . . Cramp Bark
Kiss Her in the Buttery . . . . Heart's Ease
Kit Run About . . . . Heart's Ease
Kit Run in the Fields . . . . Heart's Ease
Knight's Milfoil . . . . Yarrow
Knitback . . . . Comfrey
Knitbone. . . . . Comfrey

Ladder to Heaven . . . . Lily of the Valley
Ladies' Meat . . . . Hawthorn
Lady's Purse. . . . . Shepherd's Purse
Lemon Balm. . . . . Balm
Lily Constancy. . . . . Lily of the Valley
Live in Idleness . . . . Heart's Ease
Lizzy Run Up the Hedge. . . . . Ground Ivy
Love Idol . . . . Heart's Ease
Love In Idleness. . . . . Heart's Ease
Love Leaves . . . . Burdock
Love Lies Bleeding . . . . Heart's Ease
Loving Idol. . . . . Heart's Ease
Love Man . . . . Cleavers
Lurk In the Ditch. . . . . Pennyroyal

Male Lily . . . . Lily of the Valley
Mallard . . . . Marshmallow
Mandragora . . . . Mandrake
Manzanilla. . . . . Chamomile
Mary Gowles . . . . Marigolds
Mauls . . . . Marshmallow
May . . . . Hawthorn
Mayblossom. . . . . Hawthorn
May Lily . . . . Lily of the Valley
May Rose. . . . . Cramp Bark
Maythen . . . . Chamomile
Meadow Cabbage . . . . Skunk Cabbage
Meet Me In the Entry. . . . . Heart's Ease
Milfoil . . . . Yarrow

384

Monk's Rhubarb . . . . Dock
Monk's Hood . . . . Aconite
Moose Elm . . . . Elm, Slippery
Mortification Root . . . . Marshmallow
Mother's Heart . . . . Shepherd's Purse
Mountain Tea . . . . Wintergreen
Mullein Dock . . . . Mullein
Mutton Chops . . . . Cleavers
Myrica . . . . Bayberry
Mystyldene . . . . Mistletoe

Nerve Root . . . . Lady's Slipper
Noah's Ark . . . . Lady's Slipper
Nosebleed . . . . Yarrow

Old Man's Flannel . . . . Mullein
Old Man's Pepper . . . . Yarrow
Old Wife's Hood . . . . Aconite
Orange Root . . . . Golden Seal
Oregon Grape Root . . . . Mountain Grape
Our Lady's Gloves . . . . Foxglove
Our Lady's Flannel . . . . Mullein
Our Lady's Tears . . . . Lily of the Valley

Paddock Pipes . . . . Horsetails
Papoose Root . . . . Blue Cohosh
Partridge Berry . . . . Wintergreen
Passerina . . . . Chickweed
Pearl Barley . . . . Barley
Pepper & Salt . . . . Shepherd's Purse
Perlatum . . . . Barley
Personata . . . . Burdock
Peter's Staff . . . . Mullein
Pewterwort . . . . Horsetail
Philanthropium . . . . Burdock
Phu . . . . Valerian
Pick Pocket . . . . Shepherd's Purse
Pick Purse . . . . Shepherd's Purse
Pilewort . . . . Celandine, Lesser
Pink Eyed John . . . . Heart's Ease
Pink o' the Eye . . . . Heart's Ease
Pipe Tree . . . . Elder
Plants' Physician . . . . Chamomile
Poisonous Gum Thistle . . . . Spurge
Polar Plant . . . . Rosemary

Polecat Weed . . . . Skunk Cabbage
Poor Man's Parmacettie . . . . Shepherd's Purse
Poor Man's Treacle . . . . Garlic
Pot Marigold . . . . Marigold
Priest's Crown . . . . Dandelion
Prunella . . . . Self Heal
Pudding Grass . . . . Pennyroyal
Pulegium . . . . Pennyroyal

Quack Grass . . . . Dog's Grass
Quick . . . . Hawthorn

Raspis . . . . Raspberry
Rattle Pouches . . . . Shepherd's Purse
Rattle Root . . . . Black Cohosh
Ray Paper . . . . Mullein
Red Elder . . . . Cramp Bark
Red Elm . . . . Elm, Slippery
Red Pucoon . . . . Bloodroot
Ripple Grass . . . . Plantain
Robber Grass . . . . Cleavers
Robin Run In the Hedge . . . . Cleavers
Robin Run In the Hedge . . . . Ground Ivy
Rose Elder . . . . Cramp Bark
Ruddes . . . . Marigold
Run by the Ground . . . . Pennyroyal

Saint John's Plant . . . . Mugwort
Sanguinary . . . . Shepherd's Purse
Sanguinary . . . . Yarrow
Satan's Apple . . . . Mandrake
Sawge . . . . Sage
Scabwort . . . . Elecampagne
Scaldhead . . . . Blackberry
Scratweed . . . . Cleavers
Schloss Tea . . . . Marshmallow
Set Wall . . . . Valerian
Shavegrass . . . . Horsetails
Shepherd's Bag . . . . Shepherd's Purse
Shepherd's Club . . . . Mullein
Shepherd's Scrip . . . . Shepherd's Purse
Shepherd's Sprout . . . . Shepherd's Purse
Shepherd's Staff . . . . Mullein
Silver Bells . . . . Cramp Bark
Skunk Weed . . . . Skunk Cabbage

Slan Lus. . . . . Plantain
Slippery Root. . . . . Comfrey
Small Celandine. . . . . Celandine, Lesser
Smallwort. . . . . Celandine, Lesser
Snakebite . . . . Bloodroot
Snakeweed. . . . . Plantain
Snapping Hazelnut . . . . Witch Hazel
Snowball Tree . . . . Cramp Bark
Soldier's Woundwort. . . . . Yarrow
Solidago . . . . Golden Rod
Spotted Alder. . . . . Witch Hazel
Squaw Root . . . . Black Cohosh
Squaw Root . . . . Blue Cohosh
Star Chickweed . . . . Chickweed
Starweed. . . . . Chickweed
Staunchweed . . . . Yarrow
Stellaire . . . . Chickweed
Stepmother. . . . . Heart's Ease
Sticadore. . . . . Lavender
Sticklewort. . . . . Agrimony
Stinging Nettles . . . . Nettles
Sunkfield. . . . . Chickweed
Sweet Balm. . . . . Balm
Sweet Bay. . . . . Bay Laurel
Sweet Slumber. . . . . Bloodroot
Swine's Snout . . . . Dandelion
Synkefoyle . . . . Cinquefoil

Tallow Shrub . . . . Bayberry
Teaberry. . . . . Wintergreen
Tetterwort . . . . Bloodroot
Thorn . . . . Hawthorn
Thorny Burr. . . . . Burdock
Thoroughwort. . . . . Boneset
Thousand Weed . . . . Yarrow
Three Faces Under a Hood . . . . Heart's Ease
Torches. . . . . Mullein
Trefoil . . . . Clover
True Laurel. . . . . Bay Laurel
Turn Hoof. . . . . Ground Ivy
Tun Hoof . . . . Ground Ivy

Velvet Dock . . . . Elecampagne
Velvet Dock . . . . Mullein

Velvet Plant .... Mullein
Virgin's Glove .... Foxglove

Water Elder .... Cramp Bark
Wax Myrtle........................... Bayberry
Way Bennet .... Avens
Waybread............................. Plantain
Waybroad............................. Plantain
White Man's Foot .... Plantain
White Mullein .... Mullein
White Thorn .... Hawthorn
Whitsun Bosses .... Cramp Bark
Whitsum Rose .... Cramp Bark
Wild Curcuma .... Golden Seal
Wild Ice Leaf .... Mullein
Wild Pansy .... Heart's Ease
Wild Rye............................. Avens
Wild Sunflower .... Elecampagne
Winterbloom .... Witch Hazel
Witches' Gloves .... Foxglove
Witches' Pouches .... Shepherd's Purse
Woolen............................... Mullein
Woundwort .... Golden Seal

Yellow Root.......................... Golden Seal

BIBLIOGRAPHY

Bethel, May, *The Healing Power of Herbs,* California: Wilshire Book Co., 1968.

Beyerl, D.D., Rev. Paul V., *The Holy Books of the Devas, Vol. I,* Minneapolis, Minn.: The Rowan Tree, Inc., 1980.

Christopher, Dr. John R., *School of Natural Healing,* Provo, Utah: BiWorld Publishers, Inc., 1976.

Conway, David, *The Magic of Herbs,* New York: E.P. Dutton & Co. Inc., 1976.

Culpeper, Dr. Nicholas, *Astrological Judgement of Diseases,* Tempe, Ariz.: American Federation of Astrologers, Inc., 1959.

Culpeper, Dr. Nicholas, *Complete Herbal,* Buck, England: W. Foulsham & Co., Ltd.

Cunningham, Scott, *Magical Herbalism,* St. Paul, Minn.: Llewellyn Publications, 1982.

Gerard, John, *The Herbal or General History of Plants,* New York: Dover Publications, Inc., 1975.

Grieve, Mrs. M., *A Modern Herbal,* New York: Dover Publications, Inc., 1971.

Hartman, Franz, *Occult Science in Medicine,* England: Whitstable, 1975.

Hausman, Ethel, *Beginner's Guide to Wild Flowers,* New York: G.P. Putnam's Son's, 1948.

Hurley, Phillip, *Herbal Alchemy,* U.S.A.: Lotus, 1977.

Huson, Paul, *Mastering Herbalism,* New York: Stein and Day, 1974.

Huxley, Anthony, *Plant and Planet,* New York: Viking Publishers, 1974.

Kloss, Jethro, *Back to Eden,* Coalmont, Tenn.: Longview Publishing, 1939.

Leek, Sybil, *Sybil Leek's Book of Herbs,* New York: Thomas Nelson, Inc., 1973.

Meyer, Joseph, E., *The Herbalist,* U.S.A., 1918.

Muir, Ada, *The Healing Herbs of the Zodiac,* St. Paul, Minn.: Llewellyn Publications, 1959.

Rose, Jeanne, *Jeanne Rose's Herbal,* New York: Grosset & Dunlap, 1972.

Twitchell, Paul, *Herbs: The Magick Healers,* San Diego: Illumined Way Press, 1971.

Wren, R.C., *Potter's New Cyclopedia of Medicinal Herbs and Preparations,* New York: Harper and Row, 1972.

RESOURCES

APHRODISIA   This is an excellent source of a variety of mail order herbs. They also offer oils and other things to delight the herbalist. A catalogue is available, and with it you may order herbs by the quarter pound or pound. There is a cost for the catalogue, which varies, so check ahead, and send a S.A.S.E. (self-addressed stamped envelope). 28 Carmine St., New York, N.Y., 10014

MOON MAGICK   A small catalogue listing many herbal mixtures, oils, and wonderfully fun things for the practitioner. Drop a S.A.S.E. in the mail for price of the catalogue. P.O. Box 395, Littleton, Co., 80160

THE ROWAN TREE HERB SHOP   A small catalogue listing herbs. Many are cheaper than major sources, some are more expensive. Profits are minimal, and go to support part of the cost of the Mystery School. Send a S.A.S.E. and one dollar for a catalogue, and also for sample issue of the newsletter with Beyerl's regular herb column, "The Unicorn." P.O. Box 8814, Mpls., Mn., 55408

DR. MICHAEL'S HERB CENTER   A nice catalogue available for a dollar, listing many herbs. Some of the prices are high, but small quantities are available. 1223 Milwaukee Ave., Chicago, Ill., 60622

CIRCLE SANCTUARY HERBS   Quality dried herbs grown and harvested at a Pagan Sanctuary by magickal people. Free details. P.O. Box 219, Mt. Horeb, WI., 53572

NOTES

1. (page 8) "In the past couple of decades there have been instances in which plants have led to the apprehension of criminals." The Wall Street Journal (Feb. 2/72) reports that a precedent has already been set for the use of plants in an actual police case in New Jersey.
2. (page 26) I would like to add that you may make balms by using beeswax as one of the prime ingredients in an ointment preparation. Further information on the preparation and use of balms is found in "The Herbalist as Magickal Practitioner," pages 195-6.
3. (page 28) An original statement of this adage is "Let need, not reason, determine the season."
4. (page 36) "Mary Cook's Remedy..." This was a recipe found in the recipe box of my Grandfather Bitter's second wife, Ivy Buck Bitter, after her death. We are uncertain of its origin, other than that it is likely to come from Iowa; however, it is a good formula, and deserves preservation.
5. (page 66) A note on the use of Bay leaves in the kitchen. Though a wonderful Greene Herbe, of late there has been caution expressed in the news, for the unsuspecting dinner guest may choke upon a Bay leaf. Swallowing a leaf is highly dangerous. Warn your guests that there is a Bay leaf in the stew...better yet, tell them there is a Bay leaf in the dinner (specify the course) and tell them that whomever finds it gets a wish...true 'kitchen magick.'
6. (page 84) "Flying ointment" is one of those herbal preparations which appears in print in many books. Many of the herbs associated with this mixture are of a poisonous nature, and include symptoms which leave the user feeling as if he/she were flying. It could also, if properly prepared and administered, enable the experience of astral projection. There are many myths and legends about 'flying ointments': study them with several grains of salt, yet search within those tales for the grains of truth.
7. (page 100) "Useful in the treatment of diarrhea and are also used as a laxative." This may at first seem like a troublesome dichotomy, yet we find similar situations in the Remedial Herbal. Another example is the use of valerian as a sedative, yet an excessive dose will act as an unpleasant stimulant. It is important to fully understand the dosage (see Dosage Guide to the Remedial Herbal), and to be extremely careful.
8. (page 125) One theory which explains the function of an herb working by application to the temples, is that it stimulates trace chemicals in the brain. With luck, this could be an area of scientific investigation in years to come.
9. (page 178) Liquorice...From 5-7% of the root is made up of a compound called 'glycerrhizin' which is described as fifty-times sweeter than sugar. If taken to excess, it could seriously lower your potassium level, and cause various symptoms, including weakness.

Index

Page numbers in italic represent major entries.

395

396

carpenter's weed 380
caseweed 380
castor oil 367
catarrh 38, 47
catch weed 85, 380
cathartic 37, 38, 44, 46, 95, 109, 155, *367*
cathartic expectorant 30
Catholics, Roman (see also Roman Catholics) 300
Catholic Cardinals (see Cardinal)
catmint 380
catnep 380
catnip 36, 38-41, 43-48, 61, *75*, 174, *206*, 276, 277, 343, 366, 367, 368, 372, 373
cats 206
cat's foot 114, 381
Cauldron of Cerridwen (see Cerridwen) 208, 323
cayenne 35, 38, 40, 44-48, 65, *76*, 102, 174, 343, 370, 372, 373
cedar 193, *206*, 276, 277, 315, 324 343
celandine 36, *207*, 329, 336, 369
celandine, greater 37, 39, 40, 42-46, 49, 77, 174, 343
celandine, lesser 42, *78*, 174, *207*, 343
celebrations 122
celery seed 207, 343
celibacy 294
Celts 68, 79, 146, 204, 210, 243
Centaury *207*, 343
ceremonial rituals 201, 248, 300
Ceres 208, 300, 360
Cerridwen 208, 225, 282
chakras 192, 210, 244
chalcedony 241, 304
Chaldeans 220, 298
chaledony 295
chalice 276, 285, 307, *316*
chamomile 35, 36, 38, 40, 42-45, 47-49, 63, *80*, 90, 175, 193, *208*, 328, 331, 335, 343, 365, 371-373
change 268
charcoal 42, 193, 194
Chariot card 200, *206*, 254, 276
charity 300, 305
Charon 139
chaste tree *208*, 328
chastity 294, 298
checkerberry 381
cheeses 381
chemical dependency (see dependency, chemical)

chervil *208*, 308, 323, 343
chest 62, 90, 92, 107, 371
chickweed 35, 38, 39, 41-44, 46-49, *81*, 175, 343, 372
childbirth 38, 135, 142, 145, 298, 300
childhood 264, 267
children 38, 75, 145, 157, 236, 261, 324
chillies 381
chills 38, 65, 77, 138, 141, 150, 163
China (Chinese) 162, 254, 300
Chinese Anise 381
Chiron 166, 207, 255, 360
chloride 38, 94
cholorophyll 6 (manufacture of)
choloroplast 7
cholera 38, 302
Christ 250, 260, 304
chrysolite 295
chrysoprase 296
church steeples 55, 381
cinqulum sancti johannis 381
cinnamon 36, 38, 41, 42, 47-49, *82*, 175, *209*, 276, 343, 366, 373
cinquefoil 36, 39, 41, 43, 46-48, 83, 175, *209*, 329-331, 371
Circe 231, 237, 360
Circle (Magickal) 283, 285, 313
circulation 68, 77, 110, 132, 138
citrus 343
city avens 381
clairaudience 192
clairvoyancy 192, 211, 214, 223, 231
clary *210*, 343
cleansing (see also purification) 106, 120, 146, 150, 242, 246
clear thinking 211, 214, 218
cleavers 35-38, 40, 43, 44, 46-48, *85*, 175, 343
clivers 85, 381
clot 381
clover 35-37, 45, 46, 48, 49, *86*, 175, *210*, 276, 316, 343
clove root 381
clover, red 35-37, 39, 45-49, *86, 145*, 180, *243*, 343, 364
clove(s) 35-42, 45, 47, 48, 175, *210*, 276, 364-367
clown's lungwort 381
coal 301
coca (leaves) 364
cockleburr 381
cockle buttons 381
coffee 85, 157 (tansy as substitute for), *211*, 343
cohosh 35, 45, *88*, 343, 365

399

401

402

403

405

411

412

verbena (vervain) 36, 37, 39-49, *160*,
181, *252*, 316, 317, 332, 350,
368, 371, 373
verility 218
verobyerite 394
vertigo 49, 131
vervain (see verbena) 232, *252*, 350
Vesta 296
vigor 292, 373
violets 115, *253*, 324, 330, 350
virginity 208, 250
Virgin Mary 129, 205, 212, 227, 228,
233, 250
virgin's glove 388
Virgo 250, 261
(herbs of) 358
virility 105, 224
Vishnu 202, 361
vision 228, 231, 264, 292, 293, 298
visionary dreams 295
Visionary Herbes 67, 79, 88, 104,
118, 123, 128, 129, 132, 135,
142, 159, 195, 197, 199, 202,
207, 211, 212, 228, 234, 235,
241, 251, 252, 254, 268, 271,
377
vitality 65, 105, 147, 262
vitamins 19, 69, 90, 137, 371
(A) 49, 94, 367
(B) 367
(B-12) 49, 92, 367
(C) 49, 77, 90, 367
(D) 367
(E) 49, 94, 367
volatile oils 21, 22, 149, *367, 374*
vomiting (see also emetic) 66, 149,
155, 368
(to induce) 41, 49, 100, 128
(to induce in an emergency) 71
(to stop) 83
von Hohenheim (see Paracelsus)
vows 215
vulnerary 37, 47, 49, 91, 97, 106,
112-114, 117, 122, 136, 139,
145, 146, 153, *374*

Wales 76, 225
wallet 65
Walpurgis Night 237
wands 198, 201, 206, 216, 221, 235,
253, 254, 276, 299, 303, 306,
315
waning moon 28
war 306
warmth 76, 77, 307
warrior (see soldier)
warts 49, 78, 155, 174, 181, 201, 234

washes (herbal) 26, 81, 101, 131,
132, 148, 150, 172, 192, 291
wastefulness 262
wasting diseases 111, 299
water 230, 283, 285, 316
water creatures 230, 254
watercress 254, 276, 316, 350
water elder 388
water fern 107
waxing moon 28
wax myrtle 388
way bennet 388
waybread 388
waybroad 388
wealth 301
weather magick 94
weavers 219
weddings 75, 122, 147, 166, 205,
206, 243, 245, 255, 295, 297,
325
(cake) 59, 75, 200, 206
whale 293
wheat 332, 350
Wheel of Fortune (of Tarot) 276
Wheel of the Year 313, *328*
Whig Plant 80
white man's foot 388
white mullein 388
white oak root 366
white thorn 388
white willow (see willow, white)
whitsun bosses 388
whitsun rose 388
whooping cough 49, 87, 111
Wicca 241
Wiccaning 324
wild cherry 371
wild curcuma 388
wild guelder rose *92*
wild ice leaf 388
wild pansy 116, 388
wild rye 388
wild sunflower 388
willow *254*, 315, 324, 350
willow, white 35-37, 39, 40, 42, 43,
48, *161*, 181, 193, 364
wind (God of the) 199, 226
winterbloom 388
wintergreen 36-40, 44-48, *162*, 181,
350 364, 373
Winter Solstice 224, 318, *335*
(Saturnalia)
Wisdom 200, 227, 246, 295, 300,
304, 306, 308
wishes 66, 166, 203, 255
wisteria *254*, 350

414

Notes